MARCHING ON TOGETHER

My Life at Leeds United

MARCHING ON TOGETHER

My Life at Leeds United

EDDIE GRAY

with Jason Tomas

Hodder & Stoughton

Copyright © 2001 by Eddie Gray

First published in Great Britain in 2001
by Hodder and Stoughton
A division of Hodder Headline

The right of Eddie Gray to be identified as the Author of
the Work has been asserted by him in accordance with the
Copyright, Designs and Patents Act 1988.

2   4   6   8   10   9   7   5   3

A CIP catalogue record for this title
is available from the British Library

ISBN 0 340 81975 8

Typeset in Plantin Light by
Rowland Phototypesetting Ltd,
Bury St Edmunds, Suffolk

Printed and bound in Great Britain by
Mackays of Chatham plc, Chatham, Kent

Hodder and Stoughton
A division of Hodder Headline
338 Euston Road
London NW1 3BH

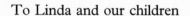
To Linda and our children

CONTENTS

ACKNOWLEDGEMENTS

I would need another book to thank all the people who have helped me produce this account of my life in football.

One person to whom I owe a particular debt is Jason Tomas, the London-based football journalist who spent countless hours with me at my home in recording my recollections and views and, of course, also had the job of helping me to express them in this form. One reason why it was so good to work with him is that Jason's affection for Leeds dates back almost as far as mine. In his case, it started in 1964, when he took on the job of assisting Don Revie in the writing of Don's weekly columns – a role which was maintained for the rest of Don's remarkable career at Leeds and also included his spell as England manager. This is the fourth Leeds book with which he has been involved.

In this particular venture, we consider ourselves fortunate to have had an unrivalled publishing team behind us. As in my career as a Leeds player, the people supporting me at Hodder have made my job so much easier. Among those to whom Jason and I owe a great deal are Roddy Bloomfield, the team leader, Marion Puall, the copy editor, and Gabrielle Allen, the picture researcher.

For our general research, and checking on details I had forgotten, we are grateful to David Hartshorne, head of the *Yorkshire Evening Post* library, not to mention books including *The Leeds United Dream Team* (Jason Tomas), *Leeds United, A Complete Record* (Martin Jarred, Malcolm Macdonald), and *The Official history of Leeds United 1919–1996* (Andrew Mourant).

Last but not least are my thanks to all the people I have worked with throughout my career in football. There really would not have been an Eddie Gray autobiography but for them.

Photographic Acknowledgements

The author and publisher would like to thank the following for permission to reproduce photographs:

Allsport, Colorsport, Gerry Cranham, Empics, *Hull Daily Mail*, Hulton Getty, Mark Leech, Mirror Syndication International, Popperfoto, Press Association, Peter Robinson, *Rochdale Observer*, Sport & General, Sporting Pictures, Topham Picturepoint, Andrew Varley, *Whitby Gazette*, *Yorkshire Post*.

All other photographs are from private collections.

INTRODUCTION

W HEN Howard Wilkinson brought me back to Leeds as a coach in 1995, he told me, 'I want our players to excite me.' I cannot say to what extent, if any, I have carried out the job he expected of me. But the Leeds squad to have emerged in recent seasons – featuring a group of outstanding youngsters I have worked with since the start of their Elland Road careers – certainly excite me. That excitement reached a higher point than ever in 2000–01 when Leeds became the most talked-about club in Britain by reaching the European Champions League semi-finals at their first attempt. It has taken some time to rekindle the magic that surrounded the team in which I played under Don Revie, but there can be no doubt that the team built by David O'Leary has done just that.

How have we managed to get this far? In the Champions League, it has to be admitted that we had some slices of luck, and that we were helped by not having any real pressure on us to do well. We were not expected to get beyond the first group stage, let alone the second. Almost all the teams we had to face in the league section – Barcelona, AC Milan and Besiktas and then Real Madrid, Lazio and Anderlecht – were regarded as being in a different class from us. It suited us to be the underdogs. The players were able to relax and enjoy the experience, to play without any inhibitions.

I should imagine that most Leeds followers will particularly relish the memory of the win over Lazio in Rome. But the performance that gave me the most enjoyment was the one against Anderlecht in Brussels when we became the first English team to beat them on their ground in a European tie since the Leeds team in which I played did it in the European Cup quarter-final in 1975. It was that 4–1 victory that put us through to the quarter-final knock-out stage. No less thrilling to me was the manner in which it was achieved.

In their first-round group, Manchester United, Lazio and PSV Eindhoven had all failed to win at Anderlecht, and that did surprise me. Although Anderlecht had given us a hard time at Elland Road, where we had to come from behind to get our 2–1 win, what I had seen of them on their own ground convinced me that we would beat them comfortably there. I told David O'Leary that I would be very disappointed if we did not win both matches against them.

Anderlecht struck me as being a prime example of a team who, as a result of not having much competition in their own country, had allowed themselves to become over-confident. At home especially, it was rare for them to be fully tested – a lot of matches were little more than half-paced training games for them – and on the basis that habits cannot be changed overnight, I felt that if we set our stall out to go at them, we could destroy them. That is the way it turned out. Amazingly, Anderlecht did not have any cover for the two defenders marking Mark Viduka and Alan Smith; it was just two against two. With our strikers being told to get after them, keep hounding them, Anderlecht hardly knew what hit them. You do not often see teams at this level taken apart as Anderlecht were in the first half. If I had to pinpoint a Leeds display that most reminded me of the team I played in, our performance during that period – which brought a 3–0 half-time lead – would be it.

The third goal, which effectively settled the tie, was my favourite one from our Champions League campaign. It all started with a long clearance from Lucas Radebe, which was won in the air by Alan Smith. The ball broke to Olivier Dacourt in the middle of the park, and from there the sequence of players getting touches was Smith–Batty–Dacourt–Viduka–Batty. The memory of the *coup de grâce* is also one to savour – Alan, from David Batty's pass, cut inside a defender and chipped the keeper. At that moment, I was transported back to the Revie era. Batty could easily have been Billy Bremner or John Giles, and Smith was a dead ringer for Allan Clarke.

I am not sure that our boldness did not ultimately rebound on us. There was a naivety about our play, and this is what caused us to go out of the competition at the hands of Valencia. There were times when it would have been more advisable to hold back for maybe five or ten minutes and concentrate on keeping the ball, instead of playing with our foot flat down on the accelerator all the time. Our cavalier approach was seen in some of our scoring attempts. For example, when Lee Bowyer had it in mind to have a crack at goal, you knew that nothing was going to stop him, no matter how much the odds were stacked against him. He, like others, was not bothered in the slightest about giving the ball away.

In some ways, it is a wonderful attitude, and nobody likes to see players taking chances more than I do. But at the highest level, you do need a balance. Valencia underlined this. They beat us because there was greater variation in their play.

However, Valencia, in common with most of the other teams we faced, are considerably more experienced than we are at this level and we can only get better.

While addressing the problem of what we need to go further, and recognising that we cannot begin to look upon ourselves as a great team until we have won a trophy, the 2000–01 season has to be seen as one of the most satisfying in the club's history.

I am grateful to Howard Wilkinson for bringing me back to the club and to his successors, George Graham and David O'Leary, for retaining and promoting me. The thanks must also be extended to those who helped bring Leeds United and me together almost forty years ago.

1
WHY LEEDS?

DESPITE having spent all but ten of the last thirty-eight years with Leeds United, I would probably nominate something that had nothing to do with the club as my most cherished football memory. It happened on 4 January 1995 when my occasional stint as a match summariser for BBC Radio Five Live took me back to my home city of Glasgow to watch Celtic against Rangers at Ibrox, and my son, Stuart, make his Old Firm derby debut in the Celtic defence.

Being selected for a match of this importance was a big step up for Stuart. It is one of the greatest club fixtures in the world, and certainly the one that means the most to fans in the west of Scotland. Then twenty-one, he had made just a handful of first-team appearances. It was special for him, helping Celtic come from behind to achieve a 1–1 draw, and it was even more special for me. The reason concerns the memory of my father, Edward, who died aged fifty-one in September 1972. It is one of the biggest regrets of my life that he did not see that match.

He was an avid Celtic supporter, as were my brother Frank and I – indeed Celtic meant so much to us that on the rare occasions they were beaten, we would be almost in tears. I am still a big Celtic supporter, as anyone who is in my company when I am watching their matches on television will readily confirm. My father was proud of the progress Frank and I made in the game but I think, deep down, he was disappointed that we did it with other clubs.

As schoolboys, Frank and I both made our mark in the Glasgow and Scotland representative teams, and having trained with Celtic, we both had the opportunity to sign for them after leaving school. Frank's link with the club even extended to his being employed as one of their home-match ball boys. But, with me having started my professional career at Leeds in the summer of 1963, Frank followed in 1970. While I spent all of my career at Elland Road, Frank had two spells here as a professional player – from 1971 to 1979 and 1981 to 1985. In between, he played for Brian Clough at Nottingham Forest, where he won a European Cup winner's medal. He also played for Sunderland, and then Darlington. Frank also has a son in professional football; Andrew started at Leeds and is now with Nottingham Forest. Stuart, who moved from Celtic to Reading, is now at Rushden and Diamonds, and completing the Gray family football picture is my other son, sixteen-year-old Nicholas, who as been training at Leeds.

Stuart, too, trained at Leeds as a schoolboy. Then John Kelman, Celtic's chief scout, invited him for a trial when he was fourteen, and before long, Stuart was going up to Celtic almost every week. The arrangement worked out perfectly for him because he could stay with my mother in Glasgow and it did not detract from his schoolwork. He flew to Glasgow after school on a Friday, played for the Celtic Boys Club team on the Saturday and came back that night or Sunday morning.

How my father would have loved that. Stuart found it difficult to establish himself in his six seasons as a Celtic professional, but I daresay that my father would have been prouder of him than of any of us if he were around today.

Apart from Frank, who at forty-seven is six years younger than me, I have another brother, David, fifty, and a sister, Carol, forty. David, a buyer for a Glasgow building supplies company, also attracted the interest of professional clubs as a teenager, but he was not as committed to the game as Frank and I were and drifted out of it after breaking an ankle. He had not started playing until he was fourteen – much later than Frank and I did – and as if to emphasise his sense of independence, and willingness to risk being labelled the black sheep of the family, he even professed to being a Rangers fan.

In our family circle, he was not alone in stating an allegiance to a club other than Celtic. All my mother Helen's family were staunch Clyde supporters, which perhaps was only to be expected considering that she was brought up with her seven brothers and six sisters around the corner from the club's Shawfield ground. But it was unusual, to say the least, for anyone in a Catholic home to sing the praises of Rangers. The best thing that can be said about David is that he has since seen the error of his ways and become more Celtic-daft than the rest of us.

I owe a lot to my father. I am told that he was an excellent footballer. When I was a lad, a number of the people who had seen him said to me, 'You are a good player, but you have a long way to go to be as good as your dad was.' According to them, he was similar to me in technical ability but was inclined to be hot-headed.

My mother, who was much the more placid of the two and came from a closer-knit, more harmonious family, appeared to have a steadying influence on him. There seems little doubt that I have inherited her nature and temperament. I was never one to give referees a hard time over their decisions – I never saw the point – and in 557 matches for Leeds and twelve for Scotland, I was never booked or sent off. The only time I can recall losing my rag on a football field was during a match against Stoke, following a foul on me by their right-back Jackie Marsh. We both fell to the ground and I was so incensed by his challenge that I actually had my hands around his throat, much to the amusement of the other Leeds players. I don't think they could believe I was capable of an action like that.

My father, a welder by trade, was a left-half in junior football – semi-professional football as it would be known in England – but was forced to stop playing as a result of a shrapnel wound in the right thigh incurred while serving with the Highland Light Infantry in the Netherlands in December 1944. He was declared unfit for combat duty and was taken from the front to Ostend in Belgium where he was made up to the rank of corporal and put in charge of the officer's mess until his release in 1946. His most traumatic war-time experience was seeing his best friend shot dead. They were standing next to each other. My mother believes that it affected his nerves and caused him to start smoking. He became a heavy smoker and that is what ultimately killed him. In May 1972, he was taken ill at Wembley after Leeds' FA Cup final win over Arsenal. I was in the dressing room when I was told that he had collapsed by his seat during the presentation of the trophy and medals, and been taken on a stretcher by the St John's Ambulance attendants to the dressing-room tunnel. He had had a mild stroke some time previously and, initially, we thought that this time he might have suffered a slight heart attack. He seemed OK when I got to him and although it was intended to take him to hospital, it never occurred to me – or my mother, who was with him – that the problem might be more serious than it appeared.

Leeds had a great chance of clinching the championship and we had to travel straight to the Midlands after the Cup final to prepare for our last league match of the season at Wolves on the Monday. The telephone conversations with my mother on Sunday indicated that my father was recovering well. I later discovered that he had suffered a relapse, and she and Don Revie decided it was best to keep it from me until after the game. Thus, within an hour of the final whistle, with Leeds' dreams of the double having been destroyed by a controversial 2–1 defeat, I was on my way back to London.

Over the next couple of days, while the hospital tests on my father were being completed, I stayed with my mother at her hotel. We both continued to be under the impression that my father had heart trouble. Then we were called in and told that he had lung cancer, and that it was too advanced for us to hold out any hope for him. Four months later, he was gone, but memories of him, and the manner in which he helped shape me as a person, will stay with me forever.

My upbringing was dominated by football – both playing and watching it – just as it was for thousands of other youngsters living in the deprived inner-city areas of Glasgow. My parents set great store by bringing us up with good manners and respect for other people. It is down to them that throughout my adult life, I have never used bad language. Swearing was always frowned upon in our household, and the habit of not using it has stuck with me. In a profession in which industrial language is commonplace, I am quite proud of having been able to maintain those standards.

One thing I particularly remember about my father is his protectiveness. I am sure that stemmed from the violence and degradation he witnessed almost from day one. He was born and raised in the heart of the infamous Gorbals, once arguably the most deprived inner city area in Britain. The suburb of Castlemilk, where he and my mother spent most of their lives – and where my mother, aged seventy-nine, still lives – was not exactly the most genteel of places either.

Before my wife Linda and I got married in 1968, we would often go to Glasgow after a Leeds match on a Saturday, and spend the rest of the weekend at my parents' place. If we went out for a walk, it was not unusual for my father to follow us up the road, without our knowledge, to make sure we were safe.

I was only six or seven when he started taking me to matches – mainly Celtic matches, of course. He loved to kick a ball around with me and discuss my performances, so I suppose he was my first coach. I could not have had anyone better to guide me in those early years. He had a tremendous knowledge of the game for a man who had never been a professional, and he never allowed me to rest on my laurels. No matter how well I had played, he always balanced his praise with reminders of how I could improve. This is the essence of coaching young players. So many fall into the trap of thinking that the attributes they were born with will be enough to see them through, and lose sight of the need to keep working hard.

The environment in which I learned the game was also an important factor in helping me establish a successful career. To an extent, it was a throw-back to the circumstances from which so many great footballers in Britain sprung just before and after the war.

The common denominator among them was that they came from poor backgrounds and football was by far their main source of entertainment, if not their only one. In those days, when there was no television or computer games, and far fewer organised matches at schoolboy level than there are today, kids would spend hours playing football in the streets or on wasteground. These informal kick-abouts were a perfect way for boys to develop their ball skills.

Things are different now. Impromptu football has become less prevalent, partly because the choice of leisure activities for youngsters has become much wider and partly because of the increase in road traffic and the omnipresence of residential and office developments. There is plenty of organised football, but whether those who supervise teams at schoolboy and youth levels give their players enough encouragement and freedom to play their own game is another matter. There is no doubt that a lot of these people tend to put the emphasis on team systems and winning trophies instead of the development of individual skills.

The introduction of schoolboy academies at league clubs – the main part of the wide-ranging Charter for Excellence player-development programme initiated by the former Leeds manager Howard Wilkinson in his capacity as the Football Association's Technical Director – should help overcome this problem. In broad terms, it means that the responsibility for the coaching of youngsters has been taken out of the hands of those who run their school teams and put into the hands of the professionals. Boys can join the academies from eight or nine, and while they are attached to them, the number of formal matches for which their school teams can select them is limited.

It is a question of learning to play before they learn to compete, not the other way around. Andy Roxburgh, the Scottish Football Association's former Director of Coaching, sums it up best when he talks about the importance of player-development programmes that replicate the street-football culture.

I consider myself fortunate to have been immersed in that culture naturally. The area in which I was brought up – in a two-bedroomed flat on the second floor of a tenement building – might not have been the best place in Britain to live. But this, and other areas like it in Glasgow, were great breeding grounds for footballers. In lives that were nothing if not basic and straightforward, football provided the greatest excitement and pleasure.

For boys like me, much of that excitement revolved around fantasising about being in the shoes of the stars we watched on a Saturday. In terms of the career I was able to establish in football, the hours I spent with a ball at my feet when I was a boy unquestionably proved one of the most important factors. I cannot stress enough that natural ability counts for little unless it is honed in practice; the more you play, the better you become. I appreciate that I was fortunate to be born with greater ability than a lot of other players, but at the same time, this in itself would not have been enough to give me the success I achieved. The point was summed up perfectly by golfer Gary Player who, when told that he was lucky to be able to hit such great shots, replied, 'The more I practise, the luckier I get.'

One of the many stars of my generation who endorsed this message was Jimmy Johnstone, the brilliant winger who started his illustrious career at Celtic at the same time that I began with Leeds. His ball-playing tricks took the breath away, and led to him being looked upon as a footballing genius. He was, but part of his success could be attributed to the fact that he had an insatiable appetite for practising his skills. He said that when he was twelve, he was galvanised by the gift of a book which described the relentless practice with which Sir Stanley Matthews refined his ability. Johnstone was quoted as saying, 'I used to go into the school playground at night and practise for hours on end, running with the ball, sprinting, twisting and turning. There was a wall about a hundred yards long, and as I went up and down, I played one-twos off it. Then, when I went home, I would spend another hour or two dribbling around milk bottles.'

I can relate to this – I had similar routines. I got so much enjoyment from playing football that it was virtually the only thing I thought about. In retrospect, I sometimes wonder how I managed to maintain my enthusiasm. My school team did not have many good players. We often turned up for matches with nine or ten boys, a number of whom did not have the proper kit; and the rag, tag and bobtail image of the side was further heightened by the fact that our goalkeeper – a wonderful character by the name of John Gavin, who once did a bit of scouting in Scotland for Leeds – had a glass eye.

Although our home matches were staged at a place called Glasgow Green, they took place on shale or red-ash pitches, which made tumbles painful to say the least. It was rare to play on grass; and when I was at school, it was rare to play with a proper football.

Conventional balls, even tennis balls, were banned in the concrete jungle that was our playground – it was bang in the middle of the school buildings, framed by high walls with windows on all sides – so we had to make do with balls comprising a rolled-up piece of paper inside a sock. The bonus was that if you could consistently achieve mastery of the ball in such circumstances, you had good cause to feel that you could do it in any circumstances. After a while, my control of the ball – first touch, dribbling and passing – was something that I took for granted. I felt comfortable on the ball in most areas of the field. I became so confident that, without wishing to appear conceited, there was not one player throughout my entire career to whom I felt technically inferior.

My favourite position as a schoolboy was wing-half, and as my Leeds performances at outside-left indicated, I liked nothing better than to hold the ball and take on opponents. To do that, I had to learn to shield the ball and make it difficult for opponents to knock me off balance. Much of my boyhood football was played in tight, enclosed areas in which bruising contact with an opponent – or a wall – was par for the course, and I got into the habit of using my arms to hold off opponents. This explains the running style for which I was noted – the hunching of my shoulders over the ball with my arms held out like those of a high-wire artist.

I have always been a great believer in players taking opponents on when they have the opportunity to do so, as opposed to playing in front of them. So much so that it could even be said to be an obsession with me. As a boy, I was often told that I held the ball too long and I was greedy. But this is one aspect of my play that my father never criticised. I was also encouraged by the example set by the former Celtic and Scotland forward, Willie Fernie, my favourite player.

Fernie, who won twelve Scotland caps (the same number as I did) between 1954 and 1958, was also labelled greedy. But for me, there was no more exciting sight than Fernie picking up the ball and gliding past three or four players. Perhaps the most memorable of his performances was when he helped Celtic beat Rangers 7–1 in the 1957 Scottish League Cup final – the most famous Old Firm derby victory in Celtic's history and one that I will always feel privileged to have seen.

In addition to his skill, I also admired Fernie's strong-mindedness – or should it be courage? – in resisting the pressure on him to change his approach. He played the percentage game, inasmuch as he would keep trying to go past opponents with the ball on the premise that even though it might come off for him only three or four times out of ten, the overall result would be worth it. There were quite a few occasions when, having lost the ball, he would make you think, 'Oh, he should have passed it.' But then he would go on a run again, take three or four defenders out of the game and it was a goal.

There are many ways in which to define the word courage in professional football. The sort Fernie showed was no less pertinent than its other forms. It had a considerable impact on me.

Don Revie drew my attention to this aspect of the game. During the early part of my Leeds career, he would tell me that to realise my potential, I would need to think of the three cs – confidence, concentration and courage. He was referring to moral courage. When I was manager at Rochdale, some of the players remarked, 'It must have been easy to perform well in a team like the one you were in at Leeds.'

'Well, yes and no,' I replied. 'It was easy in the sense that I had so many great players around me. But the other side of the coin was that Leeds were under enormous pressure to keep winning. In some matches at Elland Road, if we were not a goal or two ahead after about twenty minutes, the crowd would become restless and have a go at you.'

That is when you needed the courage that Don was referring to, and that Fernie displayed, to keep playing in the right way.

Watching great players is the best football education a youngster can have. I was only six when England were humbled 6–3 by Hungary at Wembley in 1953, but I saw a film of the match a few years later, and the goal scored by Ferenc Puskas when he beat England's captain, Billy Wright, with that superb drag back, absolutely captivated me. As with countless other soccer-mad boys who saw it, I couldn't wait to learn how to do it.

I was reminded of this recently when I was sent a video of a goal I once scored against Burnley following a dribble through half their team. The run started when I beat someone with a drag-back wide on the left, close to the Burnley goalline. As soon as I saw it again, I immediately thought 'Ferenc Puskas'. It just goes to show how much you can be influenced by such players.

Apart from Fernie, the other Celtic players I particularly liked were centre-half Bobby Evans, midfielder Bobby Collins (with whom I later played at Leeds), and centre-forward Billy McPhail. Collins moved from Celtic to Everton in September 1958; Fernie and Evans also went on to play in England, with Middlesbrough and Chelsea respectively. I wish others could have done so to show people south of the border what good players they were.

The strange thing was that while I strove to match their skills, it was some time before I thought about the possibility of becoming a professional footballer myself. In those days, the schoolboy recruitment system in British professional football was not as exhaustive and intense as it is now. Until the age of fourteen, when I first became aware of clubs showing an interest in me, the prospect of a career in professional football seemed to me to be too distant a dream to think about. I did not have a clue how to go about becoming a professional footballer anyway. I was just happy to keep playing with my friends, and let the question of what I was going to do for a living take care of itself.

The first contact involving league club scouts arose from my performances in the Glasgow Schools representative team. It was through that team that I initially established my close friendship with Jimmy Lumsden. We had been regular members of the side from the age of nine – he was the inside-right, I was the left-half – and as we lived close to each other, we became virtually inseparable.

We were like two ragamuffins. One of my fondest memories of those days concerned the night when the Glasgow Schools squad was invited to train at Hampden Park. Jimmy and I, having got off school early, were the first to arrive at the stadium. As we were looking around, we stumbled across a room with a large table of sandwiches and cakes. Thinking that they must be for us, we started tucking in like a pair of hungry wolves. There was plenty of food left, but needless to say, we made the most of getting the first pick. We thought nothing more about it until an official of Queen's Park, the club who owned the national stadium and have always trained and played their home matches there, came into our dressing room to ask who had eaten the food. Imagine the embarrassment for Jimmy and me when we were told that we had scoffed the Queen's Park players' tea.

Jimmy came to Leeds with me – we shared the same digs – and he was my assistant when I was manager of the club and then of Rochdale.

We are from similar backgrounds and have so much in common we are more like brothers than friends. His father died prematurely too, at forty-six because of stomach cancer. Jimmy was out with his girlfriend when the call came through at our digs, and I was the one who had to break the news to him.

Jimmy, who also played for Southend, Morton, St Mirren, Clydebank and Celtic, did not make a bigger impact at the highest level only because he lacked a bit of pace. It says much about the knowledge he acquired in striving to get the best out of himself that he has forged a good career as a coach. Currently the coach at Preston, his other roles have included assistant-manager and manager at Bristol City and youth-team coach at Celtic.

Of all the players I have played with, he is the one with whom I have the strongest bond. We are so close that I have derived as much pleasure from his achievements as I have from my own. The one regret that I have about my schoolboy career is that we did not play together in the Scotland Under-15 team. We took part in the same trial matches, and overall he probably performed better than I did. But in the final trial, when we were both in the 'probables' line-up, he had the misfortune to have a stinker. He was taken off at half-time and that was it.

By the time of the Scotland matches against Wales, England and Ireland in May 1963, the trickle of English and Scottish League clubs who had made approaches to sign me had become a flood. At the final count, the total was thirty-five, and included Everton, that season's First Division champions; Tottenham, the 1961 championship and FA Cup double winners, who were runners-up; Manchester United, the FA Cup winners; Liverpool, Arsenal and Chelsea. The only clubs I had visited were Arsenal and Leeds. I had gone to each with my parents the previous year, and had made up my mind then that Leeds were the club for me. Nonetheless, as Leeds were not allowed to sign me until I left school, a number of other clubs still felt it was worth the attempt to persuade my father and me to have a rethink. It reached the stage where Don Revie deemed it necessary to send assistant-manager Maurice Lindley to Glasgow as a sort of minder for me.

One manager of whom Don and Maurice were particularly wary was Tommy Docherty, then in charge of a Chelsea team that had been relegated to the Second Division. Of all the managers who wanted to snatch me from Leeds' grasp, the Doc's bid was probably the one that worried Don the most. So it was not coincidental that when Docherty came to our flat once, and was talking to my parents and me in the living room, Maurice was actually listening to the conversation while hiding in the bedroom.

On a couple of occasions, there were two or three rival scouts or managers at our home at the same time. Needless to say, the conversation was somewhat stilted.

I am sure they were all surprised that I was going to Leeds, and I cannot say I blame them. The choice did seem incongruous, considering that Leeds were in the Second Division when I joined

12

them in May 1963 – they had finished that season in fifth place after nearly being relegated to the Third Division the previous season – and had no tradition as a top club. They had never won the championship or the FA Cup, and their highest league position had been fifth in the First Division way back in 1930.

When my father first told me of their interest in me, I am ashamed to have to admit that I did not even know where they were situated. For some reason – possibly because I got their name confused with the word 'leeks' – I was under the impression that they were a Welsh club. My father was no expert on the subject either.

So why did I join Leeds? Cynics might argue that the decision was based on what I could earn there. The usual procedure for clubs signing players from school was to give them a two-year contract as apprentice professionals at fifteen (then the official school-leaving age in Britain) and, depending on progress, their first full professional contracts at seventeen. Clubs could not have more than fifteen apprentices on their books at any one time, and could not pay them more than £7 a week for the first year and £8 a week for the second.

But Leeds signed me as an amateur player and arranged for me to be 'employed' by a local printing company. It is such a long time ago that I forget how this was put to us; if memory serves me right, Don Revie told my father that it had to be done this way because the club had reached its apprentice quota. But I cannot deny that I benefited from it financially. It meant that I was paid three times what I would have received on an apprentice pro-fessional agreement – a lot of money in those days for someone of my age. For obvious reasons, there was some sensitivity about the arrangement, as Don Revie confirmed when he stressed, 'On no account should you tell anyone what you are earning.'

I think a number of clubs bent the rules in this way. As far as Leeds were concerned, I was not the only Scottish schoolboy player who was signed by the club as an amateur. The others were Jim McCalliog and Peter Lorimer, in 1961 and 1962 respectively. After he had joined Leeds, Peter actually played for the Scotland amateur team on a tour of Kenya.

Signing players as amateurs, rather than apprentices, struck me as quite a risky arrangement for the club. As an amateur, a player had the freedom to leave and go somewhere else whenever he wished. This is what happened with McCalliog. Just before his seventeenth birthday, when he was poised to sign professional forms with Leeds, he changed his mind and signed for Chelsea.

There was never any danger of me following his example, even though Celtic tried to get me to do so. There were never any doubts in my mind that Leeds were ideally suited to me. The money was relatively unimportant – I could have got better deals elsewhere. My attraction to the club was based on other consider-ations.

For one thing, Leeds worked exceptionally hard to sell them-selves to us. This is where Celtic fell down – despite the competition to sign me, they were disconcertingly laid-back in their dealings with us. Most Catholic boys in Scotland who are interested in football would give anything to play for Celtic, and I think the club took it for granted that I would want to start my career there. Leeds projected themselves superbly as a progressive club with a strong family spirit, a place where I would be well looked after; and they were the first English club to show an interest in me, via their famous Scottish scout, John Barr.

John, a former Partick Thistle and QPR centre-half who had become associated with Leeds in 1961, immediately made a big impression on my parents and me. He was a gentleman, a quiet, unassuming man whose life revolved around football, his family and caravanning. He made a big impression on many other people too, Sir Alex Ferguson among them. Sir Alex was once quoted as describing John as someone he had learned a lot from as a young manager with St Mirren. Referring to his relationship with John and another Scottish scout, John Dickie (who worked for Manchester United), Fergie said, 'I learned about scouting by watching games with them. They were of the old school. They always treated people with respect and went about their jobs with integrity.' That said it all. I was one of a number of Scottish youngsters whom John helped to bring to Leeds. Others included Peter Lorimer, Gordon

McQueen and Joe Jordan. They all talk about him as warmly as I do.

Another reason for my decision to join Leeds was Don Revie. He had tremendous physical presence and personality. He told my father, 'I know you don't know much about Leeds United now, Mr Gray, but in the not-too-distant future, this club is going to be one of the best in Britain.' He was not the only manager who sang that type of tune, but his enthusiasm and drive were such that it was difficult to dismiss his claims. His persuasiveness was underlined even more forcibly by our belief in his assertion that Leeds could become the English equivalent of Real Madrid; an assertion he supported by changing the club strip from blue and gold to Real's famous all-white.

His appreciation of the art of PR – winning friends and influencing people – was outstanding. When it came to making people feel special, he thought of everything; he thought about things that I daresay would go over the heads of a lot of other managers. It was typical of him that to celebrate the decisions of Jimmy Lumsden and myself to join Leeds, Don and the club chairman, Harry Reynolds, came up to Glasgow and threw a party for us and our families in the Central Hotel.

It was a relief when the signing was completed because our tie-up with Leeds could easily have ended in tears.

Clubs could not sign a player while he was still on the roster of a school, but Don persuaded me to sign a contract in advance on the understanding that it would be kept in his desk and only be registered when the rules allowed. However, he became so anxious about the number of clubs chasing me that he panicked and registered the agreement prematurely, before my last Scotland Under-15 match against Ireland. This led to the threat of the Scottish Schools FA banning me from the team. My mother, upset that I should be caught in the middle of a controversy like this, was furious with Don. The night before the game, with no decision having been made about whether I would be allowed to play, she was adamant that if I was dropped, I would not be going to Leeds.

I was in the dressing room before the kick-off when members

of the committee who ran the team called me into a small ante room and asked me to confirm that I had signed for Leeds. When I did so, someone said, 'You know it's against the rules, and that we could stop you from playing today?' With that, I went back to the dressing room and waited for them to make a decision.

Half an hour before the kick-off, with no one having told me what was happening and my No. 6 shirt not having been taken by anyone else, I assumed that the committee had settled for an easy life and were not going to carry out their threat. So I put the shirt on and went out and played. I heard nothing more about it.

Because of exams, I was not officially due to leave school until the summer. But Don stayed on in Glasgow after the Ireland game, and the following Monday morning, he went to my school and persuaded my headmaster that it would be in everybody's best interests for me to be released early. That afternoon, Jimmy Lumsden and I travelled with Don back to Leeds in his blue Ford Zephyr – a journey that was to lead to a career that even someone with my confidence could hardly have anticipated or even hoped for.

2

SYD, BOBBY AND ALBERT JOHANNESON

A LOT of people contributed to my success as a Leeds player. For obvious reasons, the figure at the top of the list has to be Don Revie. But others to whom I have to give special thanks are Syd Owen and Bobby Collins.

Syd was part of a wonderful backroom team at Leeds under Don. The others were assistant-manager Maurice Lindley, trainer Les Cocker, physiotherapist Bob English and coach Cyril Partridge. I thought the world of all of them, but I have to single out Syd because as the youth and reserve-team coach during the two years that preceded my first professional contract with the club and my first-team debut at seventeen, he was the person who did the most to help me acquire the necessary football knowledge and professional habits. Bobby, the Leeds captain, also had a hand in this process, but the main reason why I will always be grateful to him concerns his work in steering Leeds back into the First Division. Whether Leeds would have got out of the Second Division when they did without him is open to doubt as far as I am concerned; it could be argued that, but for him, they would have ended up in the Third.

In the case of Syd, my thoughts about what he did for me are tinged with embarrassment. He was out of football when I became Leeds manager in July 1982, and I brought him back to the club as chief scout. But I then sacked him – the most difficult decision

I have ever had to make. The reason was that I felt he was too much of a perfectionist.

Syd was Luton's centre-half and captain in their FA Cup final defeat by Nottingham Forest in 1959, when he won the Footballer of the Year award. He was a brilliant judge of players. It was easy to see why Syd, in tandem with Maurice Lindley, had been deployed by Don Revie to compile the dossiers on the strengths and weaknesses of opposing teams; and why, to ensure there was as little as possible in our own play for the opposition to exploit, Don occasionally instructed Syd and Maurice to do a breakdown on us. The problem of having Syd in the role I gave him, however, was that he was too critical. Leeds had just been relegated to the Second Division when I landed the job, and were short of money to spend in the transfer market. We were in no position to subject prospective signings to the level of scrutiny that Syd favoured. We no longer had a dressing room bursting with international-class players and our guidelines concerning players who could improve our team had changed considerably – but not to Syd. The players to whom he was prepared to give his seal of approval were very few and far between, and because we badly needed strengthening, I had to let him go.

The irony in this is that it was largely because of Syd's ultra-high standards that I went from strength to strength as a Leeds player. The extent to which he made me aware of parts of my game that he felt needed to be improved reminded me of my father – but Syd was even more demanding.

His appearance alone said a lot about him. He was a bit like an army officer in that he was immaculately groomed (we used to joke that you could use his shoes as a mirror) and put a great emphasis on discipline. When playing with him in training matches, it was noticeable that everything he did was done cleanly and precisely. He treated the game very seriously and if any players gave the impression that they didn't – something they could do just by laughing in training – he would come down on them like a ton of bricks. One player who was clearly disconcerting to him was Peter Lorimer. Peter could seem somewhat casual and unfocused; half an hour before a match, while others might be think-ing about what they had to do, he was liable to be trying to get a bet on a horserace. This did not fit Syd's perception of how a professional footballer should conduct himself. Thus, unsurpris-ingly in view of Syd's intransigence in the matter, he and Peter never got on professionally.

Peter and I had numerous debates about Syd, with me accentuat-ing his positive traits and Peter the negative ones. Peter did have a point when he said that man-management was not one of Syd's strong points. I would say that the older and more experienced the players he dealt with, the more that this quest for perfection, and his frustration when he had to accept less, was inclined to create friction. I suspect that this side of him might have been one of the reasons why Don switched him from coaching the first team to coaching the youth and reserve-teams.

Syd, who'd had a short spell as Luton's manager before being brought to Leeds (by Don's predecessor, Jack Taylor) in 1960, seemed to recognise the logic behind this himself. Recalling his initial work as first-team coach, in tandem with Les Cocker, he once said, 'It was frustrating because there was only a limited amount of work we could do with the senior players. They were too set in their ways. It was different with the youngsters, although Jack Taylor sometimes felt that we were inclined to push them too hard. I couldn't see that – I just felt that a lot of really hard work at the start of their career was bound to stand them in good stead in the long run.'

To say that Syd was hard on me would be an understatement. He told me, 'I probably pick on you more than I do the other players because I know you are capable of doing all the things I want you to do.' Despite such back-handed compliments, there were times when he almost reduced me to tears.

Don was aware of this. Occasionally, if he felt that Syd had gone too far, he would put an arm around my shoulders and say, 'Don't let it get to you, Eddie. Just concentrate on expressing your ability, and enjoying your football, as much as you can.' To Don, that meant holding the ball and taking on people, as he once did in his days as a Manchester City and England centre-forward. When he felt that Syd, through his attempt to broaden my ability, might be taking me too far away from that, he would have no compunction about stepping in and telling me to carry on doing what I was best at.

But the education Syd gave me was the best I could have had. I picked up a lot of knowledge from him about every position and role, not just my own. That's why, apart from the positions in which I made most of my Leeds appearances – outside-left and left-back – I was also played in midfield, at centre-forward and as a sweeper.

Syd was a great believer in players doing extra fitness work outside their usual club training sessions, as Jimmy Lumsden and I found when we stayed with him and his wife Trudie for a while. One of the drawbacks in this arrangement was Syd's insistence on taking us for a jog around his local golf course each day before we had our tea. Through Syd's influence, it was not unusual for me to set aside some time on most days for a five- or six-mile run – something that I have kept up to this day.

Syd and Don often singled out the example of Stan Matthews, with whom they had both played in the England team, as the perfect one for us to follow. I still remember the stories they used to tell us about Matthews' training methods – his one-day-a-week diets, when all that would pass his lips was water; his deep-breathing exercises; and his runs along the promenade or the beach at Blackpool.

To build up our physical strength, Don insisted on the young players at Leeds taking a drink of sherry and eggs before training each day. He actually prepared it himself and although some of the players hated it – including Jimmy and me – there was no escape. Don also regularly gave us expensive steaks to take back to our digs for our landladies to cook for us.

In view of all this attention to our physical well-being, it was perhaps significant that a number of the youngsters at Leeds in those days went on to play professional football until they were way into their thirties. If any player epitomised the messages that the club strove to get across, it was Paul Madeley. I am sure that if Syd had been pressed to pinpoint his ideal professional among the Leeds players with whom he was associated, it would have been Paul. He really was a coach's dream. The remarkable versatility that enabled him to play for Leeds in every position except that of goalkeeper may have worked against him – without one specific position or role that he could call his own, he did not attract the same attention as other players – but that was the way he seemed to prefer it. Paul, who came from a comparatively well-to-do family, was an exceptionally quiet, undemonstrative person. He was interested in doing a good job for the team. At his best as a defender, he was happy to do whatever was required of him with the minimum fuss and bother.

One aspect of his approach was seen in the fact that, in an Elland Road career spanning seventeen years and 725 first-team appearances (a match record bettered only by Jack Charlton, Billy Bremner, Paul Reaney and Norman Hunter) he was booked just twice. Off the pitch as well as on it, he was a man of few words. His image as the strong silent type was best illustrated by the fact that he was looked upon as the Leeds player who made the least fuss when undergoing painful treatment for injuries.

Paul, like so many of the other players with whom I was brought up at Leeds, showed the importance of mental strength in professional football. Although I did not appreciate it at the time, there can be no doubt that this was another sphere in which working with Syd Owen was good for me. Handling his demands stood me in good stead for being able to handle anything.

The two-year period from being signed by a club as an apprentice professional or amateur after leaving school to becoming a full professional is a difficult one. This is especially true of youngsters starting their careers with clubs outside their home towns. My short visits to Arsenal and Leeds as a schoolboy were the only times I had been out of Scotland; apart from that, the furthest I had ever stayed from my Glasgow home was when we went to Arbroath on the east coast on summer holidays. Those couple of years can make or break you – you have to adjust to your new life quickly, otherwise the opportunities just pass you by. You realise that having the ability to make the grade is one thing – having the character, the mental toughness, to express it while living away from your home and family is another.

During that period, when I was alternating between the youth team and the reserves, and also for my first few years as a professional, I was helped by having Jimmy Lumsden with me. Moreover, Leeds were such a friendly club. They put a great deal of effort into ensuring that young players felt at home.

A lot of the players in my age group must have thought that I had been born under a lucky star. They all envied the digs that Jimmy and I found because the landlady – a charming woman by the name of Mrs Lazenby – treated us like royalty. Unfortunately, we were eventually forced to leave as a result of her forming a romantic attachment with a local widower. My feeling that the writing was on the wall for us was finally confirmed one day when Jimmy and I returned from a trip to the cinema to find our suitcases outside the front door. 'You are not staying here any more,' the gentleman told us. 'Mrs Lazenby wants you to go.'

By far the best bit of good fortune I had was that Leeds took me off the groundstaff after a year – much to the annoyance of Jimmy and one of his other pals, Terry Hibbitt, who had to remain on it for the full two-year period. Whereas I could leave the ground after our morning training sessions, they had to stay behind and continue doing jobs such as helping to sweep the stadium terracing and stands, clean the toilets and weed the pitch.

Terry, who went on to have an excellent career with Newcastle, tragically died of cancer at the age of forty-seven in 1994. Most of his colleagues remember him fondly, not just because of his midfield passing skills, but also for his moaning. He never seemed to stop. However, I have to acknowledge that his complaints about the way I was being treated in comparison with Jimmy and himself were perfectly justified. The irony of the situation was that Terry and Jimmy, while finding those groundstaff chores as irksome as everyone else, were probably the hardest workers among the whole group.

It was a different story with me. My working partner was Mick Bates. I use the word working loosely because we were always looking for ways to dodge our duties. One way in which this was achieved, at least for a while, was to creep into a small hiding place that we found at the back of the West Stand from where we could watch the first-team players train.

Our groundsman, Cecil Burrows, who had the unenviable task of supervising us, was so pernickity he could drive you crazy, although I have to admit that he had a lot to put up with when it came to his dealings with Mick and me. Mick had been an excellent javelin-thrower at school, and when I attempted to demonstrate my own ability one day – using one of Cecil's pitchforks – I propelled the missile into his knee. I do not think I have ever breathed a bigger sigh of relief than I did when learning that Mick's injury was only superficial.

Cecil always had a struggle on his hands in trying to motivate us for the weeding jobs. I hate gardening and Linda, who has never had much success in getting me to do any at home, often jokes that it can all be attributed to my experiences with Cecil Burrows. 'That man has a lot to answer for,' she says. I was the bain of his life, and he complained to Don Revie about me a few times. But although Don felt duty bound to call me into his office and give me a ticking-off, his reprimands were of the tongue-in-cheek variety.

'Look, Eddie,' he said, 'just do a little bit to keep Cec happy.'

When I was relieved of my groundstaff responsibilities, it must have been one of the happiest days of Cecil's life. For me, the other good part about it was that I started training with the full-time professionals – some feather in the cap for a sixteen-year-old – and those full-time pros included Bobby Collins.

As Bobby played for Celtic – he was there from 1948 to 1958 and picked up all the honours in the Scottish game – my views on him are bound to be seen as prejudiced. Nonetheless, I really do believe that, among all the figures acknowledged as having contributed to Leeds' rise under Don Revie, Bobby has not been given the praise he deserved. He was arguably the most influential player in Leeds United's history.

The facts concerning Leeds' transformation when Bobby was there, and the personal honours he achieved at the time, speak for themselves. When Leeds bought him from Everton for £25,000 in March 1962 – twelve months after Don Revie's appointment as manager – they were in a seemingly hopeless situation at the foot of the Second Division. Bobby was thirty-one, and as implied by Everton's decision to release him, he was generally looked upon as past his best. This was not a view shared by Bobby himself; according to Don, he had initially baulked at the idea of stepping out of the First Division and, in fact, within a few weeks of joining Leeds, he asked for a transfer. But the challenge of proving himself in such a difficult situation as the one that existed at Elland Road then, gripped Bobby to the point where it represented almost a personal crusade.

Bobby was a midfield player who could do virtually everything. He was only 5ft 4ins tall and weighed little more than 10 stone but he dominated almost every match – physically, mentally and technically. He was very much the general, and his leadership qualities were especially necessary with all the young players Leeds were bringing into the team. Bobby did much to stop Leeds being relegated in that 1961–62 season. They finished fifth in the Second Division in 1963, the year I came to Elland Road, won the title in 1964, finished second in the championship in 1965, and also reached the final of the FA Cup that year, all with Bobby playing a captain's part. His role was recognised when he was chosen as Footballer of the Year in 1965 and recalled to the Scotland team after a six-year absence.

As I have said, I reaped the benefit of his influence when I came into the team in 1966 because they were on such a high.

Bobby was a strange person in some ways. He was very aggress-ive and confrontational – even to his own team-mates or those who professed to be close to him. Sometimes, you were tempted to suggest that he was capable of starting a row in an empty house. In recent years I have played in a few charity matches with him for the Leeds United former players team, and even in his sixties, he still showed a propensity for getting into fights. Forget the fact that he was hardly built like a giant, when he was riled – a situation that could be sparked by literally anything – he was not a man to mess with. Bobby attributed this aspect of his game to the general macho nature of professional football in his impressionable development years. 'It was a hard game in those days,' he would say, the sub-text being that if players did not learn to look after themselves, they would go under. I remember him talking about the first time he played against Tommy Docherty when he was with Everton and Docherty was with Arsenal. The Doc was one of his closest friends but, according to Bobby, this counted for nothing during the game. When they challenged each other for the ball near the touchline, Bobby found himself being propelled by the Doc towards row Z of the stand. Thus Bobby was brought up in football with what he described as a 'kill or be killed' mentality.

To an extent, the respect he had from the younger players at Leeds was based not just on his skill and his record in the game, but also on the fear factor. Whenever he instructed us to do something, we would jump. As soon as you saw his finger go up, pointing at someone, you knew that person was in trouble.

I got on well with him although I was left in no doubt that this could change dramatically if he ever had cause to feel that I had let him down. One of my most embarrassing experiences at Leeds was when, at fifteen or sixteen, I was in Bobby's team for pre-season training. There were four teams in all, each comprising eight or ten players. Points were awarded for our performances in various fitness exercises and the sessions were extremely competitive. As I was regarded as one of the best runners at the club, Bobby felt that victory for the team in the cross-country race – and with it a score of 10 points – was virtually a foregone conclusion. The only threat came from Jim Storrie, the Scottish striker bought from Airdrie in 1962. Sure enough, half a mile from the end, Jim and I were at the front; it was between him and me. I felt I had loads of power in reserve but as I was thinking of unleashing it, Jim said, 'Eddie, we don't need to race. If we stay together, we will both get the ten points.' I fell for it hook, line and sinker – how naive can you get? About 100 yards from the line, Jim, a real character with a tremendous sense of humour, sprinted flat out to win. Bobby was not amused. When he heard what had happened, he strode over to me and gave me a cuff around the head, like a father admonishing a naughty child. That tells you something about how much winning meant to him.

This clash was mild compared with the ones he had with other players. Take his altercations with big Jack Charlton. Don Revie often recounted the story of a half-time row between Jack and Bobby over a mistake Jack made in the first half of a tour match against AS Roma in the 1962 close season. While the pair were arguing in the dressing room, Jack decided to take a cold shower. Bobby tore after him, punches were thrown and Don had to dash into the shower cubicle, in his suit, to separate them.

Another favourite Collins–Charlton anecdote among Leeds insiders concerns the team's stay at a Harrogate hotel on the eve of a match against Burnley in March 1965. Jack knocked on Bobby's door and threw a jug of water over him, and Bobby, in chasing Jack down the corridor to get his own back, accidentally put his arm through a glass door. Bobby had to be taken to hospital and, having had sixteen stitches inserted into the wound, it seemed doubtful to say the least that he would play. But, according to Don, who had not been in the hotel when the mishap occurred and did not find out about it until the following morning, Bobby begged him for the chance to atone.

Don recalled, 'I finally gave in, and to protect the injury, Les Cocker used so much bandage on Bobby's arm that it was almost twice the size of his other arm and impossible for him to bend it.' But Bobby had an outstanding game, scoring two goals and making two others in a 5–1 win that lifted Leeds to the top of the First Division. 'When he came into the dressing room afterwards,' Don said, 'he was covered in mud, and blood was dripping through the bandage on his arm and on to the floor. He just grinned at me and said, "There you are – I told you I would not let you down."'

If anything, Bobby's relationship with Billy Bremner, who was of a similarly diminutive build and could be described as Bobby's apprentice, was even more highly charged. Billy had joined the club in 1959 after leaving school in Stirling and broken into the team the following year, aged seventeen. He was also a dominating personality who seemed to thrive on aggro. He was not scared of anybody. Even in those days, he was no shrinking violet when it came to asserting himself, so he and Bobby clearly had cause to look upon each other as kindred spirits.

When they were on opposite sides in training matches, a situation encouraged by the Leeds management in order to ensure that such games were as competitive as possible, they looked more like enemies than friends. Billy was fond of recalling the time when he beat Bobby with a cheeky dummy, which made the other players laugh. Billy had not known it was Bobby – he had his back to the captain – but he was made well aware of the dangers of denting Bobby's pride on the next occasion he was in possession. As Billy said, 'He came in with a tackle that nearly killed me.'

When I watched them in opposition for the first time, I could not believe my eyes. They were kicking lumps out of each other. I thought there was always an edge to their relationship, just as there was an edge to the relationship between the two of them and John Giles when John arrived from Manchester United in 1963. While they all admired and respected each other, there was something in their personalities that made it important to them to be seen as the top dog.

Such training-ground sparks are nothing new in professional football, of course. It's a game in which emotions run high, as Leeds fans saw in 2000–01 with the astonishing bust-up between Bradford City's Stuart McCall and Andy Myers during the 6–1 win over our Yorkshire neighbours at Elland Road. While that was obviously taking things a bit far, this is a game in which some needle among team-mates is only to be expected.

I had one direct experience of this with goalkeeper Gary Sprake. It came about as a result of Peter Lorimer and myself breaking clear of the defenders in front of Gary in a training match and, with only him to beat, milking the situation for all it was worth by teasing him with dummies and feints. I was the one who eventually put the ball past him and Gary, upset at having the mickey taken out of him, responded with a head-butt that left me with a gashed nose. Among others with painful memories of what it was like to light Gary's notoriously short fuse was his goalkeeping colleague, David Harvey. During one argument between them, Gary was so riled that he lifted David off his feet and somehow managed to hang him on a dressing-room peg. Still, in any confrontation between Gary and Bobby Collins, there could only have been one winner.

I would say that if any one man was responsible for influencing the players' ideas on how the game should be played, it was Bobby, so it was perhaps unsurprising that Leeds should be looked upon as an over-physical team. I think Bobby took the view that, with the players we had then, we were never going to get out of the Second Division on skill. Instead of playing our way out, we were going to have to claw our way out.

I have to admit that as a young player watching matches from the stands, some of our tackling in those days caused me to cringe. I would think, 'How are they being allowed to get away with this?' Deep down, even Don was embarrassed by it, as he confided to me when he was no longer connected with the club. We were talking about the old days when he said, 'Eddie, even I used to wince at our approach.'

Having gained the reputation as an over-physical team, and therefore established this as a guideline for the approach of other teams against us, Leeds found it difficult to go the other way. Therefore, while the quality of our players improved when we reached the First Division in 1964, our matches became ever more fractious.

I think that our approach then has to be put into the perspective of English football in general. Almost every team had a core of hardness and abrasiveness; you knew before you went on to the field that someone would try to kick you, and you were rarely proved wrong. One or two teams were more interested in kicking you than in playing football. Those were the days when a player would clog an opponent in the first minute, and then try to dissuade the referee from taking action against him by reminding the official that it was his first foul. It is amazing how many times players were able to get away with this.

One factor that helped change this mood and bring the emphasis on to skill again was possibly the lead given by Brazil's 1970 World Cup-winning team and then the Johan Cruyff-inspired total football of the Ajax and Dutch national teams. It cannot be merely coincidental that at the time those fabulous Brazilian stars – Pele, Rivelino, Tostao, Gerson and Jairzinho – were making such a big impact on millions of football lovers throughout the world, Don Revie took the decision to take his players 'off the leash' (his words) and give them greater scope to express their creative talents.

But up to the start of the 1970s, and for a while afterwards, a lot of matches in Britain resembled open warfare and you just accepted this as part of the game. John Giles, who eventually took over from Bobby as Leeds' midfield general and also inherited his role of giving the team its ruthless competitive edge, is very enlightening on the subject:

You had to establish a reputation that would make people think twice about messing with you. I felt that Bobby Collins sometimes created a bit more space because of that, because people [the opposition] were wary of him. I have certainly done things on a football field that I am embarrassed about now but one has to put them into the football climate that existed then. It was a different game then, much more physical than it is today – vicious even – and people like Bobby and myself were targets. Before teams played against us, the first thing they'd say in the dressing room was, 'Get hold of these guys – get stuck into them and put them out of the game.' Now you either took it or you responded to it, and Bobby and I responded to it. Nothing would have suited us better than for everybody to go out and play fair, to give us space and not kick us. But it didn't work that way and you had to get respect in the sense that people could not clog you without knowing they would be clogged back. People might say, 'Oh, that's not right – it's not sporting,' but that's the way it was, a fact of life.

When I look back on what the game was like then, one of my most vivid memories is of the great Dave Mackay marking me in a Leeds–Derby match in the late 1960s. The players had to change ends before the kick-off and as Mackay and I walked past each other, he grinned and held out his hand. I thought, 'What a nice guy.' He was still grinning as we shook hands, and he muttered, 'Eddie, if you try and take the mickey out of me today, I will break both your legs.'

Another image that sums it up is that famous photograph from a Leeds – Tottenham match, of Mackay grabbing Billy Bremner by his shirt collar.

That sort of thing was not for me. I was just not made that way. I expressed my passion, my competitive instincts, in other ways. At the same time, I could not help but admire Bobby Collins and Dave Mackay because their aggression was allied to fantastic ability and, equally important, they took on so much responsibility in trying to get good performances out of the players around them, not just themselves.

I had to wait a long time to play with Bobby in the Leeds first team. By the time I had broken into the team, in January 1966, he was out of action having suffered a fractured thigh three months earlier in an Inter-Cities Fairs Cup tie against Torino in Italy. When we did play together in the 1966–67 season, it was for a handful of matches only and at the end of that season, he left the club. Even so, I could well appreciate how others would have been helped by him. One notable example was Albert Johanneson, my predecessor as Leeds' first-choice outside-left. Albert, a very talented footballer (and a very likeable person), was not the strongest of characters. Bobby was probably able to get more out of him than anyone else at the club could have done.

Most professional footballers can look back and see where they might have come close to taking a wrong turning and ended up not making the most of themselves. I was no different, especially in my early days as a professional when I was adjusting to having a lot more time on my hands. We generally trained in the mornings only and, not being interested in much outside football, I tended to get quite bored. Jimmy and I still laugh over the memory of our attempts to learn to play the guitar. After just a few days, the guitars we bought were stashed away in a cupboard and our musical ambitions were forgotten.

After training, most of the players would spend the afternoons in a local snooker hall; and none of the members of the younger brigade were immune from doing stupid things. Peter Lorimer, for example, bought an old Austin Westminster car from full-back Willie Bell and drove it around – or rather attempted to drive it around – for some time without having passed his driving test. This created all manner of awkward situations for the lads who mixed with him socially, including me. One day when Peter was attempting to park the car outside my digs, he went straight into a beautiful MG sportscar that belonged to a middle-aged man making a visit to a neighbour. The guy was almost in tears because the car was brand new – he had just taken delivery of it.

We got into numerous situations of this kind with Peter. It is no secret that he liked gambling and that his betting habit ultimately caused him major problems. It could easily have been the same with me. I also liked a wager and by the time I was about nineteen, it was getting out of hand. I was in the bookmakers almost every day and it was not unusual for me to lose most of my wages and have to ask Linda for the money to pay for my digs. For Linda, the final straw was when I reneged on a promise to keep out of the bookies. We had a major bust-up and she told me that if I did not stop, she would break off our relationship. That brought me to my senses.

The case of Albert Johanneson remains one the most poignant examples of how a footballer can mess up his life. He joined Leeds in 1961, having come over from his native South Africa on a three-week trial. He was a wonderful player for Leeds when the club were in the Second Division. Some of the things he did with the ball in training took the breath away. Quite apart from the chances he created, he was our joint top scorer when we won the Second Division title in 1964 and the following season he became the first black player to appear in an FA Cup final (Leeds' 2–1 defeat by Liverpool). It was some success story, given that English football was such a big culture shock for him. When he first came to Leeds, Albert, having been conditioned to apartheid in South Africa, believed that he would not be allowed in the team bath with the white players. He was subjected to a lot of heavy tackles, not to mention racial abuse.

This is where the strong leadership of Bobby Collins was good for him. But it is widely acknowledged that Albert, for all his ability, still found it increasingly difficult to handle the pressure of the big First Division matches. As the expectations of Leeds increased, he seemed to undergo a complete personality change, becoming as quiet and introverted as he was previously boisterous and outgoing.

Things went from bad to worse for him as he struggled with alcoholism. Following his move from Leeds to York in 1970 and his retirement in 1972, he lost his house and possessions. With his wife having left him and taken their two children abroad, he lived in squalor with his brother, Trevor. In 1995, at the age of fifty-three, he was found dead in a Leeds tower block.

To the other Leeds players, one of the first signs of his reliance on drink had come in a match against Stoke in the 1966–67 season. Don Revie always kept a bottle of whisky in the dressing room for Bobby Collins, who had long been in the habit of taking a small swig of the hard stuff before a match as a kind of psychological performance-booster. Albert, who was substituted at half-time in that match and remained in the dressing room when we went out for the second half, got his hands on it. By the time we came back into the dressing room after the match, he had drunk the rest of the bottle and was comatose.

When I was Leeds manager, he would sometimes come to visit me at the ground. He would tell me that he wanted to start training again, but could not afford to buy any boots. I would give him all the equipment he needed,but I always knew that he really wanted it so that he could sell it and use the money to buy drink.

It was difficult not to be moved by the story of Albert's decline. One day when Linda came to pick me up at the ground and we spotted Albert by the main entrance, we gave him a lift into town.

During the journey, Albert talked about all the things that had gone wrong in his life. I'd heard it so many times that I had become emotionally immune to it, but it had a big effect on Linda. By the time Albert left us, tears were rolling down her cheeks like a waterfall.

Any problems I have had, either professional or personal, pale into insignificance when compared to those of Albert Johanneson. This is something I keep telling myself when I look back on my Leeds playing career.

3

WHAT MIGHT
HAVE BEEN

O N the face of it, I have a playing record that anyone would
be proud of. From January 1966 to May 1984, when I played
my last match against Charlton, I made 561 full first-team appearances for Leeds, including 441 in the League. For eight of those
years, I was in one of the most consistently successful sides in
Britain since the war and all but the last couple of years of my
career were spent in the top division.

When I was at my peak, some people handed me the ultimate
compliment of comparing me with the great George Best. I gained
two championship medals, FA Cup and League Cup winner's
medals and two in the Inter-Cities Fairs Cup. I played in three FA
Cup finals, a European Cup final, a Cup-Winners' Cup final and
was capped by Scotland. It seems hard to believe that I played
regular first-team football until the age of thirty-six, given that
when I was in my mid twenties I was on the point of retirement
through injury. The other distinction was the award of an MBE
in 1983. But I always felt a measure of disappointment over my
record.

The fact is that from the very start of my professional career at
Leeds, I was never 100 per cent fit. In some people's eyes, that
will have made my achievements all the more remarkable, but I
have not found it easy to look upon it in that way. My overriding
attitude – which may stem from the way my father kept making
me aware of things I could improve upon as a boy – is that I had
the ability to do better.

At the risk of coming across as a manic depressive, I also have mixed feelings about some of my so-called greatest performances. The individual display for which I am best remembered was the one against Chelsea in the 1970 FA Cup final when I had the honour of being given the man of the match award. People described it as arguably the best individual display at Wembley since Stanley Matthews steered Blackpool to an FA Cup final victory over Bolton in 1953. Yet my pride in it is overshadowed by the fact that Leeds did not win the trophy and therefore the performance counted for nothing.

Throughout my whole Leeds career, the players' treatment room at Elland Road was virtually my second home. Brian Clough once said, 'If Eddie Gray was a racehorse, he would have been shot long ago.' Some of my team-mates, who took a dim view of Clough's confrontational style, objected to the remark. Despite the nature of his tongue-in-cheek verbal digs at players, I cannot say that I was happy about it either. I challenged him, pointing out that as someone whose own career had been destroyed by an injury when he was twenty-seven, he should have shown greater sensitivity. Still, he did have a point – I was not able to play any competitive matches for him during his controversial forty-four-day spell as Leeds manager.

Countless newspaper and magazine articles have drawn attention to this aspect of my career. A typical comment in one of the record books on Leeds United is: 'His career was interrupted by a succession of injuries that would have prompted a lesser man to quit the game long before he did.'

One of the most frustrating periods for me was during the 1970–71 season. A broken ankle sustained against Ipswich in December put me out of action until April. Then in the match against Southampton that month I started to experience major problems with an old shoulder injury. The shoulder had originally been dislocated, but had stood up well enough to prompt the club to take the gamble of delaying an operation. Even when I was out of the team with the ankle injury, it was felt I could afford to wait until the close season. However, the ligaments holding the shoulder became increasingly slack and the decision rebounded heavily on me. In the game against Southampton Les Cocker had to come on to the pitch to manipulate the shoulder back into its socket no less than three times. The following month, the shoulder went while I was playing for Scotland against Northern Ireland at Hampden – I slipped on the greasy surface, trying to evade a challenge from George Best – and yet again in the Fairs Cup final first leg against Juventus in Turin, which was abandoned because of torrential rain. I played no part in the replay a couple of days later, which resulted in a 2–2 draw, nor in the return leg at Elland Road. The 1–1 draw there meant Leeds clinched one of the greatest victories in their history on the away goals rule.

However, these mishaps were minor compared with the problems I experienced with my left thigh. They started when I was sixteen, flaring up in a reserve match at home to Sheffield Wednesday towards the end of the 1964–65 season. Despite four operations, the problems were never properly solved.

The thigh started to trouble me after training on the day before the Sheffield Wednesday game, when Mick Bates and I were spending the afternoon at Doncaster races, but it was only a slight niggle and I did not think anything more about it. The muscle felt quite tight during the game and near the end, while I was taking a corner, I suddenly felt a sharp pain. The injury was diagnosed as a slight muscle tear, but instead of taking a complete rest to give it a proper chance to heal, I tried to keep going. Four days later, I attempted to play for the youth team and, not surprisingly, caused the tear to get worse.

Even then, I kept trying to work on it in training. In order to strengthen the leg, one of the exercises I did involved standing in the communal bath with a medicine ball, and using the foot to lift it out of the water. Needless to say, that did not help matters; in the circumstances, it was probably the worst thing I could have done.

I spent quite a lot of time in water. One day, at 9.30 in the morning, Les Cocker told me to sit in a hot herbal salt bath and not get out until he instructed me to do so. Unfortunately, Les forgot about me – equally unfortunately, I did not have the good sense to realise this. I had been in that bath for something like two hours before Les gave me the nod to get out, and by that time, certain parts of my body felt as if they were on fire. Let's just say that I was due to meet Linda for lunch that day, and when she saw me walking towards her, she asked, 'Why are you walking like an old cowboy?' I was John Wayne for two days. We still laugh about it although there is not much else about my thigh problems that I find easy to smile about.

In the end, the muscle calcified and my flexibility became increasingly restricted as a consequence. Moreover, the surgery I underwent to remove the calcification had a similar effect because it made the muscle shorter. No matter how much time I devoted to stretching exercises – and I think I must have qualified for a place in the *Guinness Book of Records* in that department – my ability to use the leg as I wanted and thus to play on full power was restricted.

It was not too bad if I ran in a straight line without the ball, as I proved one day when Paul Madeley challenged me to a race over half the Elland Road pitch. Paul was acknowledged as the quickest Leeds player and was so sure he would beat me that he gave me a two-yard start. The race was taken so seriously that Don Revie and Les Cocker became involved as the judge and starter. Peter Lorimer and I ran a book on it. I think I surprised a lot of the players, not to mention myself, by winning.

However, when it came to the sudden changes of pace and direction in a game, I always felt I had to be careful. Quite often, if I was up against a quick defender, it was a case of trying to beat him more by wrong-footing him than through pace, and then letting the ball go as early as possible. I also had to be careful about how I hit the ball. I deliberately avoided having too many shots, especially when I would need to strike the ball hard to score.

I could not train as much as the other players, because of the number of times I broke down. I occasionally played in matches without doing any training at all. Some matches were better than others for me. But there was no way of knowing if I would last the full ninety minutes. I would be OK for a couple of weeks, and then it would suddenly go again.

I have to admit to getting quite sad when I look through the details of all the Leeds matches and teamsheets, season by season, and note the number of blank spaces alongside my name.

By the time Jimmy Armfield succeeded Clough as manager in October 1974, I had made just eight league appearances in fourteen months and it had been decided that I would have to call it a day. Still only twenty-six, and with another seven months to run on my contract, I was under the impression that once Leeds received their insurance money from the Football League, I would be paid up and allowed to try to establish some kind of career elsewhere.

It was while I was in that state of limbo that Jimmy asked if I could help with the coaching of the junior players. Then, having seen me taking part in small-sided training games, he suggested that I might be able to help the youngsters further by playing with them in some reserve matches. It went so well that Jimmy put me back in the first team. I made my comeback against Cardiff in the FA Cup on 4 January 1975 and then played in the 2–1 win over West Ham on 11 January, my first competitive matches for seven months. I went on to play in eighteen of our last twenty-four league and FA Cup games. From then on, I continued to miss a fair number of matches, but was certainly more at ease with my situation than I had been previously.

One reason for my new lease of life – in addition to the rest I'd had while waiting to be put in the knacker's yard – concerned my experience. By that stage in my career, I had learned to work around my thigh problem. To an extent, I epitomised the way in which players can compensate for any lack of physical power with what's in their minds. As Graeme Souness once said, 'As you get older, you find that the first two yards are in your head.'

For my last three seasons as a professional footballer, I was also helped by being used in roles that were relatively easy for me. As far as my number of league appearances is concerned, it is perhaps significant that I had my best season in 1980–81 when the manager, Allan Clarke, switched me to left-back and I played in 38 of the

42 games. The following season I played in 31 league matches and in my last full season before retirement as a player, I played in 21.

One of the big advantages of operating at the back is that you tend to get more time on the ball, and equally important, all the play is in front of you. Interestingly, one of the greatest matches Billy Bremner ever played for Leeds was when he was deployed as a sweeper in a Uefa Cup win at Hibernian. Billy, accustomed to the frenetic action in midfield, found this deep role a doddle. His tricks on the ball verged on the outrageous, and he looked as if he was playing in a practice match. I, too, thoroughly enjoyed myself when I played as a sweeper – again under the management of Allan Clarke – in a 4–1 win at Aston Villa. I found being at left-back similarly undemanding. In normal circumstances, I would not have chosen that position because I have always been a great believer in players stretching themselves.

Although I had a good reason for missing so many matches the fact that it occurred when Leeds were at the height of their success under Don Revie hardly makes it easier for me accept. The season in which I made the highest number of league appearances under Don was the 1968–69 campaign, when we won the championship for the first time and I played in 33 of the 42 matches. I made 32 appearances in 1967–68; 30 in 1969–70; 18 in 1970–71; 26 in 1971–72; 17 in 1972–73; and only eight in 1973–74, when we won the title for the second time. All this, though, was just part of the picture. Leeds invariably had a lot of matches in the other competitions and as it was always difficult for me to play two matches a week, the number of midweek games I missed was high. I believe this was the major factor in my being capped only twelve times for Scotland.

There were times when I felt as if I was almost cheating on the club. I know that Don was occasionally as frustrated as I was about it. The set-up of the Leeds team was similar to that of the Manchester United team of today. We, too, played to a 4-4-2 system and the roles of Peter Lorimer and myself as the wide midfielders-cum-wingers who provided the attacking width were not unlike those of David Beckham and Ryan Giggs. Natural left-footed players are not as common as the right-footed ones, and therefore I think Don looked upon me as being important in helping to ensure our team was properly balanced. We discussed it a few times, and although he did his best to encourage me, there was little doubt in my mind that he wanted me to play more games. The impression I got was that he expected greater things from me – greater than it was in my power to deliver.

I was realistic enough to accept that if my fitness problems continued he would have to look for players who could provide an alternative. It was no secret that one of the people he would have loved to sign for Leeds was Dave Thomas, the winger who played for Burnley from 1967 to 1972 and who was brought into the England team by Don in 1975, when Thomas was at QPR. Thomas was a naturally right-sided player, but he could also operate on the left.

Strange as it might seem, speculation linking Leeds with other wingers did not bother me. Obviously, all players are conscious of the possibility of injury wrecking their careers, and as I got married at twenty and had three children by the time I was twenty-four, it did not bear thinking about as far as I was concerned. Even so, without wishing to appear conceited, I had so much faith in my ability that even when Leeds did sign someone who might have been perceived as a potential replacement for me, my attitude was, 'Well, if you are fit, he [Revie] is going to have to find a place for you.'

One of the other wingers at Leeds during the early part of my first-team career was Mike O'Grady, who had been signed from Huddersfield in October 1965. Mike, who also suffered through injuries, was an excellent player – very quick and direct. Indeed, in 1969, he was recalled by the England team for his first cap for six years. But although Mike played for England at outside-left, I never felt threatened by his presence at the club. As it turned out, I was given preference over him for the No. 11 spot, if fit, and he played most of his games for the club either on the right or through the middle.

Far from merely hoping that I would continue as a first choice,

40

it is something I expected. My attitude never changed, even towards the end of my career when a lot of players of my age might have accepted that they were past their best and that the time was right for them to be pushed into the background. I remember Jimmy Armfield pulling me aside at the end of the 1976–77 season and confiding, 'Eddie, I am going to sign Arthur Graham [the Aberdeen outside-left].'

'That's great, Jimmy,' I replied. 'He's a good player. But what has this got to do with me?'

'He plays at outside-left, the same as you,' Jimmy pointed out.

'Well, Jimmy,' I said, 'it doesn't worry me. If I'm fit, I think you're going to have to play me somewhere.'

I like to think Jimmy knew me well enough not to look upon this as arrogance or presumptuousness. In any event, I was proved right; Arthur's presence at the club made no difference at all to my position.

Fuelled by the enthusiasm that Don Revie showed for me, my confidence was such that, even when I came to Leeds at fifteen, and throughout my time in their youth and reserve teams, I had no doubts that I would get a chance to show what I could do in the first team. Jim Storrie, one of the experienced full-time pros, challenged me on this. 'I hear you've been saying that it won't be long before you're in the team,' he said. He caught me offguard because I honestly could not remember saying that to anyone at Elland Road, not even to Jimmy Lumsden, and the last thing I wanted was anyone there to think I had got too big for my boots. But I did think it.

I was less sure about my ability to stay in the team, which is the hardest part for any young player. People view you in a different way after you have made your mark in the first team – their expectations inevitably get higher. It puts a lot of pressure on players, and I have lost count of the number of them who have found it difficult to cope and faded. But once I had made my debut, I was convinced that this would not happen to me. Don Revie made it perfectly clear that he felt this way, too. Immediately after my debut, with everybody praising me for my performance, a lot of managers in his position might have been tempted to play it down to ensure that I kept my feet on the ground and that I would not be subjected to ultra-high expectations in my subsequent games. But he had no compunction about telling the media, 'This lad can play a lot better than that.' The match was against Sheffield Wednesday at Elland Road on 1 January 1966, sixteen days before my eighteenth birthday. I was drafted into the side in midfield as a result of John Giles failing a fitness test on a thigh injury.

It was an ideal first match for me, in view of the gulf between the two teams in the table and the quality of the players I had supporting me – Gary Sprake in goal; Paul Reaney, Jack Charlton, Norman Hunter and Willie Bell at the back; Jimmy Greenhoff, Billy Bremner and Mike O'Grady in midfield; and Alan Peacock and Jim Storrie up front. At no time can I remember feeling nervous. Don Revie told me, 'Relax and play your normal game,' and that's what I did. It really was as simple as that. The afternoon was made extra special for me by the fact that Frank, then eleven, had travelled from Glasgow to see the match and stay with me over the weekend – and I scored the first goal and Leeds went on to win 3–0.

Coincidentally, Frank also scored on his full debut – a 4–0 win over Crystal Palace in April 1973 – having made his first Leeds appearance as a substitute in a 2–0 defeat by Leicester two months earlier.

One of the things that I remember about my first match was the weather. The report of the match in the *Yorkshire Evening Post* stated that this was 'not the right sort of day for Gray's debut,' pointing out that, 'heavy overnight and morning rain [had left] the pitch very heavy, and a stiff breeze made things generally unpleasant.' But it was far from unpleasant for me in the thirty-second minute when Jimmy Greenhoff provided me with a superb through ball and I hit it past the Wednesday keeper, Ron Springett, with my left foot from about twenty-five yards. I was happy with my general performance, although like Don Revie, I knew that I was capable of going to higher levels.

In terms of high expectations, the newspapers put even more

pressure on me. The most glowing report of my debut appeared in the *Yorkshire Post*, in which Richard Ulyatt wrote:

> Gray played with the flair of a born footballer. John Charles in the late forties and Denis Law in the mid fifties looked no better than Gray when I saw them make their first appearances [for Leeds and Huddersfield]. If this boy has the luck all footballers need – luck to avoid serious injury – and is not overwhelmed by the head-turning praise of himself he is likely to read and hear, he should become a brilliant footballer.

His point about the dangers of my head being turned became considerably less pertinent in March when I made my next appearances, in two First Division matches against Blackpool in the space of three days. The first of those matches was at home. I came into the side in place of Billy Bremner, and while I did not do badly, Leeds were well below their best and lost 2–1. The defeat signalled the end of our championship chances.

The match was memorable for the performance of Alan Ball. Winger Leslie Lea might have scored Blackpool's goals, but Ball, the closest equivalent to Bremner in English football then, was the real star of the show. His display was remarkable, as the Leeds crowd acknowledged with the standing ovation they gave him on the final whistle. Ball was also outstanding in the second match, scoring the goal that gave Blackpool a 1–0 win and the distinction of being the first team to do the league double over Leeds for three years.

Ball, who went on to help steer England to their World Cup triumph that summer, was a major target for the big clubs, Leeds among them. For a while, I think we were looked upon as the favourites to sign him, but shortly after the World Cup final, he elected to go to Everton where he formed an outstanding midfield partnership with Colin Harvey and Howard Kendall. A midfield partnership involving Ball, Bremner and Giles would not have been bad either. Of all the players from other clubs who could have made Leeds an even better team during those wonderful Revie years, I would put Ball at the top of the list. As Liverpool's manager Bill Shankly once said, 'If Leeds had signed Ball, then the rest of us might just as well have packed it in for ten years.'

It was against Everton that I made my next appearance that season, as a substitute for John Giles twenty minutes from the end of a 4–0 win over the Merseyside club at Elland Road on 16 April. The following week, Leeds, having marked their first season in the European arena with Inter-Cities Fairs Cup wins over Torino, SC Leipzig, Valencia and Ujpest Dozsa, decided to rest Peter Lorimer for the semi-final first leg against Real Zaragoza (even though he was our leading scorer) and put me in his place.

Although we lost 1–0, the same team went into action in the return leg, and recorded a 2–1 win, making the score 2–2 on aggregate. Peter was back for the replay at Elland Road, at my expense, but I suspect this was one contest that he would not have minded missing. Before the match, Don Revie, believing that Real Zaragoza were unhappy in heavy conditions, got the local fire brigade to pour enough water on to the pitch to turn it almost into a quagmire. It was typical of Don to think of something like that, but on this occasion his scheming came unstuck. Real, far from being unhappy in deep mud, seemed to relish it. They hit two goals in the opening ten minutes and went on to win 3–1.

So Leeds, having suffered the agonising experience of being championship runners-up and beaten FA Cup finalists the previous season, again ended up empty-handed. There were more disappointments of this nature to come. It was not until the 1968 League Cup final victory over Arsenal that the first trophy was won, and even after that breakthrough, it could be argued that we did not claim as much silverware as they should have done under Don Revie's management. Nonetheless, it was a great feeling to start every season knowing that we were almost certain to be among the leading contenders in every competition. It was marvellous to be repeatedly involved in the race for major honours. It was also a great feeling to sit in the Leeds dressing room and think about the standard of all the others players sitting there. I always felt that there wasn't a team who could beat us – we could only beat ourselves.

It was in the season after my debut, 1966–67, that I became established in the side. The season after that, with Albert Johanneson fading from the first-team scene, I settled down in his No. 11 spot.

I always looked upon myself as a wing-half – or midfield player to give it its modern name – and found it hard to be totally satisfied with playing out wide because it was more difficult to get into the game from that position. But I had far less cause for complaint than most other wide men. There was tremendous movement in the Leeds team, which meant that I had plenty of opportunities to interchange positions with other players. Indeed, whenever I look at videos of my matches, I am struck by the amount of time I spent on the ball in other areas. In any event, on the premise that it suited Leeds best to have me wide – to stretch the opposition and give us more space in which to exploit our skill – the saving grace for me was that because of Leeds' domination of most matches, and the players' passing ability, I was still able to get a lot of possession in that area.

On my side of the field, the link-up play involving Terry Cooper, Norman Hunter and myself prompted Les Cocker to describe us as the 'three-ringed circus'. He used to joke that we should be given a ball to ourselves. But it did not matter who was in possession or where – provided I made myself available for a pass, and a ball to me was the best option, it was rare that I did not get it. It was not unusual for even Peter Lorimer on the other flank to find me.

Moreover, the Leeds defenders looked upon me as an outlet, someone who could take the ball from them when they were under pressure and hold it long enough to give us a breather and get back into our team shape.

One player who did that superbly was the former Liverpool and England outside-left, John Barnes. I was interested to see what his former Liverpool captain, Alan Hansen, had to say about Barnes in his autobiography. Alan, now a successful TV pundit, was quite amusing on the subject. He wrote:

John was a key figure in the side because he could take on three or four defenders or at least hold the ball long enough to disrupt the opposition's attacking momentum and rhythm. He was great for me – he became my favourite passing target. If anything, I gave him too much of the ball. It was an easy option for me. It got to the stage where John got tired of it. I said to him, 'You have worked out how not to get the ball from me, haven't you?' He just smiled, and said, 'Too right I have.'

You can understand why Barnes generally did better for Liverpool than for England; in most matches, the England team did not have anywhere near as much of the ball as Liverpool did. At club level, he was fortunate to be in a team as strong as Liverpool, just as I was fortunate to be in a team like Leeds.

4

A TROPHY AT LAST

To appreciate why I thrived at Leeds in a way that I probably could not have done anywhere else, it is not enough to look just at the tremendous ability of the other players there. The fact that there were hardly any in the whole squad, let alone the team, who were not internationals helped, of course, but you also have to consider that the majority had joined Leeds from school and graduated through the youth and reserve teams. This is where I think any analysis of Leeds' success under the thirteen-year management of Don Revie has to begin.

In recent years, the advantages of having a youth set-up strong enough to produce groups of top-class players for first-team action have been best illustrated by Manchester United, through the part played by the likes of Phil and Gary Neville, Paul Scholes, Nicky Butt, David Beckham and Ryan Giggs in their championship success under Sir Alex Ferguson. One of those advantages is that, having been at Old Trafford from such an early age, the players have developed a strong sense of responsibility towards the club and each other. Another is that Sir Alex, having started his relationship with them at a stage in their lives when they were particularly impressionable, has had the scope to mould them and imbue them with the right professional habits. For all the wealth and fame those players have achieved, they have never lost sight of the principles that got them to that position. Sir Alex is not just their manager – he is something of a father-figure. So while he might not control their lives as much as he did when they were younger, he has continued to have a profound effect on them.

It is no secret that when Howard Wilkinson became Leeds manager, he set out to follow the Manchester United youth system blueprint as much as possible. Howard is passionate about youth development and Manchester United were his model. The high number of exciting youngsters coming through at Leeds has encouraged the view that we are on the verge of becoming the new Manchester United and that is very much a legacy of Howard's work in setting the ball rolling.

Manchester United were also the model for Don Revie. When Don took the step from player to player-manager at Leeds in March 1961, one of his first moves was to seek the advice of Matt Busby. Because of the impact of the Busby Babes on British football just a few years earlier, it was inevitable that Busby should stress the importance of Leeds trying to produce their own players, too, especially as they did not have much money to spend on established players in the transfer market. Following his meeting with Busby, Don persuaded the Leeds board to bring Maurice Lindley back to the club. Maurice had been sacked as first-team coach six months earlier, but Don felt he had been harshly treated and that he was just the person the club needed to revamp their youth system.

Having bought Bobby Collins to provide the playing staff with the guidance he was looking for, it was not long before Don started to build a young team around him. The first real sign of his willingness to give youngsters a first-team chance came in a match at Swansea in September 1962. Until then, the only regular first-team players who had been with the club since leaving school were Jack Charlton and Billy Bremner, then twenty-six and nineteen respectively. The number was increased to six at Swansea, with Gary Sprake (seventeen) making his second first-team appearance, and Paul Reaney (seventeen), Norman Hunter (eighteen) and Rodney Johnson (seventeen) being given their debuts. A few weeks after that game, which Leeds won 2–0, Peter Lorimer became Leeds' youngest-ever first-team player at fifteen years, 289 days

Above Mum with David (*right*) and me after a trip to Santa's grotto.

Left On holiday in Ayr with Dad and Mum, my brother David (*right*) and Uncle Peter.

Above Brother Frank and I showing our interest in football on another holiday.

Right David, my sister Carole, Frank and me (*back*) at home in Castlemilk.

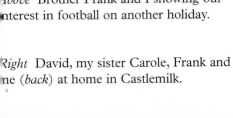

Looking confident (*back row, third from left*) in my primary school running team.

Looking even more confident (*front row, third from left*) in our football team.

Note the grubby knees, the telltale sign of my boyhood passion for playing football.

On holiday in Abroath with Dad and a lad who had joined one of our kickabouts.

The Leeds 1965–66 youth team – I'm in the back row, third from right, aged 17.

Above Celtic's Jimmy Johnstone doing what I loved to do in the 1967 World Club Championship.

Right Bobby Collins was the fellow Scot who made the biggest impression on me at Leeds.

Below Peter Lorimer and I were the Leeds wide boys'.

We celebrated our 1968 League Cup final win at London's Royal Garden Hotel.

Left to right: Jock Stein, Peter Lorimer, Billy Bremner, me and Don Revie after a friendly match against Celtic.

Above Battling for possession with Bobby Lennox during our 1970 European Cup semi-final against Celtic.

Right Trying to elude Peter Rodrigues when Scotland played Wales in 1971.

Shaking hands with the Duchess of Kent before the 1969 England v. Scotland clash at Wembley.

Linda and I announced our engagement in 1967.

Having a laugh with some nifty footwork at a media photo-call.

Back to the serious stuff against Crystal Palace.

old, when making his debut in a 1–1 draw against Southampton. Gary, Paul and Norman remained in the team, alongside Jack Charlton at centre-half, and were the main trailblazers for the other youngsters at the club.

The initial burst of encouragement created by their success led to a situation whereby there were as many as thirteen home-produced Leeds players among the seventeen who helped the club win the championship for the first time in 1969, and among the twenty-one who steered Leeds to the title in 1974.

Perhaps the best known of all Don's teams was the one with Gary Sprake or David Harvey in goal; Paul Reaney, Jack Charlton, Norman Hunter and Terry Cooper or Paul Madeley at the back; Peter Lorimer, Billy Bremner, John Giles and myself in midfield; and Mick Jones and Allan Clarke up front. Of these, only Giles, Jones and Clarke had been signed from other clubs. For obvious reasons, this was a big factor in helping Don to create a powerful family atmosphere at Elland Road.

In any discussion about our dressing-room culture in those days, I am instantly reminded of the peak winter months, when the young players would spend hours putting straw on the pitch after training on a Friday, to protect it from the ice and snow. We would spend the night in the players' lounge, where the training and coaching staff would give us bowls of hot soup and bacon sandwiches, and be up at the crack of dawn the next day to help take the straw off for the match. It was gruelling but we looked upon it as an adventure; and it helped bond us, and strengthen our emotional ties with the club.

One result of that bonding was our openness and honesty with each other – a vital ingredient in all successful teams. If you had a criticism about someone, it would be voiced openly, not behind the person's back. In most instances, we could say almost anything to each other, knowing that it would be taken in the right way and, most importantly, that it had been said for the benefit of the team.

The sense of unity among the Leeds players got to a lot of our opponents. If one of us was badly fouled, others would be almost falling over themselves in the rush to exact revenge on his behalf.

Another sign of our togetherness was the support given to the players on the ball through the positioning of other players and the information they would provide to help him make the right decision. Other teams could not believe the extent to which we all tried to look after each other. As some opposing players told me, 'Whatever happens on the field, your lot have the attitude that you are all in it together.'

On top of all this was Don's guidance as the 'family' head – the Leeds 'Godfather' as many pundits described him. He treated us exceptionally well. Our respect for him also arose from the warmth and loyalty he showed to the club's former players. Nobody who did what he considered to be a good job for Leeds United was forgotten by him.

While he was not as volatile as Sir Alex Ferguson, Don had a similarly intimidating aura. Norman Hunter, recalling the first and only time he was late for training, says, 'All Don did was to walk a couple of yards towards me and look at his watch – that really was all he did, and all he needed to do to make me feel bad about it.'

He had a very strong character and when he was angry about something, we were liable to be quite sensitive about doing or saying anything which might make the situation worse. He was a big man with big hands. I remember the hands because when he brought his fist down on a table – something that he often did when upset – the whole room seemed to reverberate. If we had not played well, the other warning signal for us was his habit of storming into the dressing room after the match, briefly combing his hair in the mirror and then going out again without saying a word. At times like that, the dressing room suddenly became quiet enough for you to hear a pin drop.

In team-talks, when addressing players who had displeased him, he had a habit of muttering, 'I'm going to need to get the cheque-book out' – meaning, of course, that if they could not do what he wanted, he would buy players who could. Despite the number of times he said it, occasionally in circumstances that made the remark seem farcical, it never totally lost its effect.

Suffice it to say that when he spoke, you listened. There was a good example of this during the Leeds match at Nottingham Forest at the City Ground in 1968, when the match was abandoned at half-time because of a fire in the main stand. We were listening to Don's interval team-talk so intently that most of us were completely oblivious to the wisps of smoke coming through the dressing-room door. Gary Sprake noticed but when he tried to draw Billy Bremner's attention to it, Billy told him, 'Shut up, Gary. The Boss is talking.'

As far as his relationship with his players was concerned, and especially those he had known as boys, some might well have described Don as something of a control freak. This aspect of his managerial style, which his critics attributed to insecurity, could be viewed as both a strength and a weakness. It certainly stood the players in good stead during the early part of their careers, when they needed strong guidance both on and off the field in order to acquire the right professional habits. Even as senior professionals, you could see the sense in his continuing in the same vein so as to ensure there was no complacency. But it is difficult to dispute that his reluctance to give us greater freedom of expression until the early 1970s could have been one of the reasons why we did not win as many trophies as we might have done.

The most notable manifestation of this side of Don was his attention to detail in his preparation for matches. He was always looking for things that could go wrong – hence his famous in-depth dossiers on the strengths and weaknesses of the opposition, and the extent to which he drew attention to the former. This knowledge was important to us, up to a point. But as his team became more experienced, it was generally felt, with some justification I have to admit, that we should be letting the opposition do all the worrying about us. The over-cautious vibes he gave out – highlighted by his superstitious nature – made it difficult to avoid the view that he was not as comfortable with the players as he should have been.

During matches, Don's fretting became something of a standing joke among those who spent the most time with him on the bench.

Terry Yorath used to say that when Don remarked that the team were too uptight, he would think, 'Looking at you, it's no wonder.'

Of course, it is easy to be wise after the event; nobody can be sure about what would have happened had Don been different. However, it is perhaps significant that when Don did make a conscious effort to be more relaxed, Leeds produced their best football.

Old habits die hard, and it was only to be expected that his proven methods of success at Leeds should be reproduced when he was England manager. This did not go down well with the stars from other clubs, many of whom felt they were being treated like schoolchildren. In addition to the dossiers, they were also irritated by having to spend so much of their spare time on international duty doing things as a group rather than as individuals. They took a particularly dim view of being subjected to his games of bingo and carpet bowls. All this was designed to create the right team spirit, and the players who had been brought up with his methods at Leeds inevitably took a different view of them.

The truth is that we would all have run through brick walls for him if he had wanted us to do so. Billy Bremner, referring to the number of times he and other players had their arms twisted to play in matches when not 100 per cent fit, summed it up perfectly when he said, 'It was typical of the gaffer [to get players to go through the pain barrier]. He could do things like that because the guys loved him.'

This was certainly no exaggeration in Billy's case; and the feelings were mutual. Of all the players raised as footballers by Don, Billy's relationship with him was the most remarkable and produced the most potent results. When Don was struck down by motor neurone disease, the illness that was to claim his life in May 1989, Billy appeared to be the player who was hit the hardest by it. Billy was very much Don's protégé. Such was the affinity between them that we used to describe him as Don's number two son (after Don's real one, Duncan). At the same time, Billy had a rebellious, independent streak that stamped him as the member of the Elland Road family who was the most difficult to control. He was the player who probably presented Don's biggest man-management challenge.

Don had been a player at Leeds for around twelve months when Billy arrived midway through the 1959–60 season. Billy joined the club with another Scottish schoolboy international, Tommy Henderson, a winger who stood out in those days as an even more exciting prospect. Both started in the youth team and as both missed their family and friends north of the border, they pledged that if they had not progressed to the reserves by the end of the season, they would return home. Billy got into the team with just three matches to go, so he stayed. Tommy went back to Scotland where he played for Hearts and St Mirren. Leeds actually brought him back in 1962, paying St Mirren a transfer fee of £1,500. I thought he was an excellent player, but Tommy made around two dozen league appearances for the club before being transferred to Bury three years later.

The early part of Billy's Leeds career was similarly uncertain. He was only seventeen when he started playing in the first-team. With Don at inside-right and Billy at outside-right, they played eleven matches together in the 1959–60 season, when Leeds were relegated to the Second Division, and seven the next season. Billy was outstanding and Don was enraptured by him. Thus, after Don was appointed player-manager in March 1961, his quest to keep him at the club in the face of offers from bigger clubs and Billy's increasing homesickness for Scotland, became top priority.

He even put his job on the line for Billy. Within a few months of becoming a manager, Don had been told by the Leeds board that the club had received a £25,000 offer for Billy from Everton and that, because of the financial position at Leeds, they would have to take it. Don told them that if Billy went, he would go, too.

In May 1962, Billy, by now desperate to go home, put in a written transfer request. The letter stated, 'I am begging the board to give me my transfer back to Scotland. I beg of you.' However, from that point, things started to get better for him.

During Leeds' summer tour of Italy, Don switched him from outside-right to midfield, which enabled him to get more involved in games – an important development for someone with Billy's assertive personality. Don, in trying to persuade Billy that he should stay at Leeds, enlisted the help of his Scottish-based girlfriend Vikky (who was to become his wife) and Alex Smith, the leading Scottish coach who was Billy's closest friend and confidant in the game there. The other factor in Billy's change of attitude was the signing of Bobby Collins to operate alongside him in the midfield area, and provide the experience and technical ability to take him and Leeds forward.

Billy became a master leader himself. He was without doubt one of the most inspiring players in the history of British football. With the possible exception of Bryan Robson, when he was the Manchester United and England captain, I cannot think of anyone I have seen who could lift a team as much as Billy could.

He often used to say that he 'didn't give a monkey's about anybody'. Reputations did not mean anything to him. The mind boggles at what some of the senior professionals in the First Division must have made of him in Leeds' first season back in the top flight in 1964–65. There was little First Division experience in the team and Leeds were generally expected to struggle to survive at this level. They gained the image of belligerent upstarts and Billy epitomised it more than anyone. A shrinking violet he wasn't. As he said, 'I never thought anybody was better than us, and I probably came across as a right cocky so and so. When we came up from the Second Division, most people thought we would go straight back down again. But in the first match, we had a 2–1 win at Aston Villa, after being a goal down; then we beat Liverpool [the reigning champions] 4–2 and it snowballed from there. After the tough matches away from home, the fans would be shouting abuse at us and I would actually be telling them to eff off. When you look back on it, you think, "Were you really like that? You're lucky you didn't get killed."'

Billy was a free spirit who worked on instinct. If Leeds were struggling in a game, he would think nothing of charging forward and playing almost like a centre-forward to change the situation. The high number of vital goals he scored for Leeds, particularly in the bigger matches, speaks for itself.

In that first season back in the First Division, it was typical of Billy that, despite his inexperience at the top level, he should get the late goal against Manchester United in the FA Cup semi-final replay that took us to our Wembley date against Liverpool. United were top of the League at the time. His ability as a big-occasion player was also seen in the final. Leeds were outplayed that day, but Billy was one of the few Leeds players who were not overawed by the occasion. It was appropriate that he should be the one to get the goal that unexpectedly put Leeds back on level terms after Roger Hunt's opener, and caused Liverpool to sweat before they finally got their noses in front again when Ian St John scored near the end of extra time.

Billy was the most extrovert of Don's players. Of all his outstanding performances, the one I remember best is the 7–0 win over Chelsea in 1967, when he set up three of the goals and scored one himself with an outrageous overhead kick that brought the house down.

I think it is fair to say that, in order to capitalise on this aspect of Billy's talents, Don allowed him greater leeway – off the field as well as on it – than he tended to give to others. Don never made any attempt to conceal his admiration of Billy, and Peter Lorimer had a good point when he said once, 'Billy would sometimes give the impression of thinking that Leeds United were all about Billy Bremner and ten others, and I'm not sure Don did not encourage him to think that way.'

Billy and Don had their fall-outs. The one best remembered by Leeds insiders occurred when Billy was late for the train journey to London on the eve of our match at West Ham during the Easter period in 1972, and only made it as a result of Don using his influence to get the train departure delayed. It had been arranged that we would all meet at Leeds Central Station, but instead of being there at the appointed time, Billy was asleep in a nearby hotel, having had a night out in the town. Fortunately, one of the players knew where he was and, after an unsuccessful attempt to reach Billy by phone, he was sent across to fetch him. We were all sitting in the dining car when Don came in with Billy behind him, looking suitably sheepish. Needless to say, Don was not happy. Usually, he played cards with Billy, Jack Charlton and Peter Lorimer on away trips, but on this occasion, he refused to join in and further emphasised his annoyance with Billy by going and sitting in another part of the carriage. Billy, now being teased about it by the other players, started to get belligerent.

'What's up with you lot?' he said. 'Do you think I won't be all right for you tomorrow? If I don't do it against West Ham, you can have a go at me then.'

Billy played a blinder and I didn't do badly either, scoring both our goals – one with the left foot, the other with the right – in a 2–2 draw.

'Thanks for that,' Billy said. 'You've got me off the hook with the gaffer.' As far as I know, Don never did take any action against Billy over his tardiness.

There was obviously a line with Don that Billy would not cross. For his part, I think Don appreciated that Billy's headstrong nature was one of his greatest strengths and that any attempts to rule him with an iron hand would have been counter-productive. For me, the way he handled Billy was great management.

Don's management ability was emphasised in a number of other ways. His appreciation of players' strengths and weaknesses was second to none. Among those who benefited from this more than most were Norman Hunter, who joined Leeds as an inside-forward but became one of the best central defenders in the country; Paul Reaney, who joined Leeds as a central defender but was turned into an England international right-back; and Terry Cooper, who had a similarly successful career as a left-back after starting at Leeds as an outside-left.

When it came to buying players to complement the ones Leeds had developed themselves, something that all clubs have to do no matter how productive their youth systems might be, his judgement was generally spot on. The ultimate example of this in my view was John Giles, who was signed from Manchester United for £33,000 in August 1963 as an outside-right. He succeeded Bobby Collins as Leeds' midfield general in the autumn of 1965 after Bobby fractured a thigh against Torino. I have already said that Bobby was probably the most important signing in Leeds' history, given the dire position of the club at the time, but when I look through all the great players I played with at Leeds, I would say that even he would have to be placed behind John.

Generally, the crucial department in any team is the midfield; the unit carries the greatest responsibility for linking the play between defence and attack and controlling the pace and pattern of a game. This particularly applies to the central area, as has been shown in recent years with the dynamic influence of Patrick Vieira and Emmanuel Petit in leading Arsenal to the championship and FA Cup double, and by Roy Keane at Manchester United.

In my day, no team had two central midfielders quite like Billy and John. This was not altogether great for me; their excellence meant that the opportunities for me to play as a central midfielder, the role to which I was best suited in my opinion, were limited. However, I couldn't quibble because, quite apart from what they had to offer the engine room of the side as individuals, Billy and John complemented each other perfectly. Of the two, I think that most of the other players would have singled out John as the key figure.

While Billy tended to play with his heart rather than his head (a heart that, it hardly needs to be said, was as big as Elland Road), it was the other way around with John. Billy was at his best when bursting forward into positions in or around the opposing box, whereas John, the more studious and calculating of the two, was essentially the playmaker. That is not to say that Billy was not an excellent passer of the ball. His speciality was the reverse pass – while running with the ball, he was brilliant at clipping it across his body in the opposite direction, without giving any indication of this by his body shape. I have never seen anyone master this art as well as he did; so many of the players who try the pass tend almost to trip themselves up.

However, John was the player who really controlled situations. Billy might have been the Leeds orchestra's outstanding soloist, but it was John who held the conductor's baton. As Billy once said, 'You could be 2–0 down, but the one person who could be relied upon not to panic was Gilesy. Me, I'd be panicking like crazy. I was always the desperate one, the one who would want to throw caution to the wind in trying to get us back into the game. But Gilesy's attitude was, "No. Keep playing normally, keep passing and it will come."'

John hated seeing the ball being given away. This was one of the facets of the game in which he set exceptionally high standards. Even if he was in difficulties, it was rare to see him get himself off the hook with a pass that put the man receiving it in trouble. More often than not, the weight of his passes was perfect.

While Billy never lost his fiery streak – it was an important part of his make-up – I do feel that operating alongside John caused him to become more mature. It comes back to my earlier point about the macho element in his partnership with Bobby Collins, with each appearing to want to show that he was the hardest. There was a macho element in John, too, but whereas Billy would sometimes lose his temper, and his concentration on the game as a consequence, this never happened with John.

The technical attributes that put him in a class of his own were his wide range of passing skills, and most importantly, his ability to hit the ball equally well with either foot. That, together with his first touch and balance, meant that he was the most difficult of players to mark. Usually, you can nullify a player who is good on the ball by forcing him on to his weaker side, but that approach was not pertinent in John's case.

The other problem for players assigned to mark him was his work-rate. He worked tirelessly to get into good positions to receive the ball in different parts of the field; he took the view that the more times he was able to get the ball, the more he would be able to influence a game. Moreover, if he couldn't get the ball himself, he was willing to drag his marker into positions that would help other players to do so. It all boils down to how much responsibility a player wants to take on; how much he wants to push himself. Sadly, a lot of talented players fall down on this; they perform too much within themselves.

During the Revie days, one of the greatest performances by any player against Leeds came from the great Scottish wing-half, Jim Baxter, then playing for Sunderland. Mick Bates was given a man-for-man marking job against Baxter that day and Mick thought it would be a doddle. We did, too, because Mick was one of the fittest players in the club and the brilliant Baxter had a reputation for being suspect in that department. However, the match against Leeds was clearly one that he was up for and Mick struggled to keep up with him. I have never seen Mick as tired after a game as he was then. In the dressing room, he just slumped on a chair and said, 'Don't let me hear anybody say that Jim Baxter does not put enough effort into his game.'

But the fact remains that Baxter was not always as committed as that, and he was in good company. This is where my admiration for John Giles really soars. For the players who had to mark John, the feeling of exhaustion that Mick Bates experienced against Baxter will have been a common occurrence. John would repeatedly come deep to take the ball off the back four and continue to be involved in the play as it moved to the other end of the field. His style of play occasionally brought him into conflict with Jack Charlton.

When big Jack was in possession, he tended to get irritated by John's habit of demanding the ball from him; he felt that he was a good enough footballer to be trusted to use the ball well himself. John took the view that this was not one of Jack's main strengths. He thought that Jack and Norman Hunter were at their best as defenders and he had a responsibility to make it as easy as possible for them to concentrate on this. During one post-match debate on the subject, Jack brought Don into the argument.

'I can do what Gilesy can, can't I, Boss?' he said.

'No you can't, Jack,' Don replied, quick as a flash. That was the end of the matter.

The unfortunate part about John's Leeds career was that much of his work was more understated than Billy's, and therefore he did not get as much recognition from the Leeds crowd. It seems incongruous that throughout his twelve years at Leeds, he was never among the top contenders for the supporters' player of the year award. But to those who witnessed his professionalism and dispassionate nature at close quarters, it was understandable why this never bothered him. In one interview on the subject, this master craftsman gave a good insight into his mentality:

> I never went out of my way to establish a good relationship with the crowd. For example, I can never understand why some players applaud the crowd. They should be applauding you.
>
> It would have been nice to get more recognition from the fans, but the thing I wanted most from football was the respect of the people I played with. That meant coming off the field knowing that, although I might not have played well, I had never bottled it. If things are not going well, it can be easy for a player to avoid getting the ball without the public being aware of it – all he has to do is take two or three steps the wrong way. If you had that mentality, then in the supporters' eyes, you would never have a bad game. But I can honestly say that I always tried to do the things that needed to be done for the benefit of the team. I was true to myself.
>
> It is important to switch off from the crowd – to keep your head all the time, not get too excited when you are up or too low when you are down. When people watch matches, they tune in to the glamour and they think, 'I wish I could be out there on the field. I wish it could be me scoring that goal.' But when it's your profession, it's different. For example, although spectators might have got a buzz out of seeing me hit a great pass, I didn't, because I had the ability to do it and I took it for granted. Instead of getting a buzz out of it, I was more likely to be disappointed that I could not do it every time. So no matter how well I played, my reaction was one of satisfaction rather than excitement – the personal satisfaction of knowing that you did your job.

Insofar as my own progress was concerned, an important change came in the 1967–68 season with Terry Cooper's emergence as England's outstanding attacking left-back. During the previous season, most of my matches were in midfield, whereas he alternated between the No. 3 and No. 11 spots. In 1967–68, we were brought together more closely, with Terry becoming the first-choice left-back at the expense of Willie Bell, and me settling down in front of him as our outside-left. I think that for both of us, it proved to be a left-wing partnership made in heaven.

Terry was poles apart from Willie Bell. Willie was a natural defender; a big, strong player who epitomised the old school of British full-backs in his discipline in sticking rigidly to the basic defensive requirements of his job. Terry, on the other hand, was a natural attacker. He could hold his own as a defender – thanks to his sharp football brain and his mastery of the little pushes and obstruction techniques that represent a defender's tricks of the trade – but his real strength was going forward. When given the opportunity to do that, it was as if he had been given a massive shot of adrenalin. There was nothing laid-back about TC when he was going forward. He attacked the space behind opponents as aggressively as anyone I have seen.

Terry, nicknamed 'The Fox', had struggled to make an impact as an outside-left because, while being clever on the ball, he did not have a lot of pace. This proved far less of a problem to him in the deeper position, where he had more space to build up momentum. Having Norman Hunter on his side of the field was a help because he knew that whenever he went forward, he could rely on Norman to cover for him. I like to think that I helped him, too, by holding the ball long enough to allow him to get into the positions he wanted to reach. Where I benefited was that Terry took a lot of the attention of opposing defenders away from me; his forward runs beyond me pushed defences back and gave me more space than I would have had in other circumstances. Our attacking double-act also enabled me to use him as a decoy. When he went on one of his runs, I would occasionally shape to kick the ball down the line to him, but cut inside and link up with someone in a better position to produce a scoring chance.

Perhaps the only criticism that could be levelled against Terry was that, for all his forays deep into enemy territory, he scored just ten goals in around 350 appearances for Leeds. However, one of the goals he scored was among the most important in the club's history – his shot in the 1968 League Cup final against Arsenal, which brought us our first major trophy under Don.

That victory provided the psychological boost that the club badly needed. Until then, the four years Leeds had spent back in the First Division had been packed with frustration. It can take time for teams to mature into trophy winners but because of the impact we made in our first season – not least in failing to pip Manchester United for the championship on goal difference – the expectations of us were inevitably exceptionally high. By the time of that League Cup final against Arsenal at Wembley on 2 March, our record of missing out on big prizes also included being championship runners-up again in 1966, and Inter-Cities Fairs Cup runners-up in 1967.

The previous year, another blow for Leeds had been our 1–0 defeat by Chelsea in the FA Cup semi-final. The result hinged on the controversial decision by the referee, Ken Burns, to disallow Peter Lorimer's equalising goal – scored direct from a free kick – on the grounds that he did not signal for the kick to be retaken and that the Chelsea players were not ten yards from the ball. We were beginning to think that we were jinxed.

The pressure on us to make the trophy breakthrough was enormous, and as Arsenal had not been a major force since the 1950s, they were under a lot of pressure to win as well. Nobody, therefore, can have been surprised that the game was a dour, spoiling affair, which was described as one of the worst Wembley finals since the war.

It was always going to be difficult for Leeds to shine, not least because Mick Jones, who had made a tremendous impact following his signing from Sheffield United earlier in the season, was ineligible while two other key players – John Giles and striker Jimmy

Greenhoff – were not 100 per cent fit. I think Don admitted after-wards that had this match not been so important, neither John nor Jimmy would have been selected.

As for the tension among the Leeds players at Wembley, we got changed into our kit so early that half an hour before the kick-off, Don and Les Cocker decided to give us a sports quiz to help ease our nerves. Terry Cooper was probably the player who needed this distraction the most. Terry could get quite nervous before big matches. On this occasion, after a sleepless night on the eve of the match, he had got up at 8 a.m. donned his tracksuit and, while everyone else was still in bed, spent an hour running around the lawn at our hotel and doing loosening-up exercises. Fortunately for Leeds, Terry was the epitome of coolness when he had the chance to put us ahead.

The opportunity arose midway through the first half, from our controversial strategy of having big Jack Charlton standing on the opposing goalline, in front of the keeper, for free kicks and corners. The idea for this ploy, which created numerous chances for Leeds, had come initially from Jack. He just happened to take up that position in a training match one day and it proved so effective we were encouraged to work on it. We paid particular attention to the service given to Jack; for corners, Peter Lorimer hit inswingers from the left while I did so from the right. Although Peter's corners were hit with more pace and had a flatter trajectory than mine, the basic aim – to get the ball as close to the bar as possible, and virtually on to Jack's head – was the same. If the ball was good enough, there was little that the keeper and his defenders could do about it. Jack was taller than most of the keepers we played against (not to mention the defenders) and when they tried to get around him, it must have seemed like trying to get around a giant octopus. Body contact and collisions were inevitable, as were the claims that Jack deliberately impeded keepers.

In this instance, Arsenal claimed vehemently that their keeper, Jim Furnell, had been fouled. I did not see it that way, although in view of how protective referees have become towards goalkeepers, I am sure that had that game taken place today, the Gunners would have been awarded a free kick, and Terry Cooper would have been denied the greatest football moment of his life.

I'd been the one to put the ball in, and although Arsenal were able to scramble it away, the clearance went as far as the edge of the area only, and straight to Terry. With a beautifully executed volley, he hit it first time into the roof of the net.

From then on, we played a game of containment. Admittedly, it did nothing to enhance the match as a spectacle, but in the context of Leeds' development, this was one match where the result really was all-important. The feeling I sensed among the players at the final whistle was quite strange. Because of that pressure to get a result, the overriding emotion seemed to me to be one of relief.

As a turning point, the importance of the match became plain for all to see. We reached the Fairs Cup final for the second success-ive year. The two matches against Hungary's Ferencvaros were held over until the start of the following season because of the chaos caused by a fixture backlog, and we went on to get our hands on that trophy as well. The story of my life at Leeds just got better and better – especially when we landed the First Division title.

5

'CHAMPIONS . . . CHAMPIONS . . . CHAMPIONS'

WHEN striving to build a successful team, and particularly one that could win the championship, Don Revie was no different from most other managers – he started at the back. After he had become manager, it was significant that Leeds became harder to beat. Although some strikers enjoyed themselves against us – and I am thinking of that famous 7–0 hiding at West Ham in the League Cup in 1967 – our defence was the foundation for everything we achieved.

When I think of the ingredients that brought Leeds the old First Division title for the first time in the club's history in 1969, the part played by the men at the back – mainly Gary Sprake, Paul Reaney, Jack Charlton, Norman Hunter and Terry Cooper – cannot be overstated. When Arsenal had their outstanding back division of David Seaman, Lee Dixon, Tony Adams, Steve Bould or Martin Keown and Nigel Winterburn, the number of times that just one goal was enough for the Gunners to win a match led to '1–0 to the Arsenal' becoming one of the most evocative crowd chants in British football. In the art of frustrating opposing strikers, we were in the same category. Coincidentally, we needed to score just one goal to lift our first two trophies in 1968; in addition to that 1–0 victory over Arsenal in the League Cup final, Ferencvaros were overcome by the same score over the two legs of the Fairs Cup final.

However, the greatest example of Leeds' defensive strength came in the championship race the following season. In finishing first, six points ahead of Liverpool, we established three records for a forty-two match season. In addition to recording the highest points total (67), we had the fewest defeats (two) and conceded the lowest number of goals (26). Since then, only one team in the top flight have conceded fewer goals over forty-two matches – Liverpool (16) in 1978–79. In any top team, the responsibility for defence, as for attack, is spread throughout all departments. Everybody did their bit in that 1978–79 Liverpool side to make it difficult for the opposition to score against them; it wasn't just down to Ray Clemence in goal and the back four of Phil Neal, Phil Thompson, Alan Hansen and Alan Kennedy or Emlyn Hughes. It was the same with Leeds. Even so, our 1968–69 defenders probably did not get quite as much protection from the men in front of them as they had in earlier seasons.

The previous season, when Manchester City won the title and Leeds finished fourth, the biggest difference between the two teams was that City, with wonderful attacking players such as Francis Lee, Mike Summerbee and Colin Bell and, most importantly, two uninhibited men at the helm in Joe Mercer and Malcolm Allison, were considerably more positive than we were away from home.

This cautious approach was typical of Don and, because it had become such an integral part of our culture under his management, it was always going to take us time to change. Don realised that we would need to take a few more chances, and the 1968–69 season was the starting point for this to be put into action. Hence the fact that we had nine wins in our twenty-one away matches, compared with five wins the previous season. Even more intriguing, at least in helping to appreciate the importance of our defence, was the difference in our goals-for and goals-against records for the two seasons. In away matches, we scored only three more goals in 1968–69 than we did in 1967–68, but this was offset by the fact that we conceded ten goals fewer.

One problem was that we did not have a lot of scoring flair, especially in the central striking positions. This was overcome with the signing of Allan Clarke in the 1969–70 close season, but in the meantime, I think it was generally accepted that the blend and balance at the front end of the team was not as potent as it was in defence and midfield. To a degree, Leeds had appeared to make themselves weaker in that department with the sale of Jimmy Greenhoff to Birmingham in the opening month of the season. Jimmy, who had initially come to the fore at Leeds as a midfield player, was one of the most talented and versatile attacking players at the club. The previous season, when he had played mostly at outside-right, only Peter Lorimer, operating as a striker alongside Mick Jones, had scored more goals than him.

The decision to let Jimmy go, which I think arose from misgivings about the level of consistency in his overall play and his ability to overcome the rough treatment opponents were starting to mete out to him, brought Don Revie a lot of criticism from the fans. It also put extra pressure on Mick Jones. Bought from Sheffield United in September 1967, Mick had not scored many goals in his first season at Elland Road – eight in twenty-five matches – but as the target-man of the side, he helped create chances for others. He had to work harder than ever in the absence of Jimmy Greenhoff and he responded to the challenge superbly. It says much about the responsibility on his shoulders in that championship-winning season that, although he scored just fourteen goals in his forty matches, he was the only player to take his league goal total into double figures.

Mick was often ribbed unmercifully by the other players. But no matter how much stick we gave him – over his absent-mindedness, his clothes, and his seemingly endless moaning about his aches and pains – his temperament was such that he just took it in his stride. It was virtually impossible for Mick to fall out with anyone.

While Mick did not have the talent of a Greenhoff, or an Allan Clarke, this was offset by his physical power, especially in the air, and his willingness to drive himself. I have never seen a centre-forward work harder than Mick did. The amount of running he did off the ball was remarkable; he did not give opposing back-four players a moment's peace. You knew that virtually whatever ball was hit to him, or into his area, he would make something of it. He gave us a physical presence that had been missing from our play up front and he was therefore vital in enabling us to push the play forward more effectively.

When Allan came to Leeds, Mick was really in his element. As with a lot of partnerships in a team, they had nothing at all in common as people. Off the field, Allan was an extrovert who hardly ever seemed to stop talking, while Mick was quiet and reserved. Allan always seemed full of confidence whereas Mick could easily give the impression of lacking it. They were very different as footballers, too, but on the premise that opposites attract – and make the best striking duos – Mick and Allan were absolutely made for each other. As John Giles once remarked, 'One was the bludgeon, the other was the sword.'

To those who watched Leeds in those days, the match in which this image of the two of them was particularly strong was the 1972 FA Cup final against Arsenal. Mick's determination in stretching Arsenal down the right and somehow getting in a cross when it seemed impossible for him to find the necessary space, set up Allan for the clinical header that brought the only goal. The other major memory of Mick from that match is of him going up to the royal box to collect his medal with his arm strapped across his chest and clearly in almost unbearable pain. He had dislocated his elbow when attempting a similar burst towards the end.

In later years, I think Mick took the view that his selflessness rebounded on him. He ended up with serious knee problems, the result of his willingness to keep playing with the help of cortisone injections and pain-killing tablets, and I have been told that he looks back on this now with a sense of resentment. It is difficult to know for sure because Mick, a quiet family man who always appeared to want to lead as normal and ordinary a life as possible when he was not involved with his job, has had very little social contact with the other players since his retirement from the game. I would like to have seen more of him. Mick was a great guy, and attracted as much respect as anyone in our dressing room.

The question of how many of us feel the same way about goal-keeper Gary Sprake is another matter. Gary is the member of the 1969 championship-winning team who has become the most remote from his former colleagues. This is mainly because of the animosity towards him engendered by his serious allegations against Don Revie in a national newspaper. A number of us, if not all, have never forgiven Gary for what he said. I see no point in repeating his comments here, but quite apart from disputing them, we were all sensitive to the fact that Don showed Gary greater loyalty than many other managers would have done.

Cynics would argue that Leeds' defensive record with Gary in our 1968–69 team was something of an anomaly and that it was achieved in spite of Gary's presence rather than because of it. No goalkeeper had greater natural ability than Gary Sprake. From both the physical and technical viewpoints, he had everything as far as I was concerned. But as everyone connected with Leeds in those days knew, Gary had problems with his temperament. This may seem a strange observation about someone who first played for Leeds at the age of sixteen when he was still an apprentice, and was first capped by Wales at eighteen. But Gary came to the fore at a time when television coverage of football had started to put the performances of the top players under increasingly close public scrutiny. Goalkeepers in particular began to find their mistakes being magnified and I think Gary found it difficult to cope with this sort of pressure. In big matches, there were times when he looked a bag of nerves. Age and experience did not appear to make much difference to him. He did have some great games for Leeds. One that stands out in my mind is his performance in guiding Leeds to a goalless draw in the second leg of the Fairs Cup final against Ferencvaros in Budapest. The Hungarians cut through our defence so often that it looked as if Gary was stopping them from putting the ball in the net virtually on his own. It was the best display I have seen from any Leeds goalkeeper. But it served to underline his unpredictability because a few months earlier, his mistake in the 1967–68 FA Cup semi-final against Everton – when

69

he kicked the ball straight to the feet of Jimmy Husband and forced Jack Charlton to concede a penalty – led to Leeds losing 1–0.

His habit of blowing up on the big occasion was seen at Arsenal on the last lap of our 1969 championship bid, when a mild clash with Bobby Gould as the pair were challenging for the ball after just four minutes, prompted Gary to lay the Gunners centre-forward out with a punch of which any boxer would have been proud. It was remarkable that he was allowed to stay on the field. It can only have been due to the referee Ken Burns – yes, the same Ken Burns who had figured in that no-goal controversy in the 1967 FA Cup semi-final against Chelsea – not having a clear view of the incident. The other stroke of good fortune for Leeds that day was that we won 2–1.

Rival crowds were quick to pick up on Gary's errors, often taunting him with the song 'Careless Hands'. It seemed that the more flak Gary took, the more stubborn Don became about being seen to stand by him. But Don could hardly ignore the fact that Gary's understudy, David Harvey, was a steadier keeper. It wasn't long before David forced his way into the Scotland team, and he took over from Gary at Leeds towards the end of the 1971–72 season. Within eighteen months, Gary was transferred to Birmingham.

When rival managers and coaches put Leeds under the microscope, I don't suppose Gary was the only member of our defence singled out as a potential weak link. Of the first-choice back four in front of him in the 1968–69 season, only Paul Reaney and Jack Charlton were what I would call natural defenders (and in Jack's case, the fact that he lives a long way from me makes me fairly comfortable about adding the rider that we often described him as a frustrated midfield player!).

Norman Hunter, like Terry Cooper, had joined Leeds as a forward player, an inside-left. He had been switched to defence by Don because he relished being in ball-winning situations. Even as an attacking player, Norman had apparently liked nothing better than to track back and put his foot in. However, he was not the cleanest of tacklers; his enthusiasm for the job could lead to rashness. Moreover, Norman did not have a lot of pace and only Gary appeared to suffer more than him with pre-match nerves. But what a defender this man turned out to be. That left foot of his was like a magic wand. He read the game well; he showed tremendous discipline in sticking to his basic job; and his will-to-win and spirit were outstanding.

His other characteristic was that he was an exceptionally honest player. By that I mean that he was always willing to own up to his mistakes, which is one of the hallmarks of all great teams. It is one of the most important aspects in developing the necessary respect and sense of unity among players, especially those who have to rely as heavily on each other as those in defence. Some players find it more difficult to show this honesty than others, probably due to insecurity, but having been schooled by Don Revie from an early age, Norman Hunter and Paul Reaney had no problems on this score. Jim Storrie, the striker who played alongside them in their early days in the Leeds team, said, 'Don was always stressing the importance of players being honest with each other and actually ended up with a situation where the likes of Norman and Paul took it too literally. If we gave away a silly goal, they would all be claiming responsibility for it. It was quite funny really, seeing the lads putting their hands up and giving all kinds of strange, obscure reasons why they should take the blame.'

There is not one Leeds player who played alongside Norman who has anything but praise for him. I think we are all agreed that he did not get the general acclaim that he deserved. The Leeds player with the fourth highest number of first-team appearances (726) behind Jack Charlton, Billy Bremner and Paul Reaney, he was arguably the one who achieved the greatest consistency. He would surely have gained more than his thirty-eight England caps but for the fact that his career coincided with that of Bobby Moore. As it was, the only Leeds defender who played more times than him for England was Jack.

Jack, ten years older than Norman, was already an established member of the Leeds team at twenty-seven when Norman started operating alongside him. He had a stronger personality than Norman and always had strong views on how the game should be played. Indeed, Jack was nothing if not stubborn, a trait that initially brought him into conflict with Don and caused him to be something of a late developer as a top-class player. Norman was the opposite.

While Norman singles out Jack as having had a major influence on him, I should imagine that Jack got a lot of help from Norman as well. Norman, talking about Jack's unwillingness to go out of the central defensive area, once put it this way:

He always had this bee in the bonnet about wanting to stay in the middle. I remember a game against Sheffield Wednesday, when he moved into a different position and their centre-forward [John Ritchie] got above me to head in a cross. Jack said, 'You see what happens when I go away? I'm staying here from now on.' Sometimes, he stood there like a policeman on traffic duty. I can see it to this day – big Jack just standing in the middle and telling everyone what to do and what positions to take up. He would have me running around all over the place.

But I tell you what, when that ball was put into the box, he didn't half clear it. When it came to attacking the ball in the air, he was the best centre-half I ever played with. There was nobody better, especially when he was fired up.

Norman's image as one of English football's serial cloggers, endorsed by those 'Norman bites yer legs' banners and placards waved by the Leeds fans on the terraces, was very misleading. A hard man he might have been, but off the field Norman was as placid and genial as anyone you could wish to meet, and would do anything to avoid trouble of a physical kind. A fighter he wasn't as he once showed when refusing to be drawn into a full-scale fight with Francis Lee after the pair had been sent off for a flare-up in a match we played against Derby. They took digs at each other as they went up the tunnel, but Norman had no hesitation in drawing the line when Lee, having lost his rag completely, tried to attack him while the teams were having a drink in the players' lounge after the match. His self-control was commendable.

As for his combativeness on the field, I think it has to be borne in mind that there was little malevolence in his challenges. The vast majority of the fouls he committed were due to anxiety and therefore challenges not being timed properly rather than any degree of malice. I know it is easy to present this defence, but Norman provided some supporting evidence for it:

> You know, you don't realise some of the things you do in the heat of the moment. I used to get quite surprised when I was booked sometimes. I remember once Paul Madeley and I were playing together in a representative match, and I was booked for a tackle that I thought was perfectly OK. When I protested to the ref, Paul came over to me and said, 'You really don't think you have done anything wrong, do you?' I said, 'No,' and he pointed out, 'You absolutely buried that fellow – you took the ball, him, the lot.'
>
> It was the same story when I was at Bristol City [at the end of his playing career]. When I was shown a film of some of the tackles I had made there, my reaction was, 'Where did you get these from?'

The real irony of Norman's 'hard-man' persona was that, in terms of his capacity to intimidate opponents, he was not even the number one at Leeds in my view, let alone in the First Division. For me, the player who really did stand out in that respect was Paul Reaney. That may surprise a lot of people because in a Leeds career spanning seventeen years, Paul was never sent off, and picked up about half a dozen bookings only. While his combativeness was not as obvious as Norman's, Paul had a more calculated, ruthless edge to his game as far as I was concerned. He had no compunction about showing this to his team-mates in training. I probably took as many little kicks from him as I did from the opposition on a Saturday. The digs were not vicious, but they were enough to let me know that in order to get the ball past him, I could not expect the process to be pain-free.

Paul was the 'money man' of the Leeds squad – the one we relied upon to work out our bonuses and other financial aspects of our contracts – and we used to joke with him, 'You would probably kick your own grandmother if there was a win bonus in it for you.' Given the choice between being marked by Norman or Paul, I would have chosen Norman every time.

I am sure that none of the wingers from other teams would echo this more loudly than George Best at Manchester United. Paul's pace, mobility, fitness and mental strength made him ideal for man-for-man marking jobs and I think Best has gone on record as saying that Paul was the defender from whom he found it the most difficult to get away. Paul's ability to stop Best settling on the ball was probably the main reason why Leeds had such a good record against Manchester United in the Don Revie era.

Apart from our league matches, Paul's mastery of Best is illustrated by United's failure to get the better of us in two FA Cup semi-final ties, in 1965 and 1970. Not long after the latter, Paul had the misfortune to suffer a broken leg at West Ham. Once he had recovered, Manchester United tried to sign him.

Paul readily acknowledged that his approach was based on establishing a physical mastery over his opponents. On his duels with Best, he said, 'I was quite physical with him. That doesn't sound very nice but any winger knows that when it's a fifty-fifty ball and he has someone as close to him all the time as I was, he is going to get cracked. I had to let him know that I wanted that ball more than he did. I think this built up in his mind – you could smell it – and I played on it.'

Paul was like that with all the men he marked. In order to gain that physical edge, he even deemed it necessary to avoid getting into conversations with his opponents. He said, 'I didn't want anyone talking to me, and especially people being pleasant to me, because I felt it might put me off doing what I had to do. For ninety minutes, I had to try and think, "I don't like you," so that if I had to dig in a little bit, I wouldn't feel badly about it.'

Of all the members of that first championship-winning team who had come up through the ranks, Paul was possibly the one who had to work the hardest to establish himself. That's where his mental toughness stood him in such good stead.

He did not attract as much attention as Norman, Jack and Terry, all of whom had the edge in various ways when involving themselves in the play in a creative way, and he was the one who scored the fewest goals. I remember that after one of Paul's rare goals in a match against Coventry, Norman told him, 'It's amazing, Paul – when I rang Sue [Norman's wife] and asked her to guess who had scored for us, she went through every player except you.'

Paul had the perfect response to these wind-ups – the number of times he helped prevent Leeds conceding a goal. His ability to stifle opposing wingers and stop them getting in crosses was not the only aspect of this. He was also noted for the number of goalline clearances he made. At Leeds, this was very much his speciality; for some reason, he tended to be the only player in our side who did it. When he produced that goalline block from a shot by Alan Ball in the 1972 FA Cup final – an action which was every bit as important to our victory as Allan Clarke's decisive goal – you did not need to have a good view of it to know that it was Paul who had saved us.

As that was the centenary final, and as Arsenal had achieved the double the previous year, I would have to nominate it as the most momentous single Leeds victory in which I was involved in the Revie years. However, on the basis that the championship is the ultimate test of a team's ability in England, Leeds' championship breakthrough in 1969 – the first of two title successes under Don – remains the club achievement which has given me the most satisfaction.

One thing in our favour was that we did not have as many distractions as in previous seasons; we were knocked out of all the other competitions at an early stage. Our defence of the League Cup ended with a fourth-round defeat by Crystal Palace in October and we went out of the FA Cup at the first hurdle against Sheffield Wednesday in January. Having started the season by beating Ferencvaros in the delayed Fairs Cup final, our defence of the trophy ended with a fourth-round defeat by another Hungarian team, Ujpest Dozsa, in March.

As for the championship, the triumph over Ferencvaros was

followed by seven wins and two draws from our opening nine First Division matches. The last of these, a 2–0 win over Arsenal at home, enabled us to take over from the Gunners at the top. Our unbeaten record was then broken with a 3–1 defeat by Manchester City, and after recovering with three wins on the trot, we were on the wrong end of one of the biggest shocks of the season as Burnley thrashed us 5–1 at Turf Moor.

It was then that the character of the team truly came to the fore. Despite the freak nature of Burnley's performance, a lot of people felt that it was bound to have an adverse effect on us. But I remember the positive way the players discussed it, and the determination they displayed to make light of it. Any damage to the confidence in defence was quickly repaired with three successive goalless draws. Another indication of how Burnley had galvanised us was that they were hammered 6–1 in the return match at Leeds. We also avenged our Manchester City defeat by beating them 1–0.

In fact, in the 28 league matches following that uncharacteristic walloping at Burnley, we produced 17 wins and 11 draws and conceded a total of just 11 goals. One match that summed up our resilience was the 1–0 win at QPR on 24 January. Mick Jones put us ahead after just two minutes and from then on it was all hands to the pump as QPR, battling for First Division survival, forced us into probably our most desperate rearguard battle of the season. The more a team attack without being able to score, the more demoralised they can become; and as if to emphasise our capacity to turn the opposition into suitable cases for treatment, Bobby Keetch missed a penalty.

During the championship run-in, which had developed into a three-horse race with Liverpool and Everton, we had other breaks. There was that win over Manchester City on 5 April when John Giles scored the only goal as a result of a glaring mistake by City's keeper, Joe Corrigan; and following a 1–1 draw at West Brom, when I scored only my fourth goal of the season to cancel out West Brom's opener, there was the game at Arsenal in which Gary Sprake should have been sent off.

Because of the rivalry between the two clubs, quite a few of the

Leeds players felt that the win at Highbury was the best of all our championship performances. Arsenal badly wanted to make up for being beaten again in the League Cup final the previous month, this time by Third Division Swindon. It was the shock of the season; and in the light of their experience against us at Wembley the previous year, their motivation to regain some of their pride by helping to wreck our championship chances could not have been greater. However, one problem for Arsenal was that Frank McLintock and Ian Ure had just started operating together at the heart of their defence and McLintock was inclined to move too far forward, beyond Ure. We felt that if we invited Arsenal to come at us, there would be times when a quick ball played through the middle would catch Ure without any cover. That's what happened after fourteen minutes, when Ure misjudged a high clearance from Mick Bates and Mick Jones was able to take it through to put us ahead. George Graham equalised, but just before half-time another mistake by Ure, this time in putting a back-pass wide of his keeper, Bob Wilson, led to John Giles restoring our lead.

This match was followed by a 2–0 win at home to Leicester, a goalless draw at Everton and the opportunity to clinch the title in our penultimate match of the season on Monday, 28 April at Liverpool of all places. We were five points ahead by that stage, but Liverpool had a match in hand. Thus, Liverpool had to beat us to keep their title hopes alive while we needed a draw to settle the issue.

Not surprisingly, there was a lot of tension in our camp before the kick-off. Even Billy Bremner was affected by it. Usually the Leeds player who probably worried the least about big games, Billy found it impossible to get to sleep on the eve of the match, and at 4 a.m. he felt the need to get up and have a cigarette. He said that he was more nervous before this match than he had been before his first FA Cup final appearance against Liverpool in 1965.

On top of that tension, the fact that the match was played on a windy night, on a pitch that was hard and bumpy, made it unsurprising that it did not produce much attractive attacking football. It was a game that suited defences, especially ours. Liverpool had the clearest scoring chances; two fell to Alun Evans, who fired wide on each occasion, and another to Ian Callaghan, who was denied by a great Gary Sprake save. But our ability to retain possession made it difficult for Liverpool to build up a head of steam and achieve their usual attacking fluency. The longer the game went on, the more it looked as if neither side were going to score.

While the match itself was far from memorable, what happened at the end of it, when we were celebrating our title success, most certainly was. I have never known a crowd give an opposing team the sort of ovation that Liverpool's supporters gave us. It was a moment that Don Revie had anticipated. In the dressing room before the match, just as we were about to go on to the field, Don had turned to Billy and said, 'If we win the title tonight, you take the lads over to the Kop.' Billy did not take the instruction seriously; none of us did.

It was well known that Don and Liverpool's manager Bill Shankly were good friends, partly because the father of Don's Scottish wife, Elsie – the former Scottish international wing-half, John Duncan – had been a contemporary of Shankly's during the latter's career north of the border. Shankly had taken over at Liverpool just two years before Don's arrival at Elland Road, when Liverpool were also in the Second Division, and as the two clubs rose to prominence at roughly the same time, we had a great deal of professional respect for each other. But the idea of making sure Liverpool could not stop us winning the title, and then taking a bow for this in front of the section of the ground that housed their most partisan fans, seemed ridiculous. We just forgot about it.

At the final whistle, however, while we were jumping around and hugging each other, Don went over to Billy and repeated the instruction. None of us wanted to do it, but Don would not take no for an answer. He was adamant. As we approached the Kop end, the feeling that the gesture was going to blow up in our faces became increasingly pronounced. The Liverpool fans there were clearly taken aback by it because you could hardly hear a whisper from them. Their silence was almost eerie and it seemed to me to be only a matter of time before we were given an earful of abuse.

To our amazement, though, they suddenly started chanting: 'Champions . . . champions . . . champions.' The whole area seemed to explode. Those remarkable Liverpool fans were so enthusiastic in their applause that it was as if we had been transported back to Elland Road.

Being cheered by a rival crowd – any rival crowd – was a new experience for us. This in itself was as much a turning point for Leeds as the championship achievement.

6

END OF THE REVIE ERA

ONE of the most common occurrences in English football in the 1960s was people letting off steam about Leeds. We were widely condemned as a team who took their will-to-win to unacceptable levels, and in most of our away matches, crowds were liable to express their animosity towards us in the most insulting manner imaginable. This never bothered me, not least because I tended to get off lightly compared with other Leeds players. I incurred the wrath of the crowd with the time-wasting ploy of keeping the ball by the corner flag, but nevertheless they seemed to view me as a man apart. The most frequent comment directed at me was something like, 'Gray, how can you play for a team like this?' I found it quite amusing. While I did not agree with some of the things we did, my overriding thought was that I was privileged to have so many top-class players around me. I used to think, 'How can I play for a team like this? You must be joking.'

However, I have to admit that I would have hated it had the negative image we portrayed not been changed by the time I retired. It has not changed completely even now; it is so ingrained in the culture of the club that it probably never will. For me, the point is summed up by the zany 'Soccer AM' programme on Sky television on a Saturday, and the habit of one of the presenters of referring to us, albeit tongue in cheek, as 'Dirty Leeds'.

At least there is greater recognition of the fact that, in addition to being the most cynical team in Britain at one time, we were also arguably the most skilful. Until Leeds won the championship in

ck Charlton showing his tremendous heading power in front of Gary Sprake and ohn Giles.

One of the runs that brought me the 'Man of the Match' award in the 1970 FA Cup final.

Above Fiona and Kirsty have another sister – Natalie was born in 1972.

Below Frank and me with Mum in 1976, when Frank followed me into the Scotland team.

Above Norman Hunter leaps for joy at Allan Clarke's decisive goal in the 1972 FA Cup final.

Below Allan Clarke (*left*) on the lap of honour with Paul Madeley, me, Billy Bremner and Paul Reaney.

Sunderland make life difficult for me in the 1973 FA Cup final.

There was even greater frustration for Peter Lorimer in failing to score with this piledriver

Frank followed in my Leeds footsteps.

Don Revie with the championship trophy in 1974.

These are the players who brought Don that success.

Brian Clough with Norman Hunter, Joe Jordan and me during his first Leeds training session.

Wembley flashpoint – Billy Bremner and Liverpool's Kevin Keegan get sent off in Clough's first match in charge.

bove There was controversy in the 1975 European Cup final when Allan Clarke was
rought down by Franz Beckenbauer but denied a penalty.

elow The Leeds fans before the riot that turned the occasion into our worst nightmare.

Above Evading a tackle against Ipswich …

Below … and staying on my feet to give myself the chance to do it again.

1969, only fellow professionals recognised that skill, and even then their respect for it was somewhat grudging. Not even Sir Alex Ferguson's Manchester United teams, an obvious target for abuse because of United's status as the richest club in the world and their domination of English football, have found it more difficult to win friends and influence people than we did.

As with Manchester United, the animosity we attracted helped bond our players together, and provide what Sir Alex refers to as a powerful 'common cause'. The more people knocked us, the more belligerent we became. We provided a perfect example of the 'nobody-likes-us-we-don't-care' mentality. Deep down, I think we all knew that the criticism was occasionally justified. But, for the sake of keeping ourselves motivated, it suited us to bury our heads in the sand and pretend that we were more sinned against than sinning. I am still not sure that we were as black as we were painted. But, with the benefit of hindsight, I can appreciate that we have to take a lot of the blame for our image.

That image arose not just from the physical edge to our play and the number of flare-ups we were involved in on the field, but also from our so-called 'gamesmanship' or 'professionalism' as we preferred to call it. We took this element of the game to the extreme, especially with feigning or exaggerating injuries and deliberate time-wasting in dead-ball situations. Leeds were probably the British team who had the most in common with the top Italian league teams of that era. In a lot of ways, one could say that we were the British equivalents of the notoriously cynical Inter Milan team who faced Celtic in the 1967 European Cup final and whose defeat was applauded by fans all over Europe. We were the team almost everyone in England most wanted to see beaten.

What may surprise a lot of people is that the habits that put us in this unenviable position did not stem directly from Don Revie. We acquired them through our European experiences. As Billy Bremner said, 'We learned a lot from the European ties. For example, we would be putting a team under pressure at Elland Road and suddenly, when we got a corner, one of their players would go down with the aim of holding up the play long enough to disrupt our momentum. We looked at things like this, and we thought, "Good idea – clever." To us, it was not a question of attempting to break the rules, but of getting switched on to the tricks of the trade and making sure that we were not caught out in matches through being naive. Don Revie did not tell us to follow the example of these teams, we did it off our own bat.'

On the other hand, Don didn't do anything to stop us. When Leeds caused rival teams and crowds, and the media, to scream blue murder at us, he was inclined to laugh about it. From the conversations I had with him after he had left Leeds, I would say that, underneath the surface, he was uncomfortable about this aspect of our game. But so strong was his desire for success – for us as much as for himself it has to be said – that it was easy for him to go along with it.

There is no doubt that the championship win in 1969 was a major turning point for Don and Leeds. He became more relaxed. He started to give the impression of having faith in our ability to win matches purely on skill. The change in our approach could also be attributed to the arrival of Allan Clarke from Leicester for a club record fee of £165,000 in July 1969. Allan was a world-class footballer in my opinion, let alone a world-class finisher. In terms of our development into the team that Don had dreamed of building, he represented the last piece of the jigsaw.

A lot of people felt Allan would have problems in adjusting to a dressing room in which nobody was looked upon as being more important than anyone else and everyone was expected to pull his weight on behalf of the team. Allan had been a big fish in a small pond at his previous clubs and had acquired a reputation for being self-centred and arrogant. But Allan and Leeds turned out to be so compatible it wasn't true. As is often the case in football, reputations can be misleading, and Allan has suggested that the one he was stuck with at Leicester was due partly to his caring more about winning than some other players did:

At Fulham and Leicester, you would sometimes see players laughing and joking in the bath after a defeat, but I couldn't do that and I reacted against things like that [by criticising his team-mates in the media]. It was different at Leeds. After about six months there, I remember the media coming up to see me in the hope that I would make another controversial comment but I just said, 'I have nothing to say. I'm happy – I'm with winners.'

Being with so many outstanding players was bound to improve my game, if only because of the way they dominated the teams and the number of chances they created. They helped me develop as an all-round striker. I can honestly say that with Leeds, I worked ten times harder than I did at my previous clubs. It was not that I did not want to do it with Fulham and Leicester, it was just that no one there said anything to me about my work-rate. At Leeds, playing flat out was expected of you; the players there demanded that you pull your weight on behalf of the team, both on and off the ball.

Significantly, when Allan started playing for England, he said that all manager Sir Alf Ramsey said to him was, 'Play like you do for Leeds United.'

To an extent, that meant showing a touch of arrogance. All strikers have to have it, and Allan reflected this as much as anyone. It was not difficult to understand why he and Billy Bremner were close friends; when it came to believing in themselves, they were kindred spirits. Allan always thought he was the best and, in my opinion, he was right. He was the best striker I have worked with. His self-confidence was mirrored by his composure in and around the box and his ability to strike shots cleanly under pressure. The bigger the stage, the bigger the game, the more he seemed to relish it. Not once did I see him looking uptight. The times when there is just the goalkeeper to beat are archetypal battles of wits, with each player – striker and keeper – waiting for the other to make the first move. Allan had the bottle to out-psyche most keepers; and he allowed himself little freedom of error, hitting his shots low and close to the keeper's body on the premise that the keeper would struggle to move quickly enough to get down to them.

When taking penalties, Allan would hit the ball to the left of a naturally right-handed keeper and to the right of one who was a left-hander. Allan maintained that, even if the keeper knew where he was going to hit the ball, there would be nothing he could do about it if the shot was struck well enough. He proved the point one day when practising spot-kicks against David Harvey. David eventually pushed himself so far towards the side of the goal where he knew Allan intended hitting the ball that he could almost touch the post. But Allan still managed to get the ball past him more times than he failed. All of this explains why Allan scored more than 150 goals in his 359 matches for Leeds from 1969 to 1978.

It is less easy to explain why his presence, and our more adventurous approach, did not propel us to as many trophies as we deserved under Don Revie. Ironically, the continuation of our remarkable record of near-misses in major competitions was possibly almost as big a factor in making us more popular among the general public as the high standard of our football. People in Britain do not take kindly to teams they consider to be too dominating. They seem to take the view that it is bad for the game for one club to win the vast majority of the major trophies, as Liverpool did in the 1970s and 1980s, and Manchester United have done since then.

However, the fact that Leeds did not get into the same position of power is something that none of the people involved with the club then find easy to accept. Perhaps our main problem was that we were too successful in too many competitions.

In those days, the first-team squads of the leading clubs were not as big and multi-talented as they are today, and the scope to rotate players was limited. For any club able to push themselves into the running to lift two or three trophies, there was always the danger of the physical and mental strain eventually catching up with them. You needed some luck to achieve success, especially on the last lap when there was little breathing space between matches for players to recover from knocks and little scope for mistakes.

The point about not getting the breaks was particularly difficult to dispute in the season after our championship breakthrough, when we reached out for the championship, FA Cup and European Cup treble and ended up with nothing. We finished second in the First Division to Everton, were FA Cup runners-up to Chelsea – after two matches in which we allowed Chelsea to fight back from behind three times – and lost to Celtic in the European Cup semi-finals.

Before winning the championship again in 1973–74 – Don's last season as manager before taking the England job – we were also second in 1971 and 1972. Those disappointments were softened by our victories over Juventus and Arsenal in the Inter-Cities Fairs and FA Cup finals. But in 1973, when we were third, our best chances of getting some silverware ended with defeats by Second Division Sunderland in the FA Cup final AC Milan in the European Cup-Winners' Cup final in Greece (where the help the Italians were given by the Greek referee led to his being suspended by Uefa).

One way of looking at it is that it showed the tremendous character of the team; I don't believe there were many teams who would have kept bouncing back from such setbacks in the way that we did. Even so, we were good enough to have achieved more. Leeds won six trophies during Don's thirteen years in charge and it should have been twice as many.

This was certainly a sore point with me in 1969–70. It was a good season for me in terms of personal recognition, but because of our failure to win anything, I found it difficult to savour the praise I received. This is one of the reasons why I have never got as much satisfaction as one might expect from the memory of being voted man of the match in the FA Cup final against Chelsea.

A match that did give me some satisfaction was our league clash with Burnley at Elland Road seven days earlier. With Leeds resting most of their first-choice players – Peter Lorimer and Paul Madeley were the only other regulars in the side – I scored both goals in a 2–1 victory. The goals, which came from a lob over the goalkeeper, Peter Mellor, from around thirty-five yards, and a dribble through half a dozen Burnley players, have been described as two of the greatest ever seen at Elland Road.

Most people who were at Elland Road that day, or who have seen the video highlights, think that the second goal was the best, probably because of the circuitous route involved. It started almost on Burnley's goalline, just outside the eighteen-yard box and initially took me away from their goal. Usually, the starting-point for dribbles past so many defenders is on or near the halfway line. This one – necessitated by the fact that the only player close enough to me to take a pass, Albert Johanneson, had been knocked to the ground – took place in the last third of the field. The sight of me weaving in and out of the Burnley defence had almost a slapstick element. Not long ago, when some of Leeds' youngsters were shown a video of the goal, they remarked that it reminded them of a scene from one of those black and white silent comedy movies.

Despite the praise that goal brought me, I prefer the first one, if only because finding the net from long-range was probably less typical of me. It came as a result of the ball breaking to me from a headed clearance by a Burnley defender, following a left-wing cross by Chris Galvin. I could see that Peter Mellor was off his line and vulnerable to a chip as the ball came to me but I was not sure I would be able to set myself up for the shot quickly enough to exploit this. The key to the goal was my first touch. There was no margin for error. I had two Burnley players closing in on me and had it not been perfect, the chance would have been lost. Of the sixty-eight goals I scored for Leeds, this was the one that gave me the most pleasure.

I nearly scored in the Cup Final too, but David Webb slipped in to block my run through the inside-left position and I hit the shot against the bar. My other personal highlights from that game include a shot from a similar position, which Peter Bonetti saved; taking the corner from which Jack Charlton put us 1–0 ahead; and, with the score at 2–2 in extra time, setting up John Giles for a shot that looked certain to find the net but was brilliantly blocked by Webb on the line.

When I see a recording of that match today, I am struck by the thought that there was less to choose between the two teams than I originally thought and that the standard of play was remarkable in view of the farcical state of the Wembley pitch. The playing surface, which had some 100 tons of sand poured on to it because of the damage caused by the wet weather and, more specifically, the staging of the Horse of the Year show on it, was a joke. Never has it been in such a bad condition for an FA Cup final as it was in 1970. Indeed, to help prevent this from having an adverse psychological effect, Leeds eschewed the traditional eve-of-match light training session at Wembley in favour of having our work-out in a park close to our hotel. The longer the game progressed, the more churned up it became. It was like a suet pudding. The ball had no bounce whatsoever. For our first goal, the ball squelched under Eddie McCreadie's foot as he attempted to clear Jack's header off the line. Chelsea equalised when Gary Sprake appeared to have Peter Houseman's shot covered only for the ball to slip under his body. All the players were hampered by the conditions, particularly defenders when opponents were running at them with the ball. It is perhaps significant that as the conditions deteriorated, I became increasingly more effective.

Another thing that strikes me when I look at the video is the openness of our play at a stage in the match when, in previous years, we would have closed up shop and concentrated on frustrating the opposition. How ironic that Leeds, having been accused in the past of being too cautious, should suddenly swing to the other extreme. There were only seven minutes left when Mick Jones put us in front again, but instead of killing the game – an art that had become one of our most distinctive trademarks – we continued to trade blows with Chelsea.

This rebounded on us four minutes later when big Jack, who'd had a tremendous game, was penalised for a shove on Peter Osgood to the left of our penalty area. The decision seemed harsh – it was only a slight push, the sort of little clash that is very common in the duels between defenders and strikers and often ignored by referees. However, a foul is a foul and I am sure that big Jack was disappointed to have given away a free kick, bearing in mind that Osgood had little chance of gaining possession.

Worse was to follow. The free kick by Ron Harris was played short to John Hollins, and from his cross, Ian Hutchinson – capitalising on the fact that we were defending too deep – got across Jack to bring Chelsea level again with a near-post header.

As far as my own Wembley performance was concerned, much was said and written about the problems I had caused Webb when going forward with the ball on the left. He was possibly better suited to a central defensive role than the right-back berth, and on this occasion, he was not helped by the fact that Tommy Baldwin, who had been drafted into the team at outside-right in place of the injured Alan Hudson, was not always in a position to provide a protective shield for him.

For the replay at Old Trafford, Webb was switched to the heart of defence and I found myself facing Harris. For those acquainted with the approach of English football's hard men of the 1960s and 1970s, I don't think I need to explain what this meant for me. In a television interview, Harris has since pointed out that he was determined to stop me, and that in order to do so, he was quite prepared to employ methods that would hardly get him an invite into the society for football idealists.

The upshot was an early Harris whack across the knee as I attempted to take the ball in-field. The knock was not bad enough to force me off, but it did restrict my mobility. I am not making this an excuse for not doing what I did at Wembley; nor do I think it had any bearing on the result. We played just as well as a team in this match as we had at Wembley, if not better, but whether we had the breaks we deserved was another matter.

After Mick Jones had opened the scoring, it was shattering that Chelsea were allowed to wriggle off the hook yet again, this time through a great Peter Osgood goal. It was hard to come to terms with the fact that Chelsea, on the first occasion over the two matches that they had been in front, managed to hold the advantage. But you had to give them credit for their refusal to accept defeat. This, of course, was particularly pertinent in the case of

Webb, whose nightmare at Wembley was pushed into the background at Old Trafford when he headed a dramatic winner from Ian Hutchinson's long throw-in.

I've met David a couple of times since then, and we have had a good laugh over our contrasting fortunes in those matches. I congratulated him once on his sportsmanship at Wembley in not trying to kick me, to which he replied, 'I wanted to, but I was never able to get close enough.' Suffice it to say that if I had to be pleased about any Chelsea player doing well against Leeds at Old Trafford, it would be David.

Whenever I talk to young players about the importance of adopting a positive attitude in the face of setbacks, and how quickly fortunes can change in this game, the experience of David Webb in the 1970 FA Cup final always springs to mind as one of the best examples.

As if the blows inflicted by Chelsea were not difficult enough to take, they coincided with two European Cup semi-final defeats by Celtic. I believe that Leeds were even better equipped to land the trophy then than we were when we reached the final against Bayern Munich in 1975. It would have been much better for us to have been drawn against either of the other semi-finalists, Feyenoord or Legia Warsaw, than being paired with Celtic. For as long as I can remember, continental teams have had difficulty in coping with the style of play of British teams – the high tempo of our play and our penchant for putting opponents under considerable physical pressure in all areas of the field. Teams in other parts of Europe, and especially the Latin countries, have improved this aspect of their game, but the principle of denying opponents the space to settle on the ball and use their skill has never been as pronounced in their football culture at league level as it is in ours. In Celtic, we had opponents who could be relied upon to play us at our own game. So while everybody was excited about our confrontation with the Scottish champions – the Battle of Britain as it was inevitably dubbed – I was also quite apprehensive about it.

I had the nagging feeling that we did not take Celtic's challenge as seriously as we should have done. Celtic had become the first

British team to win the European Cup just three years earlier, but in English eyes, the Scottish League tended to be viewed as a Mickey Mouse league; Celtic and Rangers, by far the most dominant teams in Scotland, flattered to deceive through not having much competition there. However, as a lifelong Celtic supporter, I had seen plenty of examples of their ability to raise their game on the big occasion and tear the best of teams apart, so I was quite sensitive about our degree of confidence. When the draw was made, I remember saying, 'I wouldn't get too carried away if I were you. This is going to be a more difficult hurdle for us than you might think.'

As Leeds fans will know only too well, Celtic have not been the only Scottish team to have justified such a warning in a European Cup-tie against English opposition. Leeds were also involved on the only other occasion when the competition has produced an England–Scotland duel – 1992–93, when Rangers recorded two 2–1 victories over us in the second round. Not long ago, I was discussing this and Celtic's win over Leeds with the former Rangers manager, Walter Smith, and Walter made the point that if Rangers and Celtic played in the English Premiership, their vast financial power alone would more or less guarantee that they would be among the most successful teams.

The mind boggles at the thought of what the wonderful Celtic side we faced in 1970 would have been like in the English First Division. As I had feared, we found it difficult to handle the pace and passion of their play – if anything, they were more fired up than we were. Many attributed the difference between the two teams in both physical and mental sharpness to the fact that Celtic were fresher. Our first match against them was our eighth fixture in twenty-two days and the second game took place just four days after our FA Cup final exertions on that strength-sapping Wembley pitch. However, I would not make that an excuse. Celtic had also played a lot of matches that season and I for one was full of admiration for the way they played against us.

In the first leg at Elland Road, Celtic scored the only goal of the game in the first minute when George Connelly's shot was

deflected past Gary Sprake by Paul Reaney. I came close to bringing us back on level terms in the second half with a drive that hit
the bar. We did equalise on aggregate in the return leg at Hampden
Park, with a tremendous twenty-five yard shot from Billy Bremner
after fifteen minutes. But before a record European Cup crowd of
136,000 – who generated probably the best atmosphere I have ever
known for a club match – Celtic swept us aside. The waves of
Celtic attacks just got more overwhelming. Like many full-backs,
poor Terry Cooper did not know whether he was coming or going
against Jimmy Johnstone. In addition to Johnstone, Celtic had
David Hay bombing down the right from the right-back position,
so in effect, Terry was facing two right wingers. It was only a
matter of time before Celtic regained control, which they did early
in the second half with goals from John Hughes and Bobby
Murdoch.

It would have been great to see Celtic go on to lift the European
Cup again; for someone with my emotional link to the club, their
defeat at the hands of Feyenoord in the final in Milan was yet
another disappointing aspect of that season. As for Leeds, the
frustration of not being able to realise our own European Cup
dreams was compounded by our having to wait three years for
another opportunity, by which time our team had started to
decline.

I am convinced that, had Leeds qualified, we would have had
an excellent chance of winning the European Cup in 1971 and
1972. There was some evidence to support that view when we
beat Juventus in the 1971 Uefa Cup final, after inflicting a first
home defeat in twelve months on Liverpool in the semi-finals. In
1972, when we came so close to taking over from our old adver-
saries at Arsenal as winners of the championship and FA Cup
double, Leeds produced the highest standard of football in all my
time with the club. Apart from the centenary FA Cup final victory
over the Gunners, the matches that unquestionably provided the
best exhibition of the panache in our play by then were the 5–1
win over Manchester United on 19 February and the 7–0 win over
Southampton on 4 March.

The Southampton game is generally remembered for the apparent arrogance with which Leeds underlined their superiority in the last few minutes with a sequence involving as many as thirty-two successive passes without a Southampton player touching the ball. 'Southampton don't know what day it is,' said Barry Davies in his commentary on the match on BBC TV. Indeed, as the ball zig-zagged between the two penalty areas and over the full width of the field, Billy Bremner and John Giles brought a further touch of showmanship to the proceedings – and perhaps invited the view that Southampton were being humiliated unnecessarily – by keeping the move going with cheeky flicks. The only Leeds outfield player who did not get in on the act was Jack Charlton, although this was not for want of trying. I remember Jack waving his arms to attract the attention of the players on the ball only for the players to pretend they had not seen him. As I've said, Jack always fancied himself as a centre-half who could do more than just defend, and to deny him the opportunity to take part in our passing exhibition against Southampton was fairly typical of the way we liked to tease him about it. John took particular delight in winding him up. When Jack later asked why no one had given him the ball, John replied, 'Because we wanted to keep it.'

Jack, one of the scorers against Southampton (along with Peter Lorimer, who got a hat-trick, Allan Clarke, who scored twice, and Mick Jones) had been luckier against Manchester United. Towards the end of that game, he was involved in a similarly dazzling sequence comprising twenty-three successive passes. In terms of showing his ability on the ball, this was a wonderful match for Jack. Even his brother, Bobby, would have been proud of his superb long ball which dipped over United's centre-half, Steve James, and landed at the feet of a surprised Allan Clarke, in a position from which Allan would usually have scored quite comfortably.

It was, indeed, a wonderful game for all the Leeds players – the best Leeds performance I can ever recall. United, the First Division leaders a few weeks earlier, had slipped to fifth following five defeats on the trot. But nobody could remember the last time that they had been beaten as comprehensively as they were by us. Matches between United and ourselves had always been extremely tight and in view of the top-class players in both teams on this occasion – all but two of the twenty-four who took part in the game were full internationals – there was no reason to suggest a change of pattern.

I cannot imagine any team being able to live with Leeds on that performance, especially in the second half, when all the goals were scored. Mick Jones broke the deadlock, following a shot by me that Alex Stepney pushed on to a post. Mick went on to complete a hat-trick, with Allan and Peter getting the others.

As far as I am concerned, one of the most enduring images from that match is a photograph of Peter Lorimer and me having a discussion by a corner flag during a break in the play for someone to receive treatment. We look remarkably relaxed, under no pressure whatsoever. I also remember the look on Bobby Charlton's face at the final whistle – he had driven himself non-stop in his attempts to lift United and at the finish, his feelings about the hiding they had taken were plain for all to see. Don Revie summed it up for Leeds when he turned to our substitute, Mick Bates, in the dug-out and said, 'Well, Mick, this is as good as it gets.'

The FA Cup run included victories over Liverpool and Tottenham and, of course, Arsenal in the final. The Gunners, who had beaten Liverpool in the previous year's final, and pipped us for the championship by one point following a remarkable run of eleven wins and one draw from their last thirteen matches, had changed considerably since our last big Wembley clash with them in the League Cup final four years earlier. Like ourselves, they had become more creative and entertaining. In their case, the change could be attributed to the emergence of such a gifted attacking player as Charlie George and, following the Gunners' double triumph, the signing of Alan Ball from Everton. Ball's presence meant that Arsenal, who had based their attacking approach mainly on a rather stereotyped long-ball game, now played through the midfield. Their slower, more deliberate build-up play suited us because we felt that we were the more skilful team and that, if we lost the ball deep in their half, we would have time to regroup defensively.

The match, which inevitably turned out to be far better as a spectacle than the 1968 version (it could hardly have been worse), produced a particularly happy scenario for Jack Charlton and Allan Clarke. Jack, two days short of his thirty-seventh birthday, knew this would almost certainly be his last chance of getting his hands on an FA Cup winner's medal, and admitted to feeling unusually nervous. During our training session the day before the game, he asked Don how he was feeling about the match.

'This might surprise you, Jack,' Don said, 'but I have never felt more confident in my life.'

'I don't,' Jack said. 'I'm feeling dead nervous.'

This was music to Don's ears; he felt that the big man was at his best when he was uptight, and Jack's display against Arsenal supported the view.

Allan was mentioned in Don's pre-match tactical dossier on the game. Referring to the need for us to 'keep calm and think clearly' and avoid getting involved in incidents that might affect our concentration, he wrote, 'Billy Bremner got involved [in a heated incident with Arsenal's Peter Storey] in the England–Scotland match and forgot his responsibilities towards his team. You do this at times, Allan. Don't be drawn into situations of this kind. Let your ability talk.' With Mick Jones taking a lot of the attention away from him up front, Allan's ability positively screamed against Arsenal.

After a bright start by Arsenal, we became more and more dominant. Allan caused problems by running at them with the ball. From one such burst, from inside the Leeds area to the edge of the opposing box, he set up Mick for a shot which went no more than a yard wide. Then, when Peter Lorimer miscued a shot across the face of the goal, Allan connected with a header which hit the bar. He was luckier with another header – it brought the only goal. Mick Jones crossed from the right and Allan, running towards it from the left, intended to catch it on the volley. But the ball began to drop earlier than he expected and, in the knowledge that he could not afford to wait for it to hit the ground, he threw himself at it to produce a perfect diving header into the corner of the net.

Although Arsenal came agonisingly close to equalising when

Charlie George's effort hit the bar, most people agreed that we deserved to win – and that, on our performances throughout the season, we also deserved to take over from Arsenal as the champions. What a blow for us that our last First Division match at Wolves was controversially staged just two days after the FA Cup final, because of Sir Alf Ramsey's refusal to release the Leeds players in his squad (Paul Madeley and Norman Hunter) closer to the opening Home International match against Wales in Cardiff the following Saturday.

There was no love lost between Don and Sir Alf; the two men had come into conflict a few times over the release of Leeds players for international matches when Don had held the upper hand. On this occasion, many suspected that Sir Alf dug his heels in more firmly than he might have done in other circumstances. What cannot be disputed, though, is that the timing of the match at Wolves was a major disadvantage for us.

It was strange for the players, to say the least, because it denied us the chance to celebrate what we had achieved at Wembley – something that I think we badly needed to do in order to re-charge our batteries. We left for Wolverhampton immediately after the final and apart from being allowed one drink on the Saturday night, it was business as usual. In retrospect, I feel we were forced to be too professional for our own good; it would have been better if Don had allowed us to let our hair down after the Arsenal match, and travel to the Midlands the next day.

The other problem for us was that Mick Jones, whose ability to hold the ball up front made him an invaluable outlet for us when we were under pressure away from home, was ruled out because of an arm injury sustained at Wembley. The three other players nursing injuries – Allan Clarke, John Giles and me – had to have pain-killing injections.

We did not play well that night but whether we deserved our 2–1 defeat was open to doubt. We felt that we could have had two penalties, the most blatant of which was when the Wolves defender, Bernard Shaw, appeared to handle the ball to prevent Allan pouncing on a rebound from the keeper, Phil Parkes. An equally big blow was Allan's groin injury catching up with him and forcing him to go off half an hour from the end, shortly after Billy had reduced the arrears. When Allan went, our chances of getting the equaliser went with him. An hour later I was on my way back to London to wait with my mother for the bad news about my father.

Leeds, who finished in the runners-up spot for the fifth time in eight years, were one of three teams with a chance of winning the championship. The others were Liverpool and Derby. Liverpool's failure to win at Arsenal meant that Derby, whose players had their feet up on holiday by this time, landed the title for the first time in the club's history.

It is often said that you need to have disappointments in your life in order fully to appreciate the good times. The truth in that was hardly lost on Leeds United under Don Revie; and never more so than when our FA Cup final defeat by Sunderland the following season was followed by our second championship success in 1974.

Our experience against Sunderland was the mother of all soccer blows. All credit to Sunderland for the way they worked together as a team against us; to Ian Porterfield for his wonderful opportunism in hitting the out-of-the-blue goal that put Sunderland ahead; and, of course, to goalkeeper Jim Montgomery for the magnificent save from Peter Lorimer that kept it that way. That save has gone down as one of the greatest pieces of play in FA Cup final history. Overriding all this, however, is the knowledge that, despite not being at our best, we dominated the game.

Nobody was more below his best than me. This was by far my worst performance at Wembley, and what made it doubly frustrating was that the player marking me, Dick Malone, was a right-back against whom I had previously done well. Throughout my career, the full-backs who tended to have the best games against me were those in the strongest teams because these were the teams in which players could always be relied upon to work hard for each other; the teams in which the men responsible for marking me were less liable to be isolated. This FA Cup final was one occasion when Malone, supported by Bobby Kerr, also had the right backing.

However, without wishing to detract from his performance, I

believe that I would have caused him and Sunderland problems had I been fit enough. Because of injury, I had played in just one of our previous nine matches and, right from the start at Wembley, the way I was feeling suggested to me that I should not have been selected for a match of this importance. Nevertheless, I should have done better.

Not surprisingly, while we had repeatedly recovered back from setbacks in the past, few people expected us to do it this time. For this reason, our championship triumph the following season – when we began with seven successive league wins, and did not experience our first defeat until the thirtieth league game – must surely rank among the most impressive of all time.

Sadly for me, that was the season in which I played the fewest number of league matches under Don Revie, and it was the season that almost marked the end of my career. After playing in six of the opening seven matches, a recurrence of my old thigh problem in the eighth game, a goalless draw with Manchester United, ruled me out of action until the penultimate league match against Ipswich. Our 3–2 win that day, combined with Liverpool, our closest challengers, being held to a draw by Everton, virtually clinched the title for us. But I was again missing for the last match, when we made sure of it with a 1–0 win over QPR.

It was also, of course, Don's last season at Leeds before taking over as England manger. What a way to bow out – especially when you look at the squad he left for his successor.

I always knew that we had a lot of great players, but the long time I had spent as a spectator while injured inevitably gave me a new perspective on them. This particularly applied to Paul Madeley, who filled in for me in a left-side midfield role, and Terry Yorath, who was in the starting line-up much more often than usual in place of the injured John Giles. In addition to Terry, centre-half Gordon McQueen and centre-forward Joe Jordan – bought as relatively unknown youngsters from St Mirren and Morton respectively in 1972 and 1970 – established themselves in the side.

Gordon faced a big challenge as the replacement for Jack Charlton. The gap left by Jack's departure to become Middlesbrough manager the previous season was initially filled by Paul Madeley. The decision to let Gordon have a crack at it was generally viewed inside the club as a gamble. Nobody could dispute that Gordon had the technical attributes for the job. He was outstanding in the air, as you would expect of someone standing 6ft 3ins, and had tremendous pace – he was one of the quickest centre-halves I have ever seen. However, he was very raw, a characteristic accentuated by an extremely headstrong, undisciplined nature. Whenever you mentioned Gordon's name, it was difficult to avoid the temptation to preface it with the word 'daft'. One example of this came under the management of Jimmy Armfield. Gordon was messing around with some of the balls before a training session but, because he was suffering from an injury, he was told by the trainer, Jimmy McAnearney, not to kick them. With that, Gordon belted every one off the pitch and, in some cases, out of the ground. 'If I can't kick a ball, no one else is going to,' was his explanation.

Gordon, whose opening line to strangers was, 'McQueen's the name, football's the game,' loved to show his ball skills in training. You had to laugh at his cheek when on one occasion, he turned to John Giles and said, 'Don't worry, John – your touch will improve if you work on it.' However, it was no laughing matter when Gordon tried to show how quick he was during matches by deliberately giving opponents an extra yard. Even Gordon, though, was left speechless when he took part in a race with the Irish equestrian star Paul Darragh.

Their duel was set up one Saturday night while Linda and I were having dinner with Peter Lorimer and his wife Jill and that larger-than-life Yorkshire show-jumper Harvey Smith in a restaurant in Leeds. Peter and I had become friendly with Harvey through his visits to our home matches with his sons, and while we were chatting about the game that day, Gordon and Joe Jordan came into the restaurant.

Harvey asked, 'Who is the quickest player at Leeds?' When we named Gordon, Harvey said, 'I have a little Irish guy who works for me by the name of Paul Darragh – he is five foot nothing and eight stone wet through, and I would back him against anyone. Why don't we get him and Gordon to race each other at Elland Road?'

Gordon was up for it and Peter and I, having had a few glasses of wine, agreed to take it further. In addition to betting Harvey £50 that Gordon would win, we were also drawn into a £50 wager on a handicap race that involved Peter running the full length of the Elland Road pitch, with Harvey covering half the distance carrying me on his back in a fireman's grip. The whole thing got even more bizarre. Such was our drink-fuelled enthusiasm for the idea that we decided to stage the races early the following morning. Elland Road is usually closed then, but Peter and I contacted the groundsman, John Reynolds, at his home and persuaded him to open the place up for us at 7.30 a.m.

The first race was the handicap, which Peter won – just. There was some doubt about it, but Paul Darragh had been installed by Harvey as the judge on the finishing line, and when Harvey asked who had won, his protégé admitted, 'I think they did, Boss.'

'Right,' Harvey bellowed. 'You had better win the next race, or you will be in big trouble.'

Paul seemed to have got the message. He started like a bullet exploding from a gun and Gordon ran just twenty yards before giving up.

Fortunately for Gordon, and for Leeds, on the field of play he had Norman Hunter alongside him to help him channel his individuality in the right direction. Gordon, while retaining some of his daftness, quickly became a class act.

Unfortunately for Leeds, when it came to getting someone to continue steering the club in the right direction in succession to Don Revie, they took the wrong turning.

7

A VICIOUS CIRCLE

W HOEVER had taken over from Don Revie would have found it difficult to maintain his success. Even the most powerful of clubs must expect to experience lean periods, and Don himself acknowledged that this was bound to be the case with us when he said, 'You only get a group of players like the one I had at Elland Road once in a lifetime.' While accepting that a number of those players were approaching the end of their careers when Don left in July 1974, I cannot help thinking that the subsequent Leeds decline could also be attributed to the club choosing the wrong people to succeed him, and some of his established players being released too early.

Of Don's 1974 championship squad, the players who proved to have the longest Elland Road shelf life – albeit at a lower level – were Peter Lorimer and me. I was thirty-six when I stopped playing for Leeds at the end of the 1983–84 season, a step arising from my problems in having to devote so much of my energies to my other role as manager. But for those added pressures, I genu-inely believe that I could have continued for another year or two. Peter, who was released in 1979 and re-signed by me at the age of thirty-seven in 1983, was thirty-nine when he took his final bow. I have often wondered how many others could have done what he did.

Apart from Mick Jones and Paul Madeley, who retired, the first to be transferred was Terry Cooper, in March 1975. He was followed by John Giles in June that year; Mick Bates, Terry Yorath,

Billy Bremner and Norman Hunter within the space of five months in 1976; and Joe Jordan, Gordon McQueen, Allan Clarke and Paul Reaney in 1978. Most were in their early to mid thirties at the time. John Giles was the oldest at thirty-five. Although the general consensus of opinion was that the team had grown too old together, I believe that all the thirty-somethings still had some mileage in them as top-class players. In view of Leeds' struggle to replace them, it could be argued that the club might have benefited from hanging on to some of them for a little longer.

There can be no doubt that the club were particularly wasteful of what John Giles had to offer. He should have been the manager. Don Revie, a great believer in continuity, had no hesitation in nominating John as the man best suited to replacing him. Moreover, at John's interview with the Leeds board, he was seemingly told that the job was his. I learned about this while Peter Lorimer and I were doing some work together on the training pitch. John ran over to us and said, 'I'm going to be the new manager – the club will be announcing it tomorrow.' We were delighted, as were most of the other players, because John was by far the most respected figure in our dressing room. But by the following day, the situation had changed, apparently as a result of Billy Bremner telling the Leeds chairman, Manny Cussins, that he wished to apply for the post.

Billy did have a lot going for him, as he was to show when he finally had the job almost ten years later. But at the time Don Revie left, John had the edge in my view. His ability was later reflected in his tremendous impact as player-manager of West Bromwich Albion, and his appointment to take charge of the Irish Republic national team. To me, the characteristic that made John the more influential of the two as a player – his calculating, dispassionate streak – set him apart from Billy even more as a potential Leeds manager.

I don't know if Manny Cussins and his fellow Leeds directors also felt this, but what is known is that Billy's bid for the post provoked the boardroom fear that if either man landed it, it would undermine their relationship as players. The rapport between Billy and John was the key aspect of the team, and as Leeds were due to compete in the European Cup again, it was easy to appreciate the board's sensitivity about it remaining intact. So Leeds took what they considered the safer option of hiring an outsider. In so doing, their mistake in rejecting the best man for the job was compounded by the appointment of a figure who was arguably the worst – Brian Clough.

The best way of summing up Clough at Leeds is to say that although his record before and since suggests that he was the best of all the managers we have had since Don, he shot himself in the foot by adopting the wrong approach. That approach was extremely authoritarian, and followed the premise that managers need to keep denting the egos of players and antagonising them to get the best out of them. Clough's management style, which was not dissimilar to the one followed by Sir Alex Ferguson and which has been commonly described as ruling by fear, worked well for him at Derby. They were a modest Second Division team when he joined the club, and he transformed them into First Division champions and European Cup semi-finalists. After Leeds, it worked even more spectacularly at Nottingham Forest. As with Derby, he led them from the Second Division to the First Division championship; and if this was not impressive enough for a small, unfashionable club, he also steered them to two European Cup triumphs – without doubt one of the greatest managerial achievements of all time in England – not to mention four League Cup successes.

Leeds, however, were different because we were already at the top of the tree when Clough arrived. We were a group of highly accomplished players who had become set in our ways. As those ways represented tried and trusted methods of success, professional principles that most clubs would have given anything to have, the aggressiveness with which Clough tried to put his own hallmark on the side seemed perverse. He seemed to have an obsession about cutting us all down to size and rebuilding us in his own image. In that respect, it was a pity for Clough that his assistant, Peter Taylor, did not join him at Elland Road. Taylor seemed to complement him perfectly, providing a less abrasive managerial link with the players. Taylor could also exert a controlling influence on him.

Clough, who liked to portray himself as an upholder of the moral values of football, had a particular bee in his bonnet about our gamesmanship and haranguing of referees. He might have had a point, but the way he went about making it was tantamount to professional suicide. It was silly enough of him openly to show his dislike for Don. No less self-destructive was his comment to the players that we had achieved what we had by cheating and that our medals meant so little we might just as well throw them in the dustbin.

Among those singled out for criticism was Peter Lorimer. Peter was one of the last Leeds players you would think of as being in this category, but Clough took him to task for 'making a meal' out of fouls committed against him so as to get his opponent into trouble with the referee. For his part, Peter pointed out that Clough's full-backs at Derby had given him as much stick as anyone, adding, 'Do you expect me to stand for that for the whole game?'

Billy Bremner, the player who had the closest relationship with Don, was probably the first to turn against Clough. Part of this was due to Billy's sending off with Kevin Keegan in the 1974 Charity Shield against Liverpool at Wembley. It was Clough's first match in charge and he insisted that Billy pay the resultant Football Association fine out of his own pocket. In the past, Leeds had taken care of such punishments from a fund set up by Don for that purpose.

Because of my thigh problems, that Liverpool match, which we lost on penalties, was the only game I played during Clough's ludicrously short forty-four-day spell in charge. But while my contact with him was more limited than that of the other players, it was impossible for anyone not to be aware of the change of mood within the club.

One of the culture shocks provided by Clough was that our training sessions were more relaxed. Under Don, they would start at 10 a.m. on the dot, and would be meticulously planned with the aim of getting the maximum from us. Under Clough, they were somewhat haphazard. Once we had done our warm-up exercises, under the supervision of trainer Jimmy Gordon, it was not unusual for us to have half an hour or forty-five minutes to kill before Clough arrived on the scene to implement the work he wanted us to do.

This was one of a number of small changes which, while seemingly inconsequential in themselves, had the cumulative effect of causing the players to feel that Clough was lowering our professional standards. With hindsight, I can see that this might have been unfair on Clough – there is more than one way to do a manager's job. However, I do think that the way he conducted himself at Leeds was wrong.

By the finish, the only established first-team player who seemed to me to respond to him properly was Allan Clarke. I think Allan, who also had streaks of arrogance and abrasiveness in his make-up, and was a fellow striker, of course, recognised a lot of himself in Clough. As for the team as a whole, the way we started the season, with three draws and three defeats in six matches, which put us in nineteenth place in the table, told its own story.

It was difficult not to have some sympathy for Clough's signings – John McGovern, Clough's former captain at Hartlepool and Derby; John O'Hare, another of Clough's former Derby players; and Duncan McKenzie. Of the three, McGovern had the biggest credibility problem among the fans, as one could have anticipated with someone who operated in the same area as Billy Bremner and John Giles. In fact, McGovern initially came into the team in place of Billy because of Billy's suspension following his sending off at Wembley.

He was a good player, the type of steady, unspectacular professional that all teams need to help keep them ticking. But he was bound to suffer by comparison with Billy, especially as the team was falling well below what had been expected of them. Unfortunately for him, he took the brunt of the fans' displeasure.

As for the dressing-room resentment towards Clough, it would have taken a very brave chairman to have given him longer to prove himself. Even Clough must have known that he was not going to get that chance at the clear-the-air staff meeting called by Manny Cussins to discuss the situation just before our first-leg League Cup-tie against Huddersfield on 10 September. The meeting, which involved Cussins, two of his directors, the first-team squad and Clough, was held in the Elland Road players' lounge, and Cussins kicked it off by asking, 'Why are things going wrong? Why are you [the players] not playing for the manager?' As we started to give our views, John Giles suggested that it might be best for Clough to leave the room so as to enable everybody to have his say without feeling inhibited in any way. At this point, Paul Madeley got up, turned to Clough and said, 'I just don't think you can manage.' If anything could be said to have sealed Clough's fate, it was that. Paul was the quietest member of our squad. He was a man of very few words, even at our regular team meetings. To Cussins and the other directors, Paul's short statement about Clough had a greater impact than anything else said in that room.

Clough's departure created another opportunity for the board to appoint John Giles. This time, though, John was unwilling to take the job on the grounds that the decision to offer it to him had not been unanimous. Told that two out of the five directors did not give him their vote, he took the view that he would be under enough pressure as it was without the additional burden of knowing that he could not count on the backing of all his employers.

So that continuation principle went out of the window for a second time. It was not until six years later, following the managerial spells of Jimmy Armfield (October 1974 to July 1978), Jock Stein (August 1978 to October 1978) and Jimmy Adamson (November 1978 to October 1980) that Leeds finally took it on board. Allan Clarke (October 1980 to June 1982) was followed by me (July 1982 to October 1985) and then Billy Bremner (October 1985 to September 1988).

By then, of course, all the threads of Don's great work at Leeds had been lost, and Leeds had gone back a great deal, not just in playing standards but also in financial terms. When it came to getting money to spend in the transfer market, I believe I was the member of the trio in the worst position. In fact, I would say that I was forced to work under tighter financial constraints than any of the other managers who have followed Don Revie. Jimmy Armfield was the one with the biggest advantage in that department because our average league attendance was nearly 35,000 when he became manager, more than double what it was when Allan, Billy and I had the job.

Jimmy was the opposite to Clough in every way and this was reflected in his management style. Amid the storm created by Clough's tenure, Jimmy was perfectly suited to the task of steadying the boat and steering us to better results, at least in the short term. He was one of the most decent, likeable people I have ever worked with. I will always be grateful to him for the part he played in getting me playing again for Leeds at a time when it seemed certain that my thigh problems would force me to retire. Quiet and mild-mannered, he smoked a pipe and liked nothing better than to play the organ at his local church services. The image that this side of him portrayed was endorsed by what he was like as the Leeds manager. Jimmy's temperament and personality, in addition to being his greatest strengths at Leeds, could also be said to be his biggest weaknesses.

Basically, Jimmy struck everybody at Elland Road as someone who wanted a quiet life with as few hassles as possible. He hated confrontations and upsetting people, which he tried to avoid, and I had the impression that he was uncomfortable with the pressures that you get at a high-powered club. Ironically, while Clough's managerial methods were too abrasive, Jimmy's struck me as being too weak. This is why I had mixed feelings about his ability to go beyond that initial boat-steadying task, and take the club forward.

In some ways, Jimmy reminded me of Bobby Brown, Scotland's national team manager in my first two years as an international player, from 1969 to 1971. Bobby, like Jimmy, was a wonderful person, but found it very difficult to handle the strong characters in the squad. You could say that he was too nice a person to be a manager at that level. While there was a happy atmosphere in the camp, the level of discipline in our squad was not always what it should have been. Our training headquarters at Largs could be a bit like a holiday camp at times. On one occasion, on the eve of a match against Northern Ireland, I woke up on the floor with the bed on top of me – practical jokers abounded in the squad. On another occasion, a group were playing cards in the early hours of the morning. Bobby sent the trainer, Tom McNiven, to tell them that they had to stop and go to bed. Their retort to Tom was 'get stuffed'. Bobby brushed it aside and said to Tom, 'Tell them that they can have one more hour.'

Over the years, Scottish players have built up a reputation for being particularly strong-minded and wayward. The notoriously rebellious Jimmy Johnstone is often cited as an example. He was handled brilliantly by his Celtic manager, Jock Stein, which begs the thought of what a fantastic Scotland player Johnstone would have been had he also had Stein as his international boss.

The fear factor, as demonstrated by the likes of Stein, Clough and Ferguson in their dealings with players – and Don Revie, too, for that matter – was conspicuous by its absence in Bobby's approach. It was the same with Jimmy Armfield, whose experiences at Leeds might well have prompted him to single out Billy Bremner as a typical member of that undisciplined Scottish footballer breed.

One incident which I think sums up the downside of Jimmy's laid-back management style concerned a close-season trip to Marbella, following our defeat by Bayern Munich in the 1975 European Cup final. There had been some complaints from other hotel guests about the noise that Billy and Allan Clarke had made on their return from a night out in the town, prompting Jimmy to summon all the players to a meeting the following morning. While Jimmy was reading the riot act to us, John Giles pointed out that Billy and Allan were not there, so Jimmy sent our physiotherapist Bob English to the room they shared to bring them down. After ten minutes, Bob came back alone.

'Well, did you tell them to come down?' Jimmy asked.

'Yeah, I told them,' said Bob, looking quite sheepish. It was clear that Bob did not want to go any further, but Jimmy kept on at him. Finally, with Jimmy insisting that he be told what the pair had said, Bob replied, 'Well, they said you should get lost, Boss.'

We just burst out laughing and Jimmy, seemingly believing that there was no point in invoking a full-scale row on what was virtually a holiday trip, let the matter drop.

There was an upside to Jimmy's approach, as was proved by the change in our performances and results. To finish ninth in the First Division in his first season was not bad, bearing in mind that we were just one place above the relegation zone when he took over. To reach the European Cup final, with wins over FC Zurich, Ujpest Dozsa, Anderlecht and Barcelona, was an achievement that not even our most avid supporters can have envisaged.

It was tempting for the players to believe that they had led Jimmy to these heights rather than vice versa. The older members of the team knew that this would almost certainly be their last chance of winning the trophy and, because of the general misgivings about Jimmy's approach – which prompted us to joke, 'The Boss's indecision is final' – we probably took on greater responsibility that we might have done in other circumstances. At pre-match team-talks, Jimmy would encourage this by remarking, 'There is no need for me to tell you what to do – you have been brought up in the right way and you know what is expected.' Another way of looking at it is to say that it was brilliant management on his part.

The disappointing aspect of it for me was that my European Cup appearances were limited. I was in the starting line-up for two of the eight ties leading up to the final – the quarter-final first leg against Anderlecht and the semi-final first leg against Barcelona – and I played the last ten minutes of the final against Bayern Munich in Paris, as a substitute for Terry Yorath. Nine minutes earlier, we had fallen behind, through a goal by Franz Roth, and a minute after the substitution, Gerd Muller made it 2–0.

I must admit that I did not agree with the decision to include Terry in the starting line-up instead of me, but I could understand the reasoning behind it. After all, he had played in all the previous ties and I am sure Jimmy felt that Terry's physical power and combativeness would be badly needed against a team as strong in these departments as Bayern. This was not the first time that Jimmy had taken such a decision. He left John Giles out of the quarter-final second leg against Anderlecht in Belgium because he thought John would find it difficult to cope with the heavy conditions that night. John, who had played many outstanding games in such conditions, and was still one of the fittest players in the club, was furious about it. He took it as a personal insult. But Jimmy was vindicated by the fact that Leeds won 1–0 to clinch a 4–0 aggregate victory. Against Bayern, I have to concede that the team he chose could easily have done likewise. As in the European Cup-Winners' Cup final against AC Milan two seasons earlier, Leeds were the victims of what most neutral observers acknowledged to be a poor refereeing performance. The most glaring examples of this came before Bayern scored. The French official, Marcel Kitabdjian, rejected two valid penalty appeals against Bayern's captain, Franz Beckenbauer – for handball and then a foul on Allan Clarke – and ruled out a Peter Lorimer goal because Billy Bremner was in an offside position, never mind that Billy was running out of that position when Peter hit the ball and could hardly be said to be interfering with play.

Even more of a blow to Leeds than the defeat was the riot by our fans following Bayern's opening goal. That brought the club a three-month European ban and marked the beginning of a terrible period in which the violent element among our followers repeatedly dragged the image of the club to further low points.

As for Jimmy Armfield, having helped restore a measure of self-respect for Leeds on the field, the ideal scenario for him would have been to move into another role at Elland Road, one not directly linked with the first team. I believe that a position such as General Manager, or the Director of Football role that has become so prevalent in Britain in recent seasons, would have been perfect for him. As it was, I got the impression that the longer he remained team manager, the more the stress of such a front-line post bothered him.

The season after our European Cup final appearance marked the start of the break-up of Don Revie's old team. Jimmy did well by steering us to fifth place in the League. But the pressure on him really built up over the next two seasons when we finished tenth and ninth – our lowest positions since our return to the top flight in 1964 – and our best runs in other competitions were limited to getting to one FA Cup semi-final and one League Cup semi-final.

When assessing whether Jimmy could have done better in replacing the old players he released, it is worth bearing in mind what Don confided to those close to him about his problems as England manager. Apparently, after just a few months in the England job, Don told friends that he was disappointed in the quality of many of the players available to him from other clubs. It made him more appreciative than ever about the standard of those he had at Leeds. The point was borne out by some of Jimmy's big-name signings. In view of the massive void created by the demise of the Giles–Bremner partnership, the most notable of those was the acquisition of the outrageously gifted Tony Currie from Sheffield United for £250,000 in August 1976.

Tony, who spent three seasons at Leeds during which he won eleven of his seventeen England caps, had as much skill as anyone. I enjoyed playing with him because of his passing ability. I think everybody did. But while he compared favourably with Billy and John in his technical ability, he lacked their discipline and work ethic. Both Billy and John worked hard off the ball as well as on it. If either lost the ball, he would always try to win it back or prevent his opponent doing whatever he wished with it. Tony's contribution in that department was erratic, which helps explain why Jimmy bought the industrious Bryan Flynn from Burnley to complement him. However, while accepting that no one footballer can be expected to have everything, and that the secret of all successful teams lies in their blend of players, I still feel Tony sold himself short. What made this particularly hard to accept was that he was so well built and strong.

As someone who got on well with Tony – I liked him immensely as a person – I would often nag him about it. 'You have so much more to give,' I would tell him. 'You have to change the way you think about the game.' He agreed, but old habits die hard; and quite apart from feeling that Tony could have done with a manager like Don Revie during the early part of his career, I also felt that Jimmy could have been harder on him.

I had similar reservations about Jimmy's next major signing, centre-forward Ray Hankin, who was bought from Burnley the following month. Ray was one of the most exciting strikers I have worked with. For a man of his build – 6ft 2ins and 14 stone – he was surprisingly quick. He was also skilful on the ball. However, Don Howe, whom Jimmy had brought to Leeds as first-team coach, and who was something of a perfectionist, used to tear his hair out over Ray's level of fitness. The fluctuations in Ray's weight were a bone of contention. Don would insist on him being weighed every day – if Ray had gone out the previous night, he could come in the next morning as much as nine or ten pounds over what he should have been. Admittedly, Ray was often hampered by injuries. He had a bad time in his first season, when he made just four league appearances. But I still wish he could have worked even harder to overcome the effects of his injuries on his general physical condition. When he was in the right shape, physically and mentally, he was outstanding. In his second season at Leeds, 1977–78, when Joe Jordan was his most regular striking partner and Arthur Graham was brought to the club from Aberdeen to provide the service of crosses such players need, he was the top scorer with 20 goals in 33 matches.

Another indication of what Ray had to offer came after he left Leeds and was playing for Vancouver Whitecaps in the North American Soccer League in 1981. Such was his form there that even Don Howe, who had left Leeds to re-join Arsenal, and become the Gunners' manager, expressed an interest in signing him. The two clubs agreed a fee of £400,000 for Ray, subject to his undergoing a two-month trial. But he did not play any matches for Arsenal and returned to Canada.

This subject of players not making the most of themselves has always been a hobby-horse of mine; and among those who must have got sick of hearing me going on about it is my brother, Frank.

Although Frank had a wonderful career, even he had a tendency to frustrate me. For obvious reasons, one of the most welcome of the Jimmy Armfield-induced changes at Leeds for me was Frank's emergence as a regular member of the team at left-back, following Terry Cooper's transfer in 1975. There's nothing quite like a left-wing partnership between brothers. Yet I have always maintained that his ability was wasted as a full-back. In fact, even when he operated as a midfielder, I would argue that he could and should have got more out of himself. He will always be remembered as a very good player, but with his natural athleticism and his tackling, passing and heading ability, he should have been recognised as one of the great ones. In some ways, I think Frank had things too easy, which prompts the thought that perhaps the injury headaches I had to contend with might have been as much a help to me as a hindrance.

I did not disagree with Jimmy Adamson's decision to sell Frank to Nottingham Forest in July 1979. Frank had reached the stage where he needed a new challenge, and as we received a then club record fee of £500,000 for him, the deal also made a lot of sense financially. Three years after Allan Clarke had brought Frank back to Leeds in 1981, the same reasons prompted me to sell him to Sunderland for £80,000.

If I had to pick the best of the newcomers with whom Jimmy attempted to rebuild the team, it would be Arthur Graham. Although he was a No. 11 like me, we were quite different. Arthur, quick and strong, was more of an out-and-out winger than I was, and he had a more direct, straightforward style of play. He scored plenty of goals as well as setting up chances for others; and he really did have a tremendous work ethic. It was a pity for Arthur that although he was at his peak when he played for Leeds, it coincided with the decline of the team. He would have been sensational in Don Revie's side.

One of the clearest signs of the decline under Jimmy's management was that within seven months of Arthur's arrival, Leeds lost Joe Jordan and Gordon McQueen to Manchester United. Joe went in January 1978, and Gordon, his closest pal, followed the next month. Neither player would have dreamt of making such a move in the Revie days. The pair, who were arguably Leeds' biggest playing assets, had been discontented for some time. Joe was quoted as saying, 'After that [European Cup final] team was broken up, I thought that was it. I was a bit disillusioned, as a lot of people were. I wanted to try and win things, and I really did not think we were going to do that.'

Gordon's last match for Leeds, a 2–1 FA Cup third-round home defeat by Manchester City, provided a poignant reminder of Leeds' slide. Gordon got into an argument with David Harvey, which led to an embarrassing scuffle between the two of them on the field; and there was another outbreak of crowd trouble involving Leeds fans, with one spectator attacking City's goalkeeper, Joe Corrigan, and mounted police having to be brought into the picture to restore order. The incident caused us to be banned from playing any matches in the competition at Elland Road the following season.

The transfers of Joe and Gordon were bound to provoke the charge that Leeds were now forced to settle for second best in view of the stature of the players bought to replace them. Joe and Gordon were established Scottish international stars, as was reflected in their respective transfer fees of £350,000 and £495,000. In contrast, the players signed to step into their shoes both came from outside the First Division. These were centre-half Paul Hart, who was signed from Blackpool (Jimmy Armfield's home-town club) for £330,000 the month after Gordon's departure, and centre-forward John Hawley, who was bought from Hull for £80,000 two months later.

Obviously, the fact that they were not big names did not mean that they were not capable of doing a good job for us – far from it. Paul, who played for me when I was manager (and who was to figure prominently in the second part of my career at the club from 1995), settled down well enough with us to be talked about as a potential England player. John did well, too. Although he was at Leeds for little more than two years, his record under Jimmy Adamson in the 1978–79 season – 16 goals in 29 matches – helped push us into fifth place in the League. When he was sold to Sunderland, he fetched a fee of £200,000.

However, Paul and John were always going to find it difficult to match the ability of Joe and Gordon. Inevitably, with Leeds sliding further and further from the stage we had occupied in the mid 1970s, and being left behind by our rivals in the financial sense, this problem of getting players good enough to give us a major push in the other direction just got worse. It was a vicious circle.

8
RELEGATION

I DO not think anyone connected with Leeds could believe their luck when Jock Stein agreed to step into the breach after Jimmy Armfield was sacked. I certainly couldn't. It was no secret that Stein, who had moved into the position of general manager at Celtic, had declined physically since his Parkhead glory days due to a near fatal road accident and heart problems. Even so, he was one of the great managerial figures in the history of British football, and his presence at Leeds was the biggest fillip the club could have had. I found it almost surreal, and that was definitely the most appropriate way to describe Stein's decision to resign after just forty-four days in the job – the same time that Clough had been in it.

Perhaps the biggest surprise about the appointment was that Stein was being strongly touted to take over from Ally MacLeod as Scotland's national team manager following the débâcle of the side's disappointing showing in the 1978 World Cup finals in Argentina. There had been talk of the SFA wanting to make the post part-time, and to observers of a cynical bent, it seemed that Stein, a wily tactician if ever there was one, might have been using Leeds in order to force the SFA's hand. Stein, who never signed his Leeds contract, maintained that he was at a low ebb when we came in for him and acted on impulse. What made him realise he had made a mistake was the refusal of his wife, Jean, to move south. This does make sense; those who knew Stein intimately say that he was very much a home bird. At that stage in his career, Scottish football was his habitat.

The episode was disappointing to me personally. I would love to have had a longer association with Stein. As it was, I had three matches under him and ended up knowing no more about him and his methods than I had done previously. As for Leeds, our situation when he left was not a great deal better than it had been at the time of Clough's departure.

In the circumstances, Leeds' choice of Jimmy Adamson as Stein's successor seemed sound enough. The former Burnley captain and Burnley and Sunderland manager had long been regarded as one of the most knowledgeable figures in the game. That reputation stemmed from his having been coach to manager Walter Winterbottom for England's 1962 World Cup trip to Chile while still a player himself, although not in the squad. He had actually been offered the job of manager following Winterbottom's resignation, but turned it down because he felt he did not have enough experience.

His initial impact at Leeds in that 1978–79 season was impressive. From looking no more than an average middle-of-the table team for the third season running, a sixteen-match unbeaten league run pushed us to fifth in the table, which gave us a Uefa Cup place, and we reached the League Cup semi-final, losing to Southampton. However, as had been the case with Jimmy Armfield, this surge was not maintained. The next season, we were back in eleventh position; and when Adamson called it a day after just a few weeks of the 1980–81 season – following increasingly strident demonstrations against him by the Leeds fans – we had lost six of our first seven games.

It was sad to see him take so much stick because, like Armfield, he was a thoroughly pleasant, decent person. Also like Armfield, he retired from football after managing Leeds. Jimmy Adamson was similarly laid-back in his approach to the job, and I think that one of the reasons why it all went wrong for him at Leeds was that he took too much of a back-seat during the week, leaving a lot of responsibility in the hands of his assistant, Dave Merrington. This led to some confusion. The way Merrington got us to play in training did not always tie in with Adamson's instructions to us before a match on the Saturday. It does seem strange that this should have happened, bearing in mind that the pair knew each other so well. Merrington, a former Burnley centre-half, had been Jimmy's right-hand man in his two previous managerial posts. However, I am not sure that Jimmy whom I had been led to believe was a tracksuit manager, was as much on the periphery of the training work there as he was at Leeds. In view of his coaching reputation, his role in that department was less active than I expected. He did start to get more involved when we were in trouble, but it was too late.

I have to admit that Merrington was not someone I enjoyed working with. His personality could best be described as high-octane. From all accounts, he had been a fiery player and there was evidence of this in his work as a coach. He was a very strong-minded character who seemed to see things in black and white and I felt he wanted you to do things his way or not at all. I took exception to the manner in which I felt he tried to impose his beliefs upon people.

These included his belief as a born-again Christian. One day he called a meeting of the players in one of the Elland Road bars. Two towering athletes introduced to us as leading American Football players endeavoured to give us what I interpreted as a lecture on how the Bible and Jesus had helped them achieve success. There might well have been a lot more to it than that but I did not hang around to find out. I just told Merrington that this line of approach to my job as a professional footballer was not for me, and with one or two of the other players, I got up and left.

This was not the only time that I was to work with Merrington. We became Leeds colleagues again when I was reserve-team coach under the managership of George Graham and Merrington, having been at Southampton – initially as youth-team coach, then reserve-team coach and finally as manager – was brought back to coach our Under-19 team. Unfortunately, we came into conflict again. This time, it was over the fact that a number of players in this age group were in my team, and I did not give him as many to work with as he deemed necessary in order to bring the club further success in the FA Youth Cup competition.

I was not trying to be obstructive. I felt that once players stepped up into the reserve team, it was my duty to concentrate on developing their ability to take the next step up into the first team. While it was good to win trophies at youth level, my own view was that the performances and results of the first team were far more important. I still believe that – after all, it is the first-team's results that pay everybody's wages.

What disappointed me about Merrington's displeasure was that the first I heard about it was through George Graham; Merrington had complained to him without my knowledge. When I challenged him about it and suggested he should have made his point to me, we ended up having a row. With George leaving us to sort the matter out between ourselves, we just had to agree to disagree. There was always an underlying tension in our relationship but I had mixed feelings when he left the club to be closer to his family in the south. I think he had a lot to offer as a coach of young players.

As for Adamson's spell at Leeds, his bid to build on what he had achieved in the 1978–79 season provoked a number of fans to claim that he had lost the plot. One reason for this view was that two of the players sold by him – Tony Currie (QPR) in the 1979 close-season, and John Hawley (Sunderland) in September that year – were great favourites with the crowd. The antagonism towards Jimmy because of this was a bit harsh, considering that Currie had asked for a transfer on the grounds that his wife had become unsettled in the north.

However, what harmed his cause even more was that none of his major signings – and there were as many as eight of them from March 1979 to May 1980 – made a big impact. Kevin Hird (Blackburn), Gary Hamson (Sheffield United), Jeff Chandler (Blackpool) and Wayne Entwistle (Sunderland) were always going to struggle to convince the fans that they had the ability to take the club forward. Of the others, Derek Parlane (Rangers) was past his best; Alan Curtis (Swansea) and Brian Greenhoff (Manchester United) were hampered by injuries; and Alex Sabella (Sheffield United) – the last arrival, the costliest of the group at £400,000 and the one who excited me the most – suffered by not having enough players on his wavelength.

Alex was a midfielder I rated very highly. He worked hard in training and his dribbling and passing skills were typical of those of a top player from Argentina. I am often reminded of him today when I look at Harry Kewell. Like Harry, he was superb at taking on defenders. But whereas Harry does it mostly wide on the left, Alex operated in the central midfield area, where losing the ball presents the danger of opponents being able to threaten your goal directly. Thus, while Alex brought greater individual flair to Leeds, the team was not good enough to give him the right support. With Leeds going steadily downhill, Alex was unlucky to be in the wrong place at the wrong time.

Such instances are quite common. It is inevitable that some teams will be able to accommodate great individuals better than others. One of the most notable examples in recent years is Eric Cantona when he played for Leeds under the management of Howard Wilkinson. Howard never lived down his decision to transfer the Frenchman to Manchester United. The move proved to be the turning point in propelling United into the position they are in today, but I have never endorsed the criticism of Howard over this. The reality of the situation was that, at that particular stage of Leeds' development, Manchester United were much better suited to Cantona.

If only it were possible to turn back the clock and have Cantona in the Leeds set-up that exists under David O'Leary. Alex Sabella would have enjoyed himself in our present team, too. From Leeds, he returned to Argentina, joining Estudiantes midway through our 1981–82 relegation season for a transfer fee of just £120,000. He went on to break into his national team. The sad irony in this for Allan Clarke, the man who sold him, was that during Allan's twenty months in charge, our scoring average was less than a goal a game. As if that record was not difficult enough for the fans to take, bearing in mind that the manager had been one of the greatest strikers in Britain, Allan also had to live with paying a club record fee of just under £1 million to West Bromwich Albion for Peter

Barnes in August 1981. Peter, whom Allan visualised as the ideal forward to provide the attacking flair that we needed, was so disappointing that we were able to recoup only about a tenth of our money on him when he was sold – by me – three years later.

Allan, having had an encouraging start to his managerial career at Barnsley, did not have a bad first season at Leeds. We were just one point from the bottom of the table when he took over from Jimmy Adamson in October 1980, and, with Allan concentrating on tightening the defence – something that I became very much involved in when he switched me to left-back after a 5–0 defeat by Arsenal in November – we finished ninth.

In addition the left-back role giving me a completely new lease of life as a First Division player, I enjoyed playing for Allan. In fact, I reckon that my general form under Allan was probably better than it had been under any of the other managers who had followed Don Revie. Nobody wanted him to succeed in the job more than I did, but within a few months of the following season – which started with a 5–1 defeat at Swansea and one win in the first ten matches – I started fearing the worst.

As for Peter Barnes, it seemed surprising that Allan was able to fork out so much for the England international outside-left given that the club were known to be finding things difficult financially. Reports suggested that Allan had forced the club's hand in the matter by giving the board a 'back me or sack me' ultimatum. If that was the case, Peter's form over the ensuing months must have represented Allan's worst nightmare.

Towards the end of that season, Peter produced one of the best performances I have ever seen from any Leeds player in a 4–1 win at Aston Villa. With his explosive pace and ability on the ball, he was unstoppable that night. But such displays were very rare and, for the most part, he was average. He was by no means the only Leeds player in that category, but it stood out more in his case because of what the club had paid for him. That transfer fee was like a millstone around his neck. I could sympathise with him just as I could sympathise with Allan because Peter was as nice a person as you could wish to meet. To me, he was a classic example of a player with the skill to be a world-beater, but not the necessary resolve. In that respect, a lot of the game's macho types will have found some aspects of Peter's approach disconcerting. I wonder what Bobby Collins would have made of it when Peter stopped during a cross-country training run because he thought he had a fly in his eye. Moreover, if he did not have a good match, he would tend to attribute it to such factors as the quality of the service to him. Although there might well have been some truth in these assertions, I did not think he accepted enough personal responsibility.

While I was manager, we loaned him to Spain's Real Betis for the 1982–83 season. The arrangement got him off our wage bill and provided Real with the option of buying him for £125,000. It seemed a good idea for Peter, too; we thought that Spanish football as it was then would suit him better than the physical intensity of the English game. The deal was agreed by all parties at 9.30 a.m. on a Friday, and as Peter was not due to travel to Spain until the afternoon, he spent the morning training with us. Immediately afterwards, he asked to see me privately and told me, 'I really enjoy it here – I don't want to go.' I telephoned the chairman, Leslie Silver.

'You won't believe this,' I said, 'but Peter has changed his mind – he wants to stay at Leeds.'

We agreed that there was no point in talking to him again about it; he had a contract at Leeds, and if he chose to remain at the club, there was nothing we could do about it. However, there was another surprise in store for us. At 4.30 p.m. I got a call from Peter's agent, informing me that Peter was on the plane to Spain.

The next time I heard from Peter was a couple of months later when I received a call from him telling me that he was unhappy at Betis.

'Can you get me out of here?' he asked. 'I hate it here. They owe me two months' wages and they think I'm a centre-forward.'

I persuaded him to try to stick it out, which to his credit he did. But Real Betis did not take up their option to buy him when his twelve-month loan period had been completed in August 1983, and after he had spent one more season at Leeds, Coventry took him off our hands for £65,000.

No doubt Allan did not feel too badly about having been seduced by Peter's flair when he looked at the player's following ports of call. Peter, who is the son of the former Manchester City wing-half and chief scout Ken Barnes, had started his career at Maine Road and he had another spell there. Then Ron Atkinson, who had been his manager at West Brom, signed him for Manchester United. Peter was one of the players inherited by Alex Ferguson when he took over from Atkinson, and I would think that Fergie's abrasive style exposed Peter's lack of mental toughness more than ever.

Two of Allan's other buys were both signed from Nottingham Forest – my brother Frank who was brought back to Leeds for £300,000 before the start of the season, and Kenny Burns who was purchased for £400,000 in October. In some ways, Burns, who had been voted England's Footballer of the Year three years earlier and was still only twenty-eight when he came to Leeds, was also disappointing. He did OK but without a Brian Clough over him, and in a set-up that was less regimented and disciplined in the football sense than the one he had come from, he did not look the same player.

Allan's other signing – the irrepressible Frank Worthington – turned out to be an excellent one. Frank, then thirty-three and acquired from Birmingham in March in a part-exchange deal involving Byron Stevenson, scored nine goals in seventeen matches, which made him the joint top scorer with Arthur Graham. But it was too little too late. Frank's scoring flair did not make a great deal of difference to our results, especially over the last ten matches. We had two wins over this period, and suffered five defeats.

Even so, our destiny remained very much in our own hands right up to our last match of the season against one of the other relegation-threatened teams, West Bromwich Albion. We knew that a win at the Hawthorns on 18 May would guarantee our First Division survival, but as it turned out, West Brom were much too good for us on the night; their 2–0 win flattered us rather more than it did them.

The fact that this was the nineteenth match in which we failed to score told its own story about our season. It did not help that Frank Worthington had to miss the match because of suspension, and some suggested that Allan made a mistake in putting Kenny Burns in his position instead of a more recognised striker such as Derek Parlane or Aidan Butterworth. But we were rarely able to put enough pressure on West Brom's defence to create scoring chances anyway.

The player who caused us the most problems was Steve Mac-Kenzie. He could easily have scored twice in the opening minutes, first with a shot that hit the bar and then with another piledriver that John Lukic brilliantly tipped over. When a team are on top as much as West Brom were, without scoring, there is always the possibility that they will run out of steam and become vulnerable to a counter-punch. For us, that hope was destroyed six minutes into the second half when a cross from the left by Ally Brown was deflected to Cyrille Regis. He mishit his shot and had another stroke of luck when the ball trickled into the net off me. Now forced to chase the game, we conceded the second, killer goal three minutes from the end. Again, I had the dubious distinction of being directly involved in the blow, this time through a goalline clearance from a MacKenzie shot which went straight back to him.

That had to be the most miserable day I have ever had as a Leeds employee. The memory is rendered even more depressing by the manner in which our fans reacted to the defeat. During the match, Leeds' followers tried to invade the pitch; and after it, they ran riot in the streets. In view of the mayhem they caused – and not just on this occasion – it is tempting to suggest that our First Division colleagues were far from unhappy to see the back of us.

It was partly for this reason that you would have needed to be a supreme optimist to have any faith in the possibility of West Brom getting us off the relegation hook by winning their last match at Stoke three days later. Stoke were also involved in the relegation battle, but they, too, clambered to safety at our expense. A draw would have been enough for them to do it on goal difference, but they won 3–0.

Although I still see a lot of Allan – he is at Elland Road for most of our home matches – we have never really discussed his experiences as manager in any depth. However, I did feel that Allan might not have had a strong-enough backroom team to help compensate for his inexperience in the job. His number two was Martin Wilkinson, who had also been an integral part of Allan's backroom team at Barnsley. Martin worked exceptionally hard; he never seemed to be off the training pitch. But his background in professional football has been limited, especially at the top levels. While I would never denigrate Martin over this, I still cannot help thinking that Allan needed someone different alongside him.

Allan was a supremely self-confident person, and in this instance, I am not sure that it didn't rebound on him. Throughout that season, I got the impression that Allan felt the players were too good to go down. I don't think that he recognised the danger early enough. Not surprisingly, his attitude was shared by a number of the players. I found some of the dressing-room discussions on the subject quite disturbing. On at least one occasion, I said, 'Look at Manchester United [who had been relegated in 1974]. If it can happen to them, it can certainly happen to us. We have to get a grip on ourselves.' To me, we were a very average team. Even in the matches we won, we mostly struggled. Apart from that remarkable Peter Barnes-inspired win at Aston Villa, only two of the eight other victories were achieved by more than one goal.

Moreover, as happens in most teams when results are bad, the spirit among the players was not what it should have been. Small cliques had been allowed to develop, with certain players having digs behind each other's backs. There was some friction between Paul Hart and Kenny Burns, while Paul and Trevor Cherry – who were great mates – were none too complimentary about Kevin Hird. One of the first things I did as manager was to call the four players together for a clear-the-air meeting. Trevor and Paul were sitting next to each other, and it says much about the resentment that had been allowed to build up that when Trevor denied any knowledge of players criticising one another, Kevin actually leapt across the table to get at the pair.

All of that helps to explain why, when reading some of Allan's comments about the ability of the team and our chances of avoiding the drop, I found it difficult not to think, 'He's kidding himself.'

Still, it is easy to be wise in hindsight, and I am the last person to criticise any manager. All make mistakes, and I certainly did when I was in the position. Perhaps my biggest mistake of all was taking the job in the first place.

9

THE MOST
CONVENIENT
OPTION

I WAS as surprised as anyone when Manny Cussins asked me to become Leeds' player-manager in the summer of 1982. The possibility of landing the job was something that I had never thought about. When Allan Clarke was sacked, I assumed that Leeds would revert to an established managerial figure who had no links with the club. It never occurred to me to apply for the job; I was happy to concentrate on getting all I could out of the rest of my playing career before attempting to establish myself on that side of the game. If I had given it some thought, the chances are that I would have turned the offer down, and therefore saved myself a lot of unnecessary stress and hassle.

I was never under any illusions about why Leeds chose me. It had a lot to do with the fact that the club were in financial trouble and that I represented the cheapest and most convenient option. I was already being paid £25,000 a year as a player and the managerial responsibilities meant Leeds having to fork out only an extra £5,000.

In a number of ways, it was a great challenge for me and I did get enjoyment from it. My three seasons and a bit in the post broadened my outlook on the game. Although the results and the way I ended up may suggest otherwise, I feel that with my old friend Jimmy Lumsden as my right-hand man, I generally tackled it reasonably well. So, from that point of view, I am pleased that

I had a go. But in striving to achieve what Leeds expected, or hoped for, I was in a no-win situation. I had virtually no chance. It was very naive of me ever to think otherwise.

Just the terrible behaviour of the hooligan element among Leeds' followers in those days should have been enough to make me think twice about taking on the job. This particular headache for Leeds – in part a reflection of the lost pride in the club among our fans – grew worse than ever when I was manager. It reached the point where I had to insist on most away matches being no-go areas for Linda and our elder son, Stuart. The most infamous example of this dreadful trend came on the last day of the 1984–85 season. Our 1–0 defeat at Birmingham was staged against a backdrop of a pitch invasion and riot, and was followed by the tragic death of a teenaged spectator as a result of a surrounding wall collapsing under the weight of Leeds supporters as they were leaving the ground. At one point, I was asked by a police officer to go over to the Leeds supporters' end in the hope that an appeal for good behaviour by me might calm them down. It had no effect whatsoever.

On the same day, much worse was happening at Bradford, with the fire in the main stand at Valley Parade in which fifty-six people lost their lives and 200 needed hospital treatment. But for that disaster, the trouble at Birmingham would have attracted far more publicity, not to mention much greater condemnation, than it did.

This was not the best time to be working for Leeds in more ways than one. As with all clubs who drop out of the top flight, the biggest headache in halting the slide was one of finance. The decline in income made it exceptionally difficult, if not impossible, for us to sustain the contracts of our highest-paid players. In a sense, this was not bad news for me because quite a few of the players I inherited were either past their best or had difficulty in motivating themselves in the Second Division. However, my scope to buy in the talent we needed to regain our First Division status was limited to say the least. My spell as Leeds manager coincided with the club falling £2 million in debt, and the directors having to cover the borrowing with personal guarantees. You did not need to be very clever to appreciate that we were in a lot of trouble and needed every penny we could get.

The board tried, unsuccessfully, to persuade certain players to take a wage cut, and at one point, I can remember Inland Revenue representatives coming to the ground to claim some of the tax we owed by taking away the club cars.

One of the high-earners we were keen to get off our wage bill was Derek Parlane. He was signed by the Hong Kong club Bulova on a nine-month loan agreement within a month of my taking charge. I took Derek to meet Bulova's English representative at a service station in the Midlands and when everything had been agreed and I was about to leave, the representative handed me an envelope containing £3,000 in cash.

'What this?' I said.

'That's for you, Eddie,' he replied.

My initial reaction was to hand the money back to him. But he persisted, and I decided to take the money on behalf of the club. When I returned to Elland Road, I handed it to the club secretary and said, 'Just keep this cash in the safe, and use it to help fund a new set of tracksuits and other kit for the youth team when they go abroad.'

At a board meeting I attended some months later, when we were discussing the possibility of the team taking part in an overseas competition, I said, 'There's some money in the safe for that purpose.' Suddenly, you could see all the directors' heads going down. The money was no longer there – it had been spent on clearing up one of the debts.

For me, that said everything about Leeds' plight in those days. What a contrast to the set-up for our young players today. No expense has been spared in our development programme at schoolboy and youth levels. No expense has been spared, either, in improving our first-team squad. In a 2001 newspaper survey on how much Manchester United's major rivals had spent in the transfer market since 1998, Leeds were top of the list with £74 million. I had to laugh when I compared that with the transfer-market spending I was able to undertake.

One reason for the transformation in Leeds' financial position is the formation of the Premiership in 1992, which has brought clubs at this level so much money from TV, corporate entertaining and merchandising. They are not so much football clubs any more as multi-faceted business empires. Leeds also have cause to be grateful for the influence of Bill Fotherby, who joined the board with Leslie Silver in 1981. Over the next sixteen years he took on the roles of commercial director, managing director and finally chairman. This extraordinary character, who was in the men's clothing business, was the most assertive of our directors when I was manager, and I have to admit that I did not respond to him as well as I could or should have done.

In those days, managers were liable to get very touchy about directors they perceived to be trying to exert an influence on the playing side, perhaps more so than they do now, and Bill seemed to fit that description perfectly. He meant well, and had a lot to offer, but being the raw young manager that I was, I found his attempts to involve himself on the football side, especially in suggesting players for me to sign, rather irritating. When Leslie Silver took over from Manny Cussins as chairman in 1983, Leslie asked me whether I would mind working directly with Bill. He visualised Bill taking on the role of liaison director between the board and the manager. But I said, 'Yes, I do mind, Mr Chairman.'

Billy Bremner was as wary of Bill as I had been. During his spell in the job, Billy rang me up one day and asked, 'Did the Chairman ever approach you about Bill Fotherby becoming liaison director?'

'Yes – why?' I said.

'Well,' Billy replied, 'he has just asked me as well.'

'What did you tell him?'

'I think I gave him the same reply that you did.'

Bill has said that Howard Wilkinson was also initially unwilling to work with him. However, Howard, recognising Bill's remarkable energy and drive, agreed to give it a go and the partnership between them paid tremendous dividends for the club.

One of the things I remember about my own dealings with Bill was that he had a bee in his bonnet about persuading Jimmy

Lumsden and me to try to sign Kerry Dixon before the centre-forward's move from Third Division Reading to Chelsea for £175,000 in August 1983. Jimmy and I knew that Leeds could not afford Dixon, and that, in any case, his sights were set on playing in the First Division.

Bill's enthusiasm and optimism on such matters knew no bounds. Over the years, the number of big-name transfer deals that he reportedly said he was trying to set up, but which did not materialise, was mind-boggling. Nobody could ever accuse him of lack of ambition – two of the names touted as possible Leeds signings were Maradona and Rivaldo. Still, he did achieve a number of signing successes, and it is easy to see why Howard Wilkinson, having nominated the players he was interested in, was happy to put the next steps in Bill's hands.

Bill was a super salesman – he could talk the hind legs off a donkey and he could sell almost anything to anybody. He reminded me of a sort of Yorkshire Del Boy. Leeds certainly benefited in the pre-Premiership days. For example, it was Bill who initiated their first set of executive boxes. Perhaps the best example of his impact is that in his first year as commercial director, Leeds' income from ground advertising increased from £1,800 to £43,000. According to Bill, he was on an incentive bonus scheme at Leeds and the money they paid him was a small percentage of what he brought into the club. In 1995, a report claimed that Bill was the highest-earning executive in the Premiership, on a salary of £240,000.

Bill was the instigator behind the sale of our ground to Leeds City Council for £2.5 million. This wiped out our debts at the time and provided a fair bit of money for Howard Wilkinson at the start of his Leeds managerial career. More controversially, he and Leslie Silver set up the sale of the club to our present owners, Leeds Sporting plc, in July 1996. The deal brought the two of them, and the other major shareholder, Peter Gilman, a massive personal profit. While the deal with Leeds Sporting (or the Caspian Media Group as the company was called then) led to some £12 million being made available to strengthen the team, a number of

Leeds fans were upset that the three directors had got themselves into a position to make so much money out of the club. According to reports they each received £5 million, on shareholdings initially worth £35,000.

Moreover, Gilman opposed the deal with Leeds Sporting, claiming that it breached an agreement between Silver, Fotherby and himself and that a rival company were prepared to pay more for the club. The saga ended on 25 July when Gilman's action was finally overcome in the High Court.

By this time, Bill Fotherby had become acting chairman – Leslie Silver had decided to step down in April because of ill health – and for the sake of continuity, the new owners kept him in the position. Bill relinquished it in June 1997, which was when Peter Ridsdale, who had been a director of the club for ten years, became chairman.

Nowadays, Bill's money-making skills are being put to use at Harrogate Town FC in the Unibond League. He took over the club in 2000 and has recently been joined there by Leslie Silver. The last time I saw him, he asked if Leeds could let Harrogate have some tracksuits and training kit, which I thought was rich coming from someone who had pocketed as much as he had from the sale of the club.

But this sort of cheek is what helped make Bill so successful in the game. As I said, it was a mistake on my part that I did not establish a close enough rapport with him and cultivate what he had to offer. As it was, whenever I wanted to sign a player, it was a case of having to get the begging bowl out. I was never given a budget, and no matter how small a transfer fee might be, I could not sign anyone without the board's permission. One player I was keen to sign was Neil McNab, the little Scottish midfielder who had five matches for us on loan from Bolton midway through my first season. Although Bolton's asking price for him, £65,000, was not excessive, it was still more than we could afford at the time.

While Allan Clarke had spent almost £1 million on Peter Barnes, the most I was ever able to spend on one player was the £250,000 which brought us the England Under-23 international midfielder

Ian Snodin from Doncaster in May 1985, at the end of my last full season as manager. Even then, Manny Cussins had to dig into his own pocket to enable the deal to go ahead. Doncaster, managed by Billy Bremner, wanted all the money up front, whereas we could only afford to pay in instalments. Doncaster refused to budge at the meeting between the two clubs to discuss the matter, attended by Cussins, Bill Fotherby, Leslie Silver and me, and that seemed to be the end of it. But when we returned to Elland Road, Bill said to me, 'Look, if you are that keen on signing the player, why don't you go and have another word with the Chairman?' I did, but Cussins reiterated that Leeds were in no position to fork out £250,000 in one go. Then, noting my expression of disappointment, he started to relent.

'Eddie, do you really want this player?' he asked.

'Yes, Mr Cussins,' I replied. 'And I promise you that you will not lose money on him.' With that, he picked up the phone and arranged for Doncaster to receive a banker's draft for the full amount from one of his own accounts. Quite apart from the excellent job Ian did for Leeds, I got a lot of satisfaction when he was sold two years later, again by Billy Bremner, to Everton for £840,000.

I also derived a lot of satisfaction from the number of youngsters I brought into the side and nurtured, and who went on to justify my faith in them by establishing good careers in the game; and from the football we played. One of the strange things about managers is that some of them produce teams with a totally different approach from the one they followed as players. I am proud of the fact that, despite the pressure on me to get results, I was true to myself and my beliefs on the game and that my teams were noted for trying to play in a skilful, constructive manner.

My league record as Leeds manager could hardly be termed a disgrace although I did have my bad spells. We were never able to get the boost of a really good start. The worst period for me was unquestionably the early part of my second season, the 1983–84 campaign, when we suffered four defeats on the trot in the League, against Fulham (1–2), Manchester City (1–2), Shrewsbury (1–5) and Sheffield Wednesday (1–3), and were beaten 1–0 at home by bottom-of-the-league team Chester in the League Cup. It was the club's worst run for twenty-six years, and put us in nineteenth position. As we had been ahead in three of those games, the overall view seemed to be that we had a soft centre and that this was a reflection of my temperament and personality. The idea that I was not ruthless enough to be a manager, which I am sure my players would have voted a myth, was summed up by a newspaper headline urging me to quite – 'Call it a day, Eddie, the nice guys can never win'.

I remember the defeat by Manchester City because their winning goal came from Derek Parlane, whom I had released on a free transfer the previous month, after his return from Hong Kong. Embarrassingly for me, Derek had taken on a new lease of life at Maine Road – that was his seventh City goal in as many matches. I also remember the match that brought our losing sequence to an end – the 3–1 defeat of Cambridge United. They missed a penalty when we were ahead, and gave us another helping hand with the blatant defensive errors which brought us our other goals. That season, we went on to finish tenth. We had been eighth the previous season and in 1984–85 it was seventh. The most encouraging aspect of all this was that our youngsters were getting better all the time.

In view of Leeds' financial position, putting the emphasis on youngsters who were already at the club and who clearly had a lot of potential seemed to me to be the most logical way to tackle the job of rebuilding the team. Having seen how effective this policy could be when I played under Don Revie, and directly benefiting from it by being given the chance to establish myself in the side at an early age, I was very enthusiastic about taking this road. Of those already at the club when I became manager, the first to be brought into the first team was midfielder John Sheridan, who made his debut at eighteen in November 1982. Others whom I brought into the side at eighteen were striker Tommy Wright (April 1983), midfielder Scott Sellars (May 1983) and full-backs Dennis Irwin (January 1984) and Terry Phelan (September 1985). Then there were Neil Aspin, Gary Hamson, Aidan Butterworth and Martin Dickinson, who had all played for the first team before but became established in the side under my management, and Andy Linighan, the big central defender who was twenty-two when we bought him from Hartlepool for £20,000 in May 1984.

Sheridan, Wright, Sellars and Irwin shared the same digs and were the closest of friends. Sheridan, the oldest of the group, seemed to like to get lost in a crowd. He was very quiet, and although he had signed a full professional contract by the time I became manager, he spent all his time with his youth-team pals. Jimmy Lumsden and I had received good reports about him from our youth-team coach, Keith Mincher, and we all agreed that, in order to bring him out of his shell, he might benefit from training with the first-team squad. From that point, we realised our impression of John as a shy, retiring lad was wrong. A tremendous passer of the ball, he showed a touch of arrogance in his play even at that age. John, who came from a very tough family background in Salford, had been signed by Leeds as a boy after being rejected by Manchester City. He was as strong mentally as any teenager I have worked with. Hence the fact that, after we had brought him into the first team, there was no way that we could leave him out of it. He was forced out the following season, in October 1983, when he broke a leg at Barnsley. It was typical of him that he was back by the start of the 1984–85 campaign and, if anything, looked stronger than ever.

John was one of the few youngsters in my team to keep their places under the subsequent managerial reign of Billy Bremner. In fact, he was the member of that group who had the longest Leeds career. He was at the club until August 1989 when Brian Clough paid £650,000 to take him to Nottingham Forest. But he is probably best remembered for his spell at Sheffield Wednesday, and the wonderful goal that brought them their victory over Manchester United in the 1991 League Cup final.

John played for the Republic of Ireland at all levels but his fellow international, Dennis Irwin, has made an even bigger impact. He, too, was very quiet as a lad. He started at Leeds as a central defender but, while he was a good reader of the game, we felt that he did not have the build for the role and put him at full-back. I have to admit that I did not expect Dennis to prove the most successful of those four boys who lived together. If I'd had to put money on someone to go as far as he has done, it would have been Sheridan.

However, at least I can claim to have shown more faith in Dennis than Billy Bremner did. Billy gave him a free transfer at the end of his first season as manager. Dennis then had a tremendous spell at Old-ham and has since had an even better one with Manchester United. He has been one of Sir Alex Ferguson's most consistent players.

No manager can afford to gloat over such apparent transfer boobs; all managers have had the experience of releasing players who have gone on to embarrass them by making it big elsewhere. My own major skeleton in the cupboard in that respect concerns the Arsenal and England goalkeeper, David Seaman. David, who was born and raised in Rotherham and signed for Leeds as an apprentice after leaving school, was one of the first players I let go – to Peterborough for £4,000 in August 1982. The reason was that I felt I had one young keeper too many. John Lukic, who was three years older than David, had been our first-choice keeper for three seasons, and he was still only twenty-one or twenty-two. Therefore, it seemed to me that in order to give ourselves another option in this position, we could do with someone older and more experienced. It seemed only fair to David to give him the opportunity to get first-team football elsewhere.

As it turned out, John, anxious to return to the First Division to boost his chances of getting into the England squad, asked for a transfer towards the end of the season and was sold to Arsenal for £125,000 in the summer. Ironically, his transfer request, which prompted us to drop him, led to the return of David Harvey, the player John had originally displaced in the first team in the 1979–80 season. David was signed on a free transfer from Vancouver Whitecaps in March 1983, when he was thirty-five. I was delighted to have him back, especially as it coincided with a period in which our most experienced defenders – the likes of Trevor Cherry,

135

Kenny Burns, Paul Hart and Kevin Hird – were being moved on. In the circumstances, having someone with his background at the back was so important to us that we made him team captain.

However, if this caused a stir among Leeds fans, it was nothing compared with the reaction to my signing of Peter Lorimer – also from Vancouver Whitecaps on a free transfer – nine months later. At thirty-seven, Peter was older than me. He had spent three years playing abroad, and when we offered him the opportunity to return to Leeds, he seemed as surprised as anyone. But I knew Peter well enough both as a person and a player to appreciate that it was not as much of a gamble as outsiders might have thought. While David gave us a greater degree of composure at the back, Peter, operating on the right of midfield, ensured that it was maintained throughout the other departments. As he said at the time, 'I suppose it could be taken as a sad reflection on the game to recall a player of my age, but most successful teams have one or two old pros and my role will be to help stop players running here, there and everywhere and bring a sense of order and direction to our play.' He did it superbly. Indeed, Peter's influence, and David's, made it easier for me to stop playing for Leeds at the end of the season.

Although my final match, a 1–0 win over Charlton at Elland Road on 12 May 1984, provided me with a good way to sign off – I put in the cross from which Tommy Wright scored our goal – I was not entirely happy about the decision because I felt I still had something to offer as a player. Nonetheless, I realised that the strain of my dual role was starting to catch up with me. There was no way I could continue to achieve the fitness required while I was also the team manager. Fortunately, with Peter and David back, the need for me to do so for the good of the team had become less pronounced.

Peter is one of the most remarkable players, and people, I have come across. Although we both operated wide on the flanks, Peter was more direct than me and scored far more goals. It is not difficult to understand why he is the only player to have scored more than 200 goals for the club. Part of the answer lies in his temperament; nothing bothered Peter. The other explanation is that he was the cleanest striker of a ball I have ever seen. If he was ever clear of the opposing defence with only the keeper to beat, the possibility of his failing to put the ball in the net was even less likely than it was with Allan Clarke. People assume that all professional footballers must be able to strike the ball well, but this is not so. At Leeds, Paul Reaney and Paul Madeley, great players that they were, did not have particularly good kicking techniques and tended to be quite scruffy in that department. In contrast, Peter was the master.

His ability to get goals from long-range, as summed up by his nickname of 'Hot Shot', was something else. As Peter once said, 'It [his natural kicking skill] was a great thing to have in your game. It meant that even if I was having a bad game, I could always get myself off the hook. All I needed to do was take a couple of free kicks – bang, bang, and you're suddenly a hero.' His kicking ability made him an outstanding passer and crosser of the ball. He was a better crosser than I was, inasmuch as the high balls he played into the middle usually had enough pace to alleviate the need for the player on the receiving end to stretch himself with his header.

This aspect of his game was still very much in evidence when he returned to Leeds, which was quite unusual. Due to the inevitable deterioration in the leg muscles as you get older, kicking ability is one of the first aspects of your play to suffer. I remember having a laugh and joke about this with Jimmy Armfield when Jimmy was taking part in a training session as Leeds manager. I pulled his leg over a shot of his that had clearly not been as powerful as he had intended. He just smiled and said, 'Wait until you get to my age yourself, Eddie. You will find that the hardest thing to do is to kick a ball hard.' He was right. Even when I was in my mid thirties, I noticed that my kicking generally was not as good as it had been.

Peter was different; he was almost freakish as far as I was concerned. Even in recent years, it has been quite soul-destroying to play with him in the Leeds old boys team. He has still been able to hit the ball as hard, and accurately, as he has wanted; equally galling, he has still had no need to go through any pre-match stretching and warm-up exercises.

Peter did think about his fitness more seriously as he got older, especially his diet, and we reaped the benefit of this when I brought him back to the club. He did a tremendous job for us. In terms of exerting a steadying influence on the youngsters, he was one of my best signings. Not all of them worked out so well. To varying degrees, the biggest disappointments for me were three other fellow Scots – John Donnelly, a left-side attacking player who was bought from Dumbarton in a deal which was to cost us £85,000 in March 1983; midfielder Andy Watson, a member of Alex Ferguson's squad at Aberdeen whom I signed for £60,000 in June 1983; and striker George McCluskey, who was bought from Celtic for £160,000 the following month.

Donnelly, my first signing, was a twenty-two year old with exceptional talent. He was also one of the most frustrating players I have ever dealt with because he was very undisciplined and unreliable. He had been in England before, as an apprentice with Notts County, and you could see why they did not keep him on. One could never be sure about him turning up for training on time (or at all) or even for matches. Sometimes the penny drops with players like him and they re-invent themselves, but John remained the same.

He liked a drink, and one of my big mistakes was putting a lad who had come from Northern Ireland for a trial with us in the same digs as him. After our last match of the 1982–83 season, a 2–2 draw at home to Rotherham in which John scored our second goal, I received a telephone call from his landlady. She was angry because, according to her, John had taken the triallist out for a drink on the Friday night and got him so drunk that the boy had been sick all over the house. I knew John was going back to Scotland that night, and I went straight to the station to confront him over it. I virtually pulled him off the train.

'What happened last night?' I asked.

'What do you mean?' he said.

When I put it to him that he had been out drinking, and that this was not the sort of conduct I expected from a professional footballer on the eve of the match, he looked surprised.

138

'But I only had six pints,' he said.

Eventually I lost patience with him and dropped him. One day, I got a call from Bob Stokoe, then Carlisle's manager.

'Eddie, the boy Donnelly – why are you not playing him?' he asked. 'He is such a good player – every time I see him in your reserve team, he never gives the ball away.'

'I know, Bob, but it's difficult to get him to play. To tell you the truth, he's unreliable and I'm fed up with him.'

Bob expressed an interest in signing him, and after we agreed that Carlisle would pay us what we had forked out for him, it was arranged for John to travel to Carlisle on the Sunday and meet Bob at the railway station to discuss his personal terms. On the Monday, Bob telephoned again. John had not turned up and Bob's day off had been completely wasted. When I approached John about this, he just shrugged.

'Aye, I changed my mind,' he said.

John was loaned to Partick Thistle in November 1984 and joined them permanently the following March. Later, he helped steer Dunfermline to promotion to the Premier Division. However, I was interested to note that this was followed by the club announcing that they had sacked him for failing to turn up to train or play.

As for the other Scottish buys, Andy Watson struggled to adjust to the pace and competitiveness of the Second Division and returned to Scotland eighteen months later. George McCluskey had a longer Elland Road career – three years – but did not make the impact that I expected. I have to accept much of the blame for that because George, noted for his exceptional first touch and cleverness in possession, was probably not the type of centre-forward that we needed then. He was typical of the non-physical striker whom I favoured in those days. Of the strikers I had inherited – Frank Worthington, Terry Connor, Aidan Butterworth and Derek Parlane – only Derek could be said to give us much of a physical presence up front, and he was past his best. Frank, like McCluskey, was noted mainly for his ball-playing skills, while youngsters Terry and Aidan were at their best when chasing balls hit through or behind defences.

In my first season, with Frank being sold to Sunderland in December, the similarities between Aidan and Terry inevitably mitigated against their chances of forging an effective partnership. Although Aidan was our top league scorer, his total was just 11 from 38 matches. It was difficult for us to keep the ball in the opposing half, and the impression of our attack being too lightweight was further underlined by the fact that nobody else scored more than five. The only players on that mark were Terry and my brother Frank.

By March, it was obvious that we needed someone who could give us a better blend in this area; someone who could hold the ball up, and set up chances for players in other positions. Brighton's Andy Ritchie seemed ideal. Unfortunately, we could only get him in a part-exchange deal involving Terry, who was extremely popular with the fans and who, ironically, had the best scoring record that season in terms of his goal average. In the circumstances, we believed that the sacrifice of letting him go was justified.

From then on, with Aidan Butterworth fading from the scene, our striking partnership came down to perming any two from Andy Ritchie, George McCluskey and Tommy Wright, and quite often, the choice of all three. But there was only a marginal improvement to our scoring record over the next two seasons. In March 1985, I bought Ian Baird from Southampton for £75,000, and that gave our front line a more earthy, aggressive dimension.

Ian would not have won any prizes for style, and could be very hot-headed, but he was strong and brave, and would battle all day. He was a tremendous asset in the hurly burly of the Second Division, especially away from home where defences tended to be able to establish a physical mastery over us too easily. It is one of my regrets as Leeds manager that it took me so long to sign a striker in this mould.

Some believed that I could have done with similar characters in other departments. During that dark period at the start of the 1983–84 season, Jack Charlton had said, 'They are still trying to play the type of football that they did in the great days, but don't have the quality footballers to do it.' To an extent, I can appreciate Jack's point.

At the heart of our defence, Andy Linighan, though standing 6ft 4ins, had yet to acquire the assertiveness to capitalise on his build while in the crucial central midfield area, John Sheridan and Ian Snodin, players who could look after themselves in any physical confrontations, were also at an early stage of their development.

The view that I encouraged Leeds to play too much football for our own good becomes particularly difficult to dispute when you consider the manner in which Howard Wilkinson eventually took us out of the Second Division as champions in the 1989–90 season. Leaving aside the fact that Howard had much more money to spend than I did, there is little doubt that he hit upon the right style of play.

For some time, the Second Division was looked upon as an environment in which constructive football could not flourish. To a degree, Howard's team reflected this. They did have some excellent footballers – Gordon Strachan, Gary McAllister and Gary Speed for instance – but with physically powerful men such as Mel Sterland, Vinnie Jones, Chris Kamara, David Batty and Lee Chapman, their approach could be best summed up as 'horses for courses'. They were noted for their work-rate and organisation. They got the ball from the back to the front as early as possible – they were the de luxe version of Wimbledon, if I can put it that way – and their pragmatism was further reflected in the amount of time they spent on set-piece moves in training. They probably scored more goals from free kicks and corners, and even throw-ins, than any other team.

In assessing where I went wrong, people have also been tempted to look at how Leeds fared under Billy Bremner. He adopted a different approach from me, and he propelled Leeds into a higher position than I did.

In my last full season as manager, the signing of Ian Baird had been instrumental in pushing us into the promotion reckoning with a late run of five wins and three draws from eight matches, in which Ian scored six goals. It was only on the last day, when we were beaten in that riot-torn game against an already promoted Birmingham, that our faint chance of joining them via the promotion play-offs evaporated.

We were in fourteenth position when the axe was brought down on me the following season on 11 October, six days after our eleventh league game, a 3–1 defeat at Huddersfield. A bad start had brought us just two points from our opening five fixtures, but after that we had achieved an unbeaten run of three wins and two draws. So, bearing in mind that there were another thirty-one matches to go, and that the team had started to gain the physical strength we previously lacked, I was confident that I was walking on the right lines.

Billy, like the man who sacked me, Leslie Silver, clearly thought otherwise. Within twelve months of stepping into my shoes, Billy had parted company with almost all of the youngsters I had nurtured and, with the help of the extra cash the club received through Ian Snodin's record sale to Everton in January 1986, replaced them with more experienced professionals.

When we discussed this some time afterwards, Billy explained that one of the reasons why he did this was that he felt a number of the youngsters had become too attached to me. I can understand this. When I was sacked, with seven months of my contract to run, a lot of people took it even worse than I did. Reports indicated that the board had voted six to two to dispense with my services and one of the directors against the proposal, Brian Woodward, resigned in protest. At the league match on Saturday, 12 October, at home to Middlesbrough which Leeds won 1–0, the fans staged a demonstration in the West Stand car park. Some of the players had been in tears when I told them I was leaving and, on their behalf, Peter Lorimer issued a public statement criticising the decision.

Billy took the view that it would be difficult to get those players to respond to him as they had to me. 'They talk about you all the time,' he told me. He thought that because of the pressure he was under to get Leeds back into the First Division, it would be best for all concerned for him to concentrate on building his own team as quickly as possible.

Billy had played for Hull City for two years after leaving Leeds, and been Doncaster's manager for seven, so he had more knowledge about what was required for success outside the First Division than I had. Even so, I am still of the opinion that the team I had assembled could easily have gone as far as his, if not further. Interestingly, although Billy took Leeds closer to promotion than I did, there was very little to choose between our teams in their overall records. He was given no more time to fulfil the board's expectations than I was. I thought that, like me, he could have succeeded had he been given a bit more time.

After his first season, when Leeds finished in the same position that they had occupied when I was given the boot, he steered the club to their best season in years. In the FA Cup, Leeds, with the luck of a draw which brought them relatively easy ties against Telford, Swindon, QPR and Wigan, came agonisingly close to getting to the final. In a pulsating semi-final against Coventry at Hillsborough, Leeds, who had taken the lead and then allowed Coventry to get back into the game, made it 2–2 just five minutes from the end only to concede another goal in extra time. Coventry went on to lift the trophy by beating Tottenham 3–2 at Wembley.

Even more of a feather in Billy's cap was the achievement in reaching the promotion play-off final against Charlton, after finishing fourth in the table and beating Oldham – on the away-goal rule after extra time – in the semi-final. For any Leeds fans of a nervous disposition, the clash with Charlton, which was extended to a replay at Birmingham after a 1–1 draw between the two teams over two legs, was even more painful. It went to extra time and Leeds, who went ahead with a John Sheridan free kick, were destroyed by two Peter Shirtliff goals in the last ten minutes.

The high hopes this created rebounded on Billy. The following season, Leeds finished seventh; and with only one win from six games at the start of the 1988–89 season, he was sacked.

As for my own sacking, I knew my time at Leeds was up as soon as I walked into the ground on that October morning and was told that Leslie Silver, who was rarely at Elland Road outside matchdays, wanted to see me. Twenty-two years is a long time to spend with one club and I think that Leslie, a genuine man whom

I have always liked and respected, found it very difficult to be the one to end the association.

'I'm afraid we will have to part company,' he said. We shook hands, and that was it.

I felt sad, obviously, but as I have said, a lot of people took it worse than I did. I am not an emotional person. I have always been able to keep an even keel on things – and I have always been able to appreciate that Bill Shankly was joking when he made that famous remark about football being more important than life or death. Being shown the door at Leeds pales into insignificance when I think about experiences such as the death of my father, and how close my Leeds colleagues and I came to losing our lives in March 1998. That was when a fifty-seat propeller plane taking the Leeds party home from an evening match at West Ham crash-landed after the starboard engine exploded and burst into flames on take-off from Stansted Airport.

We were 150 feet in the air when the pilot, Captain John Hackett, aborted the flight and decided that the plane would have to be brought down immediately. That decision alone was crucial because had he circled to make a fresh landing, the aircraft, loaded with one and a half tonnes of fuel, would almost certainly have blown up. The other factors that saved us were the comparatively small size of the plane and the length of the runway.

The plane was still climbing when the fire began. It was obvious to everyone that something was wrong. There was a lot of shouting and I remember hearing someone yell, 'The engine's on bloody fire. Stop, stop, get it down, stop going up.' This was followed by the sound of a buzzer and the announcement that we were going to make an emergency landing and should all adopt the brace position. It took about a minute to bring the plane down and to a standstill but it was the longest minute of my life.

David O'Leary and I were sitting together by the central emer-gency exit, and quite apart from the fear of the whole plane bursting into flames, I remember hoping that we would not hit anything. It was some ride. The plane bounced four or five times to the end of the runway and skidded for about 100 yards before coming to

Left My first day as the new Leeds manager, 1982.

Above My best pal, Jimmy Lumsden, was also my assistant.

Below My first squad.

John Sheridan was the first of my young players to blossom.

David Harvey was a signing at the other end of the age scale.

A trio of experienced Scots – Arthur Graham (*left*), me and Derek Parlane enjoy a training break.

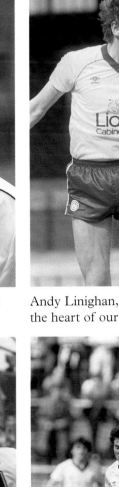

Dennis Irwin went on to establish a great career elsewhere.

Andy Linighan, at 6ft 4ins, was a giant at the heart of our defence.

Peter Lorimer was in his late thirties when I brought him back to Leeds.

Ian Snodin was my most profitable signing.

Au revoir – my last match as a player was against Charlton in May 1984.

Left Jimmy Lumsden and I maintained our managerial partnership at Rochdale.

Below The Gray team at Buckingham Palace for my MBE presentation – Linda and me with Katherine, Stuart, Natalie, Kirsty and Fiona.

Above Don Robinson was my showman of a chairman at Hull.

Above Billy Whitehurst scored some good goals for us at Hull.

Below Keith Edwards emphasises his value by completing a hat-trick with a penalty.

Above Training with the Hull players in the 1988–89 season.

Below My 1990 Whitby Town squad included top strikers Paul Pitman on (*back row, far left*) and Steve French (*front row, second from right*).

The 1993 FA Youth Cup final – Leeds' win over Manchester United helped us attract leading schoolboy players.

Spot the big names in the United wall – Paul Scholes David Beckham and Gary Neville.

rest – with its nose in the ground – a few yards from the perimeter fence.

David shoulder-charged the emergency door to open it, suffering a slight injury in the process, and with two other exits being opened by the air crew, the plane was evacuated within thirty seconds. The possibility of an explosion meant that, having jumped to the ground, in pitch darkness, we were told to run away from the plane as fast as we could. Needless to say, some people probably discovered a fleet-footedness that they never knew they possessed. When I reached the terminal, the first thing I did was telephone Linda.

'Listen, love,' I said. 'We have just been involved in an air crash, so I'm going to be home late.'

For some reason – according to her, it was the matter-of-fact way I told her about it – the words 'air crash' did not really register with her. It was only when she saw the news on TV that she realised how serious the situation had been.

One thing that helped me handle leaving Leeds was that I have never been the type to bury my head in the sand. I had seen it coming for some time and Linda and I were prepared for it. I do not think anyone takes on a manager's job thinking that it is going to last for ever. It is important to be realistic and this is something that I have always looked upon as being one of my strengths. Whatever I felt about the job I did for Leeds as manager, and all the problems I faced, the fact of the matter is that I did not deliver what the club wanted. They were paying me to take them back into the First Division. I knew that this was the yardstick by which I would be judged when I accepted the post, so on that basis, I did not feel that I could have any complaints about their decision.

The big problem for me was that, having spent all my adult life with Leeds, it was not easy to switch off from all the memories, all the Leeds habits, and pick up the threads of my career in another environment. Things did not get any better for me; they got worse.

10

REPAIRING THE LIFELINE

WHEN Howard Wilkinson gave me the chance to return to the club in 1995, after a ten-year absence, it represented something of a lifeline. At the time, I was just another ex-pro trying to make a living on the periphery of the game, and I was not exactly making a rip-roaring success of it. Financially, I was struggling, and I was still searching for something stimulating.

The period I spent away from Leeds turned into the worst of my life. I am not looking for sympathy – I would hate to give the impression that I was hard done by because I have never felt that way. Everyone goes through bad times and there can be no doubt that I have been let off comparatively lightly in that respect.

Part of this has been due to the tremendous support I have had from my friends and family. It is when things are not going well that you find out who your real friends are. A lot of people who attach themselves to football personalities quickly disappear when the personalities are no longer in the spotlight. But two friends who have come to mean the most to Linda and me, outside our pals from the soccer world such as Jimmy Lumsden, Mick Bates, Peter Lorimer and their partners, are a couple by the names of Dudley and Ruth Andjel. They were among Don and Elsie Revie's best friends and it was Don who introduced us to them. Dudley is in the textile business in Leeds and it was through him that I obtained the cloth for my suits and jackets as a young player. Since then, whatever problems Linda and I have had, he and Ruth have always been there for us.

Linda and I have even more to be thankful for with our family. In addition to Stuart and Nicholas, we have four daughters – Fiona, thirty-one, Kirsty, thirty, Natalie, twenty-nine, Katherine, twenty-three – and six grandchildren. It is impossible to exaggerate the happiness they have brought us. One of the most difficult things Linda and I have ever had to do was decide who should accompany us into Buckingham Palace to see me receiving the MBE from the Queen. We were allowed to bring in two other people and, with five children then, the only way we were able to settle the issue was by drawing straws. Stuart and Kirsty were the winners; but fortunately, the disappointment for Fiona, Natalie and Katherine was offset by the fact that Leslie Silver put his Rolls-Royce at our disposal for the day (with a chauffeur) and they were at least able to sit in the Buckingham Palace forecourt.

All our children have a lot of sporting ability, which is something that I cannot take all the credit for because Linda was an excellent athlete in her younger days – she was the Leeds schools hurdling champion three years on the trot, and was also good at netball. So, too, were our four girls, all of whom played for North Yorkshire representative teams.

Natalie and Kirsty once worked together as fitness instructors in a Harrogate gym before Natalie became a financial adviser. In February 2001, when Katherine gained a Sports Science degree at Liverpool University and elected to spend her gap year travelling around the world, Natalie quit her job to accompany her. Their absence has not made the Gray household that much quieter because the other female members of the clan – both married – live in the same area and hardly a day goes by without one or other or both popping in with their children. Fiona has five, four of whom are boys (all Leeds fans, naturally) and Kirsty has a daughter.

We are so closely knit that we still take our summer holidays together. We usually go to the South of France, and in 2000 for the family holiday in Bandol, where we were joined by my nephew Andrew and his girlfriend, the head count was sixteen.

Leeds were very good to me, not least with the testimonial match they granted me in March 1979, which put more than £25,000 in my pocket. As a player, I was always happy with what they paid me, especially in the light of my injury problems. In fact, not once did I ask for a better contract.

However, the financial positions of top-level players in my era were nothing like what they are today. Following the remarkable increase in the income of clubs as a result of the formation of the Premiership, not to mention the Jean-Marc Bosman ruling which has meant players being able to move to other clubs at the end of their contracts without their new employers having to pay a transfer fee, the modern stars are in a totally different financial league. Generally, their basic salaries have reached such a high level that most of them can set themselves up for life without winning anything or even performing particularly well. Despite Leeds' success, I was never able to accumulate enough money to alleviate worries about my financial position further down the road. It was the same with most players of my generation, especially as so many of us were not qualified to do anything else for a living.

I did not have any academic qualifications unless you include the diploma I picked up in my mid twenties when I attended a ten-week catering course sponsored by the Professional Footballers Association. I am still not sure how I got through that course; I liked the cooking side of it but struggled to maintain my enthusiasm when it came to writing notes and learning the numerous rules relating to hygiene. I was never going to open my own restaurant, or take over the family cooking from Linda. I think I have only ever made her one meal. The only lesson from that course that stands out in my mind today concerns the best way to clean wine glasses – hold them over a steaming kettle.

At one time, when I was very young (and very naive) I fantasised about becoming a millionaire racehorse owner. The people who must take the blame for this are Peter Lorimer and Mick Bates, who were both keen horse-racing fans. Mick, in particular, has a lot to answer for. He lived in Doncaster, and his friendship with local trainer Jack Berry led to us forming ourselves into a syndicate and buying a couple of horses off Jack.

Our first purchase, which cost us £200 each, was a horse by

the name of Donaire. The three of us went to watch it over the gallops at Pontefract racecourse at five in the morning. Mick and I thought it looked useless, but Peter maintained that it had tremendous potential. Mick and I were proved right, and as far as I know, Donaire ended up as a show-jumper.

Our next horse, Zemonda, cost us about the same but did better with a couple of handicap wins. It was an expensive business when you took into account training fees and the like, and it was not long before we all decided to stick to football.

Linda, who was originally employed as a personal assistant to the head of the Master Builders Association, went back to work after I was sacked. Even so, such was the drop in our income – and, more specifically, our unwillingness to let go of our six-bedroomed family home in the village of Kirkby Overblow, near Harrogate, that our financial situation grew increasingly bleaker. The property, where we have lived since 1972, means a great deal to us. Kirkby Overblow is a beautiful place and we have always felt totally contented there. But after being forced to remortgage the house two or three times in attempts to offset my low earnings, and running up debts including one of £30,000 owed to the Inland Revenue in unpaid tax and fines, we were at breaking point. We reached the stage where, in order to realise the capital to clear all the money we owed, we needed to sell the house for around £350,000 and buy another for £100,000.

The Leeds offer to become youth-team coach, which came totally out of the blue, put me on the road to financial recovery. It brought me back into professional football after a break of five years and I knew I could make something of the job. It was the happiest turning point of my life.

After leaving Leeds, it had taken me some time to find other opportunities. This was partly my fault. Leeds honoured my contract by paying me up until the end of the season and, although I did apply for one or two managerial posts, I was not pro-active enough. People close to me kept telling me, 'Don't worry – you will be offered something else,' and I spent too much time just sitting back and waiting for the phone to ring, which it didn't. It was not until ten months later that I was given the opportunity to work with another league club, Middlesbrough.

In the meantime, to keep myself fit and retain some measure of football involvement, I played fourteen matches for Whitby Town – where Dave Harvey was the player-manager – in the Northern League. The highlight of that period was that we reached the FA Cup second round where the run was terminated by a 3–1 defeat by York. The match I remember the most was a midweek fixture at Chester-le-Street, County Durham, towards the end of the season because that was when I sustained the injury that finally ended my playing career at thirty-eight. One of the problems in playing at this level for someone like me – and I think it applies to a lot of former top-level players who go into non-league football – was that you were always liable to come up against someone eager to be able to tell his friends that he had pulled you down a peg or two; and these people were none too fussy about how they achieved it. The big lad who ran towards me as I received the ball and prepared to change direction did not stand on ceremony. I saw him coming but I could not get out of the way in time, and he caught me across my left knee. The challenge left me with a ruptured anterior cruciate ligament.

Had I been playing for Leeds United, I would have been taken straight to hospital and given the best treatment that money could buy. However, this being non-league football, and my involvement in it being no more than a diversion to keep myself reasonably occupied until something more tangible came up, the scenario was different. The knee was strapped at the ground. I was given a lift to a service station on the A1, about thirty miles from Leeds, where I had left my car, and I managed to drive it home. I am still not sure how; I remember that I had to walk over a bank in pitch darkness to reach the vehicle, and was in so much discomfort that I was almost crawling to it.

After putting off the inevitable for two days, in the crazy hope that by some miracle the damage to the knee might not be as extensive as it seemed, I finally took Linda's advice (if that's the right word) and went to the casualty department of Harrogate

General Hospital. I anticipated the news that I would not be able to play competitive football again, at any level. But when the specialist told me that I would be lucky to walk properly, that was a shock. It really did get to me.

The damage was so bad that the operation to repair it took something like eight hours, and I was in plaster for seven weeks. I was determined that I was not going to be beaten by it and must have spent almost as much time at the hospital's remedial exercise centre as I did at home. The work was worth it because I made a full recovery within four months, considerably less time than the specialist had expected.

In addition to my playing commitments with Whitby, Jimmy Lumsden and I had started coaching in local schools, and decided to have a go at running our own soccer academy for youngsters in the school holidays. Linda and Jimmy's wife Val produced some advertising leaflets to be displayed in newsagents and sweetshops, and other places where they were most likely to be seen by parents and children.

These included a fish and chip shop in Wetherby, which happened to be a popular stopping off place for some league teams when they were passing through the town on away trips. It was my good fortune that when Middlesbrough paid a visit, it coincided with the club having a vacancy for a youth and reserve-team coach. Their manager, Bruce Rioch, and I knew each other quite well from our days in the Scotland squad together, and when he and his assistant Colin Todd went in to that shop to order the squad's take-away suppers, and caught sight of the poster, he hit upon the idea of asking me if I would be interested in the post.

The previous season, 'Boro had been relegated to the Third Division and when I started working there at the start of the 1986–87 season, they were on the brink of being forced into liquidation. I was paid a nominal fee, but working at Ayresome Park was convenient and I enjoyed being part of a set-up that included young players of the calibre of Gary Pallister, not to mention a managerial duo with the ability of Bruce and Colin. The pair did a tremendous job, steering 'Boro back into the Second

Division that season and then into the First the next, via the play-offs. I was at Middlesbrough for just three months before leaving to become manager of Rochdale, and in some ways I regretted not staying and being part of their remarkable success story. The tale of what happened to me at Rochdale, and later Hull, was far less uplifting, although that is not to say it was all doom and gloom.

At Rochdale it seemed quite appropriate that the owner and chairman was Tommy Cannon, of the Cannon and Ball comedy duo, because hardly a day passed without Jimmy Lumsden and me finding something to laugh about. At this level of league football, you have to laugh, otherwise you would cry.

Rochdale's greatest distinction in a largely uneventful and unsuccessful ninety-four-year history is that they are the only Fourth Division club to have reached the League Cup final, which they did in 1962 under the management of the former Leeds chief scout, Tony Collins. (They lost to Norwich City 4–0 on aggregate.) When Jimmy Lumsden and I arrived in December 1986, they were in a desperate plight. Third from bottom of the Fourth Division and with an average gate of just over 2,000, they were so short of money that Linda and Val washed and ironed all the playing kit. Jimmy and I would have to come in early when it rained to deal with the flooding in the dressing room, which had a hole in the roof.

The foundation of the Rochdale pitch was black ash, and when it rained heavily, the substance would come to the surface in lumps which were like bricks. You could actually hear and feel it crunching underfoot as you walked on to the pitch. Before matches and at half-time, we would get boys out with buckets to get rid of as many of them as possible, but a number of players who fell on that surface sustained cuts and a few clubs made official complaints about it.

In the peak winter months, we trained in a public park; and when the weather was particularly bad, in a small church hall. The M62 being the bad road that it was, I would have to leave home at 6.45 in the morning to get to Rochdale and as a number of the players lived well outside the area, it was not unusual for some of them to turn up late, or not at all.

I felt it was as difficult as any job in full-time professional football could be. In spite of this (or should it be because of it?) Jimmy and I got a lot of fun out of it. Much of the enjoyment could be attributed to the loyalty and spirit of the wonderful people who worked at Rochdale behind the scenes. I liked the down-to-earth atmosphere there. There was an honesty about the club, a lack of any form of pretentiousness, that I found very appealing.

Tommy Cannon and Bobby Ball had both been born and raised in Rochdale and once worked together as £20-a-week welders in a tractor factory there. Like a number of self-made men who get involved in their local professional football clubs, Tommy bought Rochdale FC in the hope that, through any success he could help them achieve, he would be giving something back to the community. However, he spent a lot of time away – I dealt mainly with the vice-chairman, David Kilpatrick, who is now the chairman, and another director, David Ferguson – and I think he came to realise that lifting Rochdale was going to take more energy and money than he could afford. It did not surprise me when, not long after my departure, he relinquished his control of the club.

I am sure that his dreams for Rochdale were fuelled by what Elton John had achieved at Watford in helping to steer the club from the Fourth Division to the First in five seasons, a burst to prominence that was followed by the club finishing championship runners-up in 1983 and reaching the FA Cup final in 1984. There was a reference to this in the Rochdale match programme for one of my early matches, against Tranmere. An article in it by Paul Hince of the *Manchester Evening News*, states:

Gray, the elegant wing wizard who thrilled audiences the world over during his playing career for Leeds and Scotland, has no intention of using Rochdale as a stepping stone to greater glories at one of the Football League's more glamorous clubs. In fact, if Gray follows his chairman's ambitious plans for the future,

153

the new Spotland boss will end up as a First Division manager with Rochdale. A pipe dream? Perhaps so. But stranger things have happened in soccer. Just ask the older fans of Watford. Could it be an omen that Watford have risen through the divisions with an eager young manager at the helm [Graham Taylor] and a famous show-business personality as chairman?

For obvious reasons, while I appreciated the importance of adopting a positive attitude, the vision of Rochdale following in the footsteps of Watford was something that I was unwilling to buy into publicly. For me, we had such a long way to go in order to match Watford, it just did not bear thinking about. I took the view that, far from chasing promotion, we had more than enough on our hands to stop ourselves sliding out of the League. Rochdale certainly did well to avoid that in my first season. Inside the club, it provoked a reaction that would have done a European Cup-winning team proud.

When I took over, our biggest problem was in attack. Rochdale had won two of their opening sixteen matches and scored fifteen goals. This was overcome to some extent by the signings of two former Leeds strikers – Derek Parlane and Lyndon Simmonds. Derek, one of the players I had released from Leeds, had been playing for a club called Racing Jet in Belgium before I acquired him for Rochdale on a free transfer in my first month at the club. Although he was in his mid thirties, I felt that he had the knowledge to do a good job for us in the Fourth Division. The big man, one of the major stars of Scottish football with Rangers before he moved south to Leeds, gave us a greater physical presence up front. In addition to scoring seven goals in twenty-three matches, his experience helped create space and chances for others. The obvious beneficiary was Lyndon, whose partnership with Derek was our version of the Little and Large show. Lyndon, only 5ft 4ins tall, was a quick, skilful Welsh lad who had scored many goals for Leeds' junior and reserve teams when I was there. I signed him as a professional, and gave him his first-team debut at the end of my last full season at Leeds. Initially, I brought him to Rochdale on loan, in February 1987, and with ten goals in twenty-two games, he was our top scorer. Hence the fact that at the end of the season, we bought him for £4,000.

Another player who benefited from Derek's presence was our central defender John Bramhall. Derek was like a magnet to opposing defenders at free kicks and corners, and with so much attention focused on him, John was able to find more space when he came up for set-pieces than he would have done in other circumstances. He ended up with nine goals, which put him in a higher position on our scorers' list than Lyndon if you took into account that Lyndon's total included four penalties.

I was fortunate in getting a lot of support from all the players I inherited. My approach was similar to the one I had adopted at Leeds, inasmuch as I wanted the team to play good football. Despite the club's precarious position, it seemed to me that the players liked the way they were asked to perform.

There is a tremendous enthusiasm for the game at this level. Obviously, most of the players don't have the ability of their counterparts further up the scale, but in a lot of cases, they train and play with a wholeheartedness that would put some of the highly paid stars to shame. Midfielder Shaun Reid fell into this category. He is the younger brother of Sunderland's manager Peter. Without being as good a player as Peter was in his Everton and England days, Shaun nevertheless had a similarly committed style of play and the same fiery temperament. He was forever wanting to fight with people – his own team-mates as well as the opposition – but as with Peter, his Scouse scallywag persona made this almost endearing. He is the type of player all teams need when they are in trouble, and the part he played in helping me keep Rochdale in the Football League cannot be overstated.

It was desperately close. Over the second half of the season, we spent most of our time in the bottom two and we were in the dreaded twenty-fourth spot with three matches to go. Although we had a match in hand over the other teams in relegation trouble, we were singled out by most people as the relegation favourites.

However, we moved up to twenty-second position with a 5–3

home win over Halifax and made ourselves safe in the next game, also at home, with a 2–1 victory over Stockport. Our final finishing spot was twenty-first, which was only one place higher than our position when I took over, and we were just two points ahead of relegated Lincoln. This suggested to me that, unless Rochdale underwent a major financial transformation, the task of merely keeping them in the Football League was going to be an uphill struggle.

Tommy Cannon thought otherwise. 'We have got past stage one, and now we have to get to stage two,' he said. Referring to Preston's success that season in clinching promotion to the Third Division after being in relegation trouble the previous season, he added, 'We can do the same thing. In fact, I have already backed us at 250–1.' Unfortunately for him, and for me, we never looked remotely like a team heading for promotion. Again, we spent most of the season among the teams at the bottom; and again, we finished twenty-first.

On the face of it, the claim that I did not have enough money to spend in the transfer market might seem incongruous in the light of Mark Gavin having been bought in the summer of 1987 for a club record fee of £25,000. But that was only a small amount of what I felt the club needed to spend in order to fulfil Tommy Cannon's expectations. As it was, I was generally forced to look at free-transfer players or those from non-league football – and some of those were out of our price range because of our tight wage structure.

Mark, a Glaswegian, was yet another former Leeds player. He had been released by Allan Clarke but I had brought him back to the club and put him in the team for the first time. Eventually, I transferred him to Carlisle, and he was at Bolton at the time I re-signed him for Rochdale. Mark, a smashing lad, was a left-side player who could go past opponents with the ball – which says all that needs to be said about why I had faith in him. The other side of the coin was that he could be rather casual. Hence the fact that he was erratic; so much so that he could perform like a world-beater in one match, and then look almost as if he had never kicked a

156

ball in his life the next. We discussed this a lot, and Mark appreciated that it was stopping him from realising his potential. But it was something he was never able to eradicate.

While he did not have the impact I had hoped for at Rochdale, it might have been a different story had we been able to get a few more higher-class players into the team and therefore bring him into the play more often. Mark had not been at the club long before we were hit by a financial crisis which forced us to make cuts in our wage bill. One casualty was Derek Parlane, who was released in January and joined Airdrie (where Gordon McQueen was manager). Mark, who had been signed to help provide the service of crosses Derek needed, was sold the following month to another Scottish club, Hearts, for £30,000.

As for Jimmy Lumsden and I, it became increasingly clear that Rochdale, whose average league gate had fallen below the 2,000 mark, could not afford to keep both of us; because of the team's disappointing results, it was on the cards that we would both be axed. I am blessed with sensitive antennae for moods within football clubs and, as at Leeds, I was well prepared for my fate.

I did not consider that Jimmy and I had been abject failures at Rochdale. After all, the club finished eighteenth the following season and had to wait five years before achieving promotion. Moreover, it was reassuring that we both quickly stepped into new jobs at higher levels. Jimmy became assistant-manager to Joe Jordan at Third Division Bristol City and I became manager of Second Division Hull.

It seemed a wonderful challenge. Apart from the difference between Hull and Rochdale in their league status, Hull were the bigger of the two clubs in terms of crowd potential. Even so, I had precious little money to spend, and the truth is I never felt comfortable there. Strange as it might seem, I was happier at Rochdale.

Hull was rugby league territory rather than a soccer stronghold. The club, while having had some great individuals playing for them over the years, had never been in the top flight and, at the time I was manager, the general structure led me to believe that they were far more likely to go backwards than forwards. Hull had been on the slide before I arrived. They were third in the Second Division in 1985, and over the next three seasons finished sixth, fourteenth and fifteenth. In my season as manager, 1988–89, it was twenty-first (which, being the same spot that Rochdale filled in my two seasons there, raised the tongue-in-cheek comment among my friends that at least I was consistent). As I anticipated, the Hull slide continued after I left.

One reason why I did not enjoy this job was my relationship with Hull's extrovert chairman and owner, Don Robinson. There was a clash of personalities, which was accentuated by the fact that I was in much closer contact with Robinson than I had been with Tommy Cannon at Rochdale. Robinson wanted me to move to Hull but I kept putting it off. The longer we worked together, the more I realised that our association was not going to work.

There was a lot to admire about Don Robinson. A former wrestler, boxer and rugby league player, he was an entrepreneur with a capital E. Before taking over at Hull in 1982, he had been chairman of Scarborough, and laid the foundations for the club's entry into the Football League. At Hull, he took the club out of receivership, and steered them from the Fourth Division to the Second in his first two seasons. As a figure with an acute sense of showmanship, he became even more famous for publicity gimmicks such as riding a horse around the pitch dressed in a rodeo outfit, and bringing a tame brown bear into the club. It was typical of him that when Hull played Liverpool at home in the FA Cup fifth round in the season I was there, one part of the ground was adorned with a banner which drew attention to the physical approach of our centre-forward Billy Whitehurst, and proclaimed, 'Go get 'em, Rambo'.

The Messiah of Boothferry Park he might have been, but I found him overpowering, particularly in relation to the areas of the club that I felt were my responsibility. One point of conflict between us concerned the short mid-season break he organised for the players in Bermuda. I was invited to go, too, but I felt that it would be better to remain at home and concentrate on trying to find players who could strengthen the side. That decision turned out to be a mistake because when they got back, I was amazed to learn that Robinson had taken it upon himself to give them his own training sessions and that much of their work involved running up and down sand dunes. That was the last thing they needed as far as I was concerned – it was the sort of training players did in the close season, when building up their fitness after the summer break. But when I challenged Robinson about this, he explained that he felt they needed 'toughening up'.

I also found it difficult to accept his pre-match dressing-room visits to give the players the benefit of his advice – advice that in a number of cases, I did not agree with.

Robinson typified the new breed of football club chairmen in England; men for whom football is a business, not a hobby, and who adopt much more of a hands-on approach than their counter-parts in the past. The urge to pull all the strings at Hull was one that Robinson appeared to me to find difficult to resist. I admired his drive, but as far as I was concerned, the way it was applied did not make him an easy person to work for. In common with a lot of chairmen, I think Robinson made the mistake of assuming that the principles that had made his other businesses successful were bound to work in football, too. Because of the many and varied imponderables involved, football is unique.

For someone like Robinson, Hull's results after they reached the Second Division will have been very hard to take. The fact that I could not stop the slide was disappointing for me, too, especially as we had a tremendous pair of strikers in Keith Edwards and Billy Whitehurst. Keith, a quiet, unassuming person who had played for Leeds under Billy Bremner, was one of the best finishers I have worked with. I felt he was not assertive enough at times, but his scoring record that season meant that I could never be too dogmatic about this. Then in his second spell at Hull, he was the Second Division's top scorer with 26 league goals and an overall total of 30.

Lack of assertiveness was never a problem for Billy Whitehurst, whom I signed from Sunderland and who was the perfect foil for Keith. Billy, 6ft tall and weighing 13 stone, was the strongest and most intimidating centre-forward I have worked with. He became a cult figure at Hull, as he did at his other clubs, because he made the likes of Joe Jordan and Mark Hughes seem almost genteel. Players really were scared of him. Not long ago, I was discussing Billy with Leeds' goalkeeper Nigel Martyn, who recounted a match he played against him for Crystal Palace. There was a clash between the two and Nigel, showing his recklessness in those days, tried to out-psyche him. 'I will see you after the game,' he said. Later, when Nigel was having a drink with his centre-half Andy Thorn in the players' lounge, he felt a tap on his shoulder. He turned around and there was Billy glaring at him. 'You still want to have a go then?' Billy asked him. Nigel recalled that Thorn and everybody else in close proximity to him suddenly disappeared. Needless to say, his reply to Billy was not in the affirmative.

Billy was happy to fight anyone, and from what I heard he was not too bothered about how many were against him. He knew no fear. On a couple of occasions, he would come in for training with bruises and cuts on his face, which always caused me to wonder what the other fellow (or fellows) must have looked like.

Although Billy was a very strong-minded character, I got on well with him. I knew how to handle him and he never gave me any trouble. Apart from being good in the air, his touch was not bad for someone of his build. He did a good job for me.

Not long after my sacking at the end of that season, I was surprised to get a call from him at my home on a Sunday morning. He had become the most influential member of the squad, and he put it to me that he could use this to get me back to the club. 'All the boys want you back, Eddie,' he said. 'I will lead a deputation to the chairman.' I appreciated the thought, but even if Don Robinson had changed his mind, there is no way I could have gone back to Hull. Ten months is no time in a manager's job, but those ten months had seemed like ten years to me. When Robinson sacked me in May 1989, it came as a relief. It was the right decision for both parties.

160

The experience left me quite disillusioned about full-time professional football, and especially about having to rely on the game for my livelihood. So, instead of trying to find a job as a manager or coach at another league club, I took up the offer to be manager of Whitby Town and became involved in the personal management and promotional companies run by Ken Stanley, George Best's former agent, and Ian St John junior, son of the former Liverpool and Scotland forward and ITV pundit.

Ken, the British representative for an Eastern European football, hired me to help him promote it among English clubs. It was through him that I met Ian and got involved in helping players with contracts and advertising and endorsement agreements; also in setting up summer soccer schools for youngsters from the ages of eight to thirteen. After a while, the soccer schools occupied most of my time. We had as many as 3,500 boys and girls enrolling on the summer courses and our coaching centres were spread throughout the whole of Britain.

Unfortunately, as my responsibilities with the company occasionally required me to be available to them on a Whitby training night, or a matchday, I had to resign from the club at the end of the season. It was not a decision I took lightly – I'd had a wonderful time there and achieved a fair measure of success. The club had undergone a major upheaval when I joined in September 1989, and were nineteenth in the League after taking one point from the first five games. They had scored five goals and conceded fifteen.

Here again, I encouraged the players to express themselves. I brought a striker by the name of Steve French back to Whitby from Eastfield in the Teesside League and he and our other striker, Paul Pitmann, ended up with twenty-six league goals each. The team finished twelfth and reached the final of the League Cup (in which we lost to Billingham Synthonia) and the North Riding Senior Cup (in which we beat our neighbours Guisborough Town).

One bonus of the job was that, Whitby being a fishing town, a club official would give me a huge bag of fresh fish to take home each week. Linda and I, both lovers of seafood, still joke about it – how many other managers get paid in prawns and cod? Of course, I did get money as well, but Whitby were not in a position to pay me enough to justify my staying there at the expense of my other job.

After a while, I was able to add another string to my bow with some TV and radio punditry. But I was never going to give the likes of Alan Hansen or Andy Gray any worries about their positions. My income depended on a number of small bits and pieces, and no one job truly absorbed me, and as time went by I became restless. Then came the telephone call from Howard Wilkinson which led to my return to Elland Road.

Although I did not know it at the time, the path back to Leeds started towards the end of the 1994–95 season with an application I made for the job of running the Football in the Community scheme funded jointly by Leeds United and the Leeds City Council. Paul Hart, United's Director of Youth Football, was a member of the interviewing panel. He and the others felt that I was by far the best applicant for the job on my experience as a player and manager, but they plumped for someone else because I did not have the required full FA coaching badge. Apparently, Paul discussed this with Howard, and Howard said, 'Well, could we use Eddie? Would you be happy for him to work with you?'

So Howard telephoned me and asked me to come to the ground to see him. I was surprised to put it mildly. He was not prepared to explain why he wanted to see me and my first reaction was that I had said something about Leeds during one of my radio match-summariser stints that had upset him.

I met him the following day and we agreed that I would work with Paul on a part-time basis for the rest of the season and begin the job in earnest at the start of the new season. The only stumbling block was that as Howard was a leading member of the FA coaching hierarchy, it was felt that the appointment would seem incongruous if I did not get a full FA coaching badge.

That was fair enough. I had no acquired my preliminary badge at seventeen or eighteen and had no objections about taking the

162

next step. But having booked myself on the one-week course at Lilleshall, along with a number of other pros, I walked out after the first day. I have always taken the view that one does not need a piece of paper to confirm one's coaching ability – you can either coach or you can't. In this instance, trying to get the official qualifications was a bit like taking a driving test. Some of the people on that course were schoolteachers, who had never played the game at any professional level, and it seemed to me that these were the people for whom the course was designed. The whole thing was very standardised, with the various demonstrations you had to present appearing to be assessed mainly on their organisation and timing. Everything had to be done by the FA book.

I did quite well on my first day, but among those who received the lowest marks were Peter Taylor – the same Peter Taylor who was to have so much success as coach of England's Under-21 team and is now Leicester manager – and Terry Gibson, the former Wimbledon striker now assistant manager at Wycombe. Peter and I still joke about it. For some reason, he just went to pieces on his first session and, in fact, he wanted to go home, too.

Terry had an even bigger nightmare, which worsened when he, Peter and I were having a drink at the bar that night and Dario Gradi, Crewe's manager and one of the coaching assessors, gave us our first-day reports. Maybe I was being over-sensitive, but I thought Dario's attitude to Terry was a bit like that of a school-teacher admonishing a child who had not done his homework properly. I thought, 'How can you do that to a fellow professional with his record?' I also thought, 'This is not for me.'

My departure could easily have screwed up my new position at Leeds. According to Paul, Howard told him that the club would probably have to look for someone else. Leeds' chairman, Leslie Silver, called me in and said, 'What you did was very embarrassing for the manager – it has put him in a very difficult situation.' I realised that I had probably over-reacted, and was prepared to accept the consequences.

'Look Mr Chairman, there is no need for anyone to feel bad

about this,' I said. 'If Howard does not want to employ me, that's fair enough – there are no hard feelings from my end.'

But Howard decided to go ahead with our arrangement. The lifeline was repaired.

11

DOWN AMONG THE YOUNG GUNS

A FEW weeks before the end of my first season back at Leeds,
Howard Wilkinson held a crisis meeting with his training and
coaching staff in the Elland Road boardroom. Things had not been
going well for Howard, which is putting it mildly. Our league form
had been erratic; and in the League Cup final against Aston Villa
in March 1996 – a match he was banking on to lift some of the
pressure off him – our performance in losing 3–0 was so disappointing that, unusually for an occasion such as this, Howard
left the pitch to the chant of 'Wilko out' from the Leeds fans.

It got even worse for him, with Leeds hitting a dismal league
run – we lost seven and won one of our last nine matches. I
think Howard realised that unless the situation changed quickly,
he would have to go.

Although I was involved just with the youth team then, what I
had observed about the first-team set-up surprised me. Before I
started working at Leeds again, people told me about Howard's
drive and how meticulous he was, but I had not seen much evidence
of this. For me, the tell-tale signs of a manager in decline could
be detected by the general slackness of the players in training. All
managers have a sell-by date – I think there is a limit to how much
you can keep pushing yourself with one club, especially as the
manager's job has become more difficult than ever in recent years.
With Howard having been at Leeds for eight years, I had the
impression that he had become stale.

Howard asked Paul Hart and me, among others, to go and see

him, and asked for suggestions on where things were going wrong. No one said much so I spoke up.

'Howard, do you mind if I say something?'

'No, Eddie, go ahead,' he replied. I told him that I couldn't believe the lack of discipline at the club.

'Eddie, you're right,' he said. 'It's my fault – I have let things slip. I've got to get back on top of people.'

Unfortunately for Howard, it had gone too far. In the early weeks of the next season, following another 'Wilko out' demonstration by the fans as an Eric Cantona-inspired Manchester United thrashed us 4–0 at home in our fifth match, they got their wish.

Because of the part he played in my return to Leeds, nobody can have been sadder than I was at his Elland Road career ending on such a sour note. The other reason why I felt for Howard was that I recognised what a tremendous job he had done for the club. When discussing Leeds' position today, Howard's contribution should not be underestimated. The obvious reason why nobody connected with Leeds should forget what he did is that after the struggles of eight previous managers, including myself, over a period of fourteen years, he was the one who took the club back to where they had been under Don Revie. He may have been unable to sustain that success, but his successor George Graham had a decent foundation upon which to build.

Of all the signings Howard made in producing the teams that won the Second Division championship in the 1989–90 season and the First Division title two seasons later, the most intriguing as far as I am concerned were Gordon Strachan from Manchester United in March 1989, and Lee Chapman from Nottingham Forest in January 1990. Few people expected these two to be as effective as they were. The story of Strachan's impact at Elland Road was quite similar to that of his fellow Scot Bobby Collins in the 1960s. Gordon, then thirty-two and reckoned to be a spent force as a top midfield player, took on a new lease of life under Howard.

He was not the only golden oldie Howard signed for Leeds. No doubt encouraged by Gordon's success, Howard took on other seemingly over-the-hill thirty-somethings such as Ian Rush and Mark Hateley, but they could not hold a candle to Gordon. He was a one-off.

Howard had a reputation for putting the emphasis on organisation and fitness above skill – on Route One football – so outsiders might well have expected a culture clash between him and Gordon. But it is only when you work with someone that you can really assess them and Gordon, like a lot of players who have been involved with Howard, quickly discovered that there was a lot more to him than what he had heard or read. He put it this way:

> People have certain ideas about Howard, but once you actually sit down and talk to him about his methods, you are totally blown away. As a youngster, you think there is only one way to play the game, but as you get older, you do become more open-minded. He made me appreciate that whatever style of play a team adopt, it has to create scoring chances. You can string as many lovely passes together as you want, but if it doesn't result in a scoring chance, it's a waste of time. As for the long-ball stigma, he also drove it home to me that there is a big difference between a long pass, which is what he liked to see, and a speculative hoof up the park. Howard didn't say, 'I don't want you to play.' But first, we had to pressurise teams, wear them down. Basically, he said that there was a certain way of playing that would get us out of the Second Division, provided that we trusted his judgement enough to work at it. We did trust him and it did work.

Howard boosted Gordon's self-esteem by giving him more responsibility than his Manchester United manager, Alex Ferguson, had done. Whereas Gordon felt like just another player at Old Trafford, Howard exploited his experience and know-how by appointing him Leeds' team captain and often consulting with him. At £300,000, Gordon, remarkably fit and durable, proved arguably the most inspired purchase of Howard's entire managerial career.

When Sir Alex was asked to nominate his most inspired buy recently, he singled out someone who moved in the opposite direction to Gordon – Eric Cantona. As I have said, I would not criticise Howard for letting Cantona go; in the circumstances that existed at the time, it was the right decision. It was the same with Ferguson's decision to release Gordon. It is difficult to say which manager got the better bargain – I think they were probably equal in that respect.

When Leeds won the championship – admittedly, courtesy of Manchester United losing their nerve when in a strong winning position – the midfield of David Batty, Gordon, Gary McAllister and Gary Speed was stronger than it had been since the Revie days. I had a particular interest in Speed, having signed the Welshman for Leeds as a schoolboy. It is great to see that Gary, who moved on to Newcastle, has gone on to achieve the distinction of being the Premiership player with the most appearances at this level.

However, if I had to single out anyone from that side as an example for youngsters to follow, it would have to be Gordon. In his six years with the club, he picked up more man of the match awards than any other player. The Strachan performance for Leeds that I remember best came in the season after the championship triumph, when Leeds seemed to be heading into the relegation zone. The match in question was against Blackburn at home in April. In the absence of Batty and McAllister, it appeared at times as if Gordon was playing Rovers virtually on his own. Leeds won 5–2, and his contribution included a hat-trick – which comprised two penalties and a thunderbolt of a shot from twenty yards – and a great through pass to set up Rod Wallace for one of the others. That was the sort of leadership by example for which Billy Bremner was noted. The fact that Gordon had been hailed as 'another Bremner' when he began his career as a teenager at Dundee was clearly not due just to his red hair and small build.

Howard's judgement was also vindicated by the success of Lee Chapman. He was thirty when he was bought for £400,000 and his credibility among the Leeds fans was not helped by Howard having previously sold Ian Baird, one of their favourites, to Middlesbrough. Lee was not the most polished of centre-forwards, as Eric Cantona emphasised with his somewhat arrogant, dismissive attitude towards him when the pair played together. But Howard knew Lee well, having worked with him at Sheffield Wednesday, and appreciated the manner in which the centre-forward could offset his faults – lack of pace and mobility – through his knowledge of the game, or 'tricks of the trade' as Lee described it.

Cantona's resentment over Lee's presence in the team, or rather the fact that our style of play was geared to Lee rather more than it was to him, was difficult to take seriously when you looked at how effective it was. For the system that Howard was developing at Leeds, based on stretching the opposition down the flanks, mainly through the pace of the full-backs Mel Sterland and Tony Dorigo, and getting plenty of crosses into the box, Lee was absolutely perfect. His power in the air and intelligent positioning brought him 62 goals in his 137 league matches. Leeds were top of the Second Division when he arrived and he made sure we stayed there with 12 goals in 21 matches. He was the top scorer when we finished fourth in the First Division the following season and also when we won the title in 1992.

It seems incongruous that the championship victory, in the last season of the old First Division, was followed by Leeds finishing as low as seventeenth in the Premiership the following season, not to mention being knocked out of the European Cup by Rangers in the second round. However, their approach to the game had been rendered less effective through the change in the back-pass rule.

In the championship season, the ball would often be played back to John Lukic and, with the players in front of him pushing up to the halfway line to compress the play, the next steps would be Lee Chapman getting his head to John's drop kick and colleagues moving up to win the second ball and keep the opposition hemmed into their own area. Quite often, we would be able to win a throw-in close to the goal, or a corner, without having had to make one pass. When goalkeepers could no longer handle the ball after a back-pass, it meant that defenders had to be in closer contact with them and the game became more stretched out. Instead of playing in half of the pitch, you had to use three-quarters of it. There was more space for players to settle on the ball and use their skill. As Gordon Strachan has said:

> From that point, defenders had to be able to pass and play, which is where our central defenders [Chris Whyte and Chris Fairclough] were caught out. They had been magnificent for us, but they found the change difficult. It affected Lee Chapman as well – the ball did not come through to him as early as it did previously and he had to hold the ball up longer, which was not his game. That change in the rules was what really killed our team. In contrast, Manchester United were helped by it. They had better players than we did when the rule changed, especially at the back with Gary Pallister and Steve Bruce.

Manchester United won their first championship since 1967 – the springboard that was to lead to a total of seven titles in nine years.

Howard steered Leeds to fifth place in 1993–94 and 1994–95. Then, after the slump that undermined his position in the 1995–96 season, the task of reversing Leeds' fortunes was not made any easier for him by the legal dispute over the club's change of ownership. Before the season started, Howard had wasted no time in making use of the transfer market spending money earmarked for him in buying Lee Bowyer from Charlton for £2.6 million, a British record fee for a teenager. Howard's shopping spree was halted by the High Court challenge to the take-over, and by the time he was given the green light again, the new season was less than a month away and his transfer market options had inevitably shrunk. On top of this, Gary McAllister, who had taken over from Gordon Strachan as the creative leader in midfield, and who had indicated that he would stay at the club, surprisingly left to join Gordon at Coventry.

Howard was able to make two other big signings, Nigel Martyn from Crystal Palace for £2.3 million and Lee Sharpe from Manchester United for a club record fee of £4.5 million. We did not make a bad start to the season with two wins and a draw in our opening four matches; but then came that hiding at the hands of Manchester United and Howard, who for weeks had had to contend with speculation about the new owners wanting to replace him with George Graham, was out.

As I have said, the legacy he left cannot be forgotten. Part of that legacy concerns the importance of Martyn and Bowyer in today's Leeds team; and while on the subject of signings by Howard, he also brought David O'Leary to the club as a player in the summer of 1993. David was able to play just ten matches under Howard because of injury and had retired by the time his old Gunners boss, George Graham, became manager. The two had kept in touch through playing the occasional round of golf together, and I think it's reasonable to assume that David's inside knowledge of the Leeds players, and the club, was one of the reasons why George invited him to become his assistant. The rest, as they say, is history.

The other aspect of Howard's legacy – and by far the biggest – can be seen in the youth academy set-up at our magnificent training complex at Thorpe Arch, near Wetherby, and the number of graduates from it who have become established members of our present first-team squad. It was Howard who initiated our youth system. It was part of a ten-year programme planned to put Leeds on the same footing as Manchester United and other clubs who have built outstanding teams with players they have developed themselves. In a way, it is a pity that Howard was not around to see at first hand his grand plan come to fruition. You could say that he was ahead of his time. If the youngsters in our squad now had been available to him as Leeds manager, I daresay things would have worked out differently for him.

Football club youth academies are an expensive business. They can cost millions to set up and run, especially when clubs are as committed to this facet of the game as Leeds have been. It is well known that top schoolboy players do not necessarily turn into good professional footballers and, indeed, that the failure rate among those who become attached to league clubs is exceptionally high.

For this reason, when talking about first-team players who have been with a club since leaving school, and thus not carried a transfer fee, I have always been amused to hear people describe them as having cost their clubs nothing. I am not aware of any recent financial study on the subject, but I do remember that Arsenal carried out one just after they won the championship and FA Cup double in 1971. Taking into account all their scouting and coaching costs, they worked it out that Charlie George, who had graduated through the youth system and scored the goal that brought them the double, had cost them around £100,000.

Of course, in producing players for the first team, some youth systems have better crops in some years than others and, in most cases, the leading graduates do not cost a club anything like as much as they would if they had to be bought in the transfer market. The other way of looking at it is that clubs can make money out of their youth set-ups through the sale of players. The principle that the better the education the youngsters receive, the greater their market value is likely to be worked for us with striker Noel Whelan and midfielder Matthew Jones. Noel, born in Leeds, was sold to Coventry for £2 million in December 1995 at the age of twenty-one. Matthew, who had left his native Wales to come to Leeds at fourteen – a move that meant Leeds putting him up with a family in Wetherby and arranging for him to go to a local school – was sold to Leicester for £3 million in December 2000 aged twenty.

Towards the end of 2000–01, when we were due to buy Robbie Keane from Inter Milan, it was reported that one worry for us in finding the £11 million needed to turn the loan signing into a permanent transfer was that we had a short-term debt of more than £50 million that had to be repaid. Many people might have been horrified by that, but even at a time when there was so much uncertainty about the future of the transfer market, the figure became considerably less intimidating when you looked at the market value of the home-grown youngsters in our first-team squad, and the top young players bought by David O'Leary to supplement them. That £50 million was nothing compared with what our first-team squad was worth.

All this was part of Howard's vision for Leeds' future, and he was fortunate in having people above him – notably the irrepressible Bill Fotherby, the member of the board who had the closest working relationship with him – buying into the dream. Bill did so to the extent of becoming almost as passionate about it as Howard was. Leeds were the first club in the country to have their own hostel for youngsters, which was actually Bill's old house.

Leeds were also galvanised by Paul Hart, our former centre-half. Howard brought him back at the start of the 1992–93 season from Nottingham Forest where he had been working as a coach under Brian Clough. Paul's job title was Director of Youth Football and, as that tag indicates, he was given greater power, and certainly greater autonomy, than the people running the youth development side of other clubs. Howard, who had been Paul's manager for a short while when the pair were at Sheffield Wednesday, gave Paul *carte blanche* to choose his own staff and do whatever he deemed necessary within the rules to get the best schoolboy players. Unlike some managers who are inclined to feel threatened if they do not have their fingers in every pie, Howard was happy for Paul's department to be kept separate from his and for Paul to be answerable to the chairman and Bill. In fact, Howard insisted on this, his reasoning being that the youth set-up had to be stable, and that if there was any change in his position at the club, Paul would not be affected by it.

Paul realised that in order to be successful in the fiercely competitive schoolboy footballers market, where we were up against clubs who had left Leeds behind, we needed to be bold. That boldness was reflected in the length of the contracts offered and the financial terms. On leaving school at sixteen, it was not unusual for boys to be given contracts for five or six years. In fact, in a lot of cases, Leeds were prepared to promise those contracts to the lads when they started their two-year scholarships with the club at fourteen. Therefore, even if the club had changed their minds about any of these players by the time they reached the age of sixteen, we were still obliged to take them on to the staff.

The deals Leeds offered were as lucrative as those of any other club, if not more so, and depending on the player's progress, Paul and Bill were quite happy to keep improving the terms. When I was reserve-team coach under George Graham, I remember George being taken aback to learn that on top of their normal contracts, six or seven of the youth players in my side were on an appearance bonus of £500 a match. He felt that was wrong, but as Paul's department was outside his area of responsibilities, he couldn't do anything about it.

Any outlay on teenaged players is a gamble. You could argue that the more you give young players, the greater the danger of them being spoilt and losing sight of the need to keep pushing themselves. Fortunately, in all my time at Leeds, I have never known one of our boys to be quite like the fourteen year old who came to the club for a trial – with his agent – and spent much of his time conducting conversations on his mobile phone, and asking other boys here why, unlike him, they did not have any personal kit sponsorship deals.

Paul was great at his job. While I am sure he would be the first to concede that he made mistakes, his judgement has generally proved to be exceptionally good. The hits among the players he signed have far outweighed the misses. In his first season, the need for him to find more talent for the youth squad quickly led him to signing Jamie Forrester and Kevin Sharp, seventeen and eighteen respectively, from Auxerre in France in October. Auxerre, among the smallest of France's leading clubs, have a youth system that has long been envied throughout Europe, and Forrester and Sharp, who had attended the FA National School of Lilleshall, elected to start their careers there as trainees. Paul, tipped off that they had both become homesick, moved in quickly to bring them to Leeds for £120,000.

Forrester, a talented striker, helped Leeds reach the FA Youth Cup final where, despite most people's expectations, we achieved a 4–1 aggregate victory against a Manchester United team including Phil Neville, David Beckham, Paul Scholes, Nicky Butt and Keith Gillespie. Leeds won both legs, watched by 30,000 crowds, and Forrester scored two of the goals – one of them with an audacious overhead kick which has remained one of his biggest claims to fame to this day.

Paul recognised that the triumph was achieved with organisation and astute tactics rather than flair, and that the players were not good enough to inspire much confidence in them being able to take the club further. I think half the team were released within a few weeks of the win over Manchester United, with the rest phased out of the picture more gradually.

The only member of the side who played Premiership football elsewhere was Noel Whelan, Forrester's striking partner. Even Forrester and Sharp failed to make it. Forrester, who was small and slightly built and had difficulty coping with the physical side of the game, moved to Grimsby on a free transfer in October 1995, and then on to Scunthorpe, Utrecht, Walsall and Northampton. Sharp was transferred to Wigan for £100,000 the following month.

The great thing about the win over Manchester United was that it gave our youth set-up a high profile, and led to the signing of a group of players whose technical ability took the breath away. By the 1995–96 season, the lads taking their first steps as Leeds players included the seventeen-year-old Harry Kewell, who had arrived at the club from Australia, and a group of younger trainees such as Paul Robinson, Alan Maybury, Jonathan Woodgate, Stephen McPhail and Alan Smith. Both Paul and Howard could see that these lads had the potential to be special – anyone could. Howard agreed that Paul could do with an extra coach to help him get the best out of them, and that is where I came in.

I got on well with Paul. The fact that I had sold him to Forest when I was Leeds' manager did not create any problems in our relationship because Paul wanted to go. He badly wanted to get back into the First Division and we needed the £40,000 that Forest paid for him. The thing I remember the most about that transfer was Brian Clough's reaction to Bill Fotherby being with Paul and myself at the meeting at the City Ground to finalise it. Clough, a man from the old-fashioned school of managers who believed that football club directors should be seen and not heard, told Bill that he would not deal with him and even suggested that he should stay in the car. To his credit, Bill stood his ground. He told Clough that the deal would not go ahead if he was not present, and Clough was forced to back down.

That was the first of three spells for Paul at Forest, where he became manager in the summer of 2001. After playing at Sheffield Wednesday and Birmingham, becoming player-coach at Notts County and manager at Chesterfield, he was taken on to Forest's coaching staff by Clough. Paul, who had continued to live in Nottingham, even when he returned to Leeds, recalled, 'I used to go and see Brian and ask him to put my name forward for jobs. Then one night, completely out of the blue, he telephoned me and said, "If you are as good as I keep telling people you are, you had better come and work for me."'

Paul thought the world of Clough and felt that the experience of working with him was invaluable. He was particularly influenced by Clough's discipline, especially in his dealings with young players, and this was a feature of Paul's own approach at Leeds. As Clough was renowned for his authoritarian approach and Paul was a fiery person, it was perhaps only to be expected that Paul was not the easiest of people to work for. He reminded me of Syd Owen when he was my youth and reserve-team coach at Leeds. He was very intense, which no doubt could be attributed partly to the responsibility on his shoulders, and explosive.

He was great with me, but he could be abrasive with other people. This is where we complemented each other. I had a more relaxed attitude. While appreciating the importance of players being disciplined, I felt that to an extent they needed to be allowed to make mistakes. If I felt Paul had over-reacted to a lad having done something silly, I was liable to say, 'You can't be in control of everything. These players are only young – they're bound to do silly things at times.' My attitude to their performances was the same. I wanted them to use their skills, and they weren't going to do that if they were scared of making mistakes.

So because of the differences between Paul and me, and our willingness to challenge each other, I thought we made a good team. There can be no doubt that he was good for me. He was a

My son Stuart started his senior career with twenty-two league appearances for Celtic.

My nephew Andrew in action for Leeds against Aston Villa in the 1996 Coca-Cola Cup final.

The Leeds youngsters won the 1997 FA Youth Cup.

Three of the players who played in the final against Crystal Palace – Harry Kewell (*above left*), Stephen McPhail (*above right*) and Jonathan Woodgate (*below*).

Howard Wilkinson and Gordon Strachan were central figures in Leeds' rebirth as a great club.

Paul Hart (*left*) experiences an anxious first-team break from his youth responsibilities alongside coach Dave Williams and manager George Graham.

David O'Leary, George Graham and I strive to get some points across at Tottenham in 1998.

Left David and I looking for good omens before our friendly against Celtic in July 1999.

Below Some words of wisdom (I hope) to our lads before a clash with Manchester United.

Rio Ferdinand with Peter Ridsdale when Leeds made him the world's most expensive defender.

This is my spiritual home.

Putting the irrepressible Alan Smith in the picture.

All smiles (at least from me) after beating our youngest offspring, Nicholas, at tennis during a South of France family holiday.

More potential Gray players at Leeds? My grandsons (*clockwise*) Tom, Matthew, Olive and Joseph.

The Magnificent Five – (*left to right*) Katherine, Natalie, Linda, Fiona and Kirsty on Millennium Eve.

tremendous coach and I learned a lot from him, especially through his attention to detail.

One area in which I tended to disagree with Paul concerned his quest to steer the youth team to trophies. To me, winning competitions was not that important for players of that age. I was more concerned with the way they played rather than their results. However, I could appreciate Paul's argument about the advantages for players of getting into a winning habit.

In our first season together, the youth team won the Northern Intermediate League Cup. The following season, we won the FA Youth Cup again and also the Northern Intermediate League for the first time since the youth side that I played in did it 1964. The Youth Cup trail brought victories over Sheffield Wednesday, Crewe, Manchester City, Queen's Park Rangers, Tranmere and, in the final, Crystal Palace. The team that overcame Palace 2–1 at home and 1–0 away was: Paul Robinson, Alan Maybury, Jonathan Woodgate, Damian Lynch, Harry Kewell; Kevin Dixon, Tommy Knarvik, Stephen McPhail, Wesley Boyle; Matthew Jones, Lee Matthews. It says much about the skill of the side that, at the time of the final of this Under-18 competition, the only players to have reached their eighteenth birthdays were Kewell, Maybury and Boyle. Most of the others were seventeen, or in the cases of Dixon and Jones, sixteen. It was unusual for a team as young as this to win the trophy, but in technical ability I thought we were streets ahead of our opponents. Woodgate had initially played for the side that season at sixteen. Of those who did not play in the final but contributed to our success in other matches, Alan Smith was also sixteen.

Woodgate, in fact, was only fifteen and still at school when he first started playing for the youth team. At the end of my first season, I included him in the squad I took to the United States to play in the Dallas Cup tournament in Texas. This was an Under-20 competition and as it attracted some of the best teams in the world, we viewed it as a perfect opportunity to see what our youngsters could do at a higher level. Robin Rae, the other Leeds youth coach who went on that trip, had reservations about Jonathan.

'I am a bit worried about him,' he told me. 'I'm not sure he's going to be quick enough.' Despite his tall build, Jonathan has an unusually short running stride.

'He might look slow at times,' I said, 'but if you watch him closely, you will find that he can run like the wind.'

Jonathan's pale, skinny appearance, which prompted his team-mates to refer to him as 'The Ghost', suggested that he would be blown away by any half-decent centre-forward, but he was a revelation in that competition. When we got back, I said to Paul, 'I think you have found a great centre-half.'

In training, Jonathan was one of the young players whom Paul and I tended to nag the most. As with a lot of players with an abundance of natural ability, the game was too easy for him at times and he would have lapses of concentration. This characteristic can be traced to his attitude in training. He does like a laugh and a joke, and while there is nothing wrong in that, it can be a distraction. It is important to be totally focused in training because for any player, and especially a central defender, that's what you have to be on a Saturday. Having said that, Jonathan, who played for the England team at nineteen and is still only twenty-one, has been among the best central defenders in the business at every level he has played at.

Another player Paul and I talked about a lot then was Alan Smith. Quite apart from our concern over his temperament – even in those days, Alan's temper was a problem – Paul was unsure whether he was good enough to take on to our YT staff at sixteen. Having originally been signed by the club at fourteen, Alan had left to attend the FA National School where his enthusiasm for the game was undermined by homesickness and a broken ankle. When he came back to us at fifteen, he was not the same player. Although he had not been playing well for some time, I thought that it was worth taking a chance on him; and almost immediately he came on to the staff, it was as if someone had waved a magic wand over him.

It was wonderful to be involved with young players of this cal-ibre; players who would do things on a football field that would entertain and excite you. They were all capable of it, but the ones who were really outstanding were Harry Kewell and Stephen McPhail. Harry and one of his New South Wales Soccer Academy team-mates, Brett Emerton, had come to Leeds to broaden their knowledge of the game, under a sponsorship scheme run by an Australian philanthropic body called the Big Brother movement. That was in 1995. Paul and I wanted both players, but could have Harry only because, unlike Emerton, his father was English (he emigrated to Australia at twenty) and he held a UK passport. Paul was not a bad judge. Emerton, who like Harry is a key member of Australia's national team, of which he is the captain, now plays his club football with Feyenoord in Holland.

Harry is one of the greatest players in Europe at going past opponents with the ball, and of all Paul's signings, I suppose you could describe him as the jewel in the crown. As I was noted for the same art, it should come as no surprise that he is the present Leeds player with whom I have always felt the closest affinity. Not long ago, someone asked me how I would compare Harry with myself as a player. Harry, who is exceptionally quick, has an excellent touch and is very strong, is actually quite different. He is more direct than I was. I was able to manipulate the ball in tight areas a bit better; Harry can get into difficulties if he tries to fiddle with the ball. He is at his best when he can get a run at people and beat them through pace and strength.

My coaching work with him at youth level boiled down to encouraging him to do what I did as a player – keep taking on defenders and not to worry if he lost possession occasionally. One of the two hardest things to do in football in my view is run with the ball – the other is scoring – and when you have someone of Harry's ability, it is unforgivable not to give him the scope to use it fully. The earlier that Harry can get on a run and beat people – thus giving himself a psychological edge over the opposition – the better I like it. Even now, there are times when Harry does not take the ball far enough for my liking. Sometimes he will get behind the opposing back four but cross or shoot too early instead of taking the ball through closer to the goal.

One of the things that struck me about him when I first met him was his maturity. He wanted to be one of the best footballers in the world, and was very focused on that. The only complaint that Paul and I had about him was that we thought his hair was too long. Following our nagging, he eventually got it cut, apparently much to the dismay of his mother who, according to Harry, hated his new look.

But there was nothing wrong with the way he looked with a ball at his feet. Harry's best position was either as a left-side midfielder or as a withdrawn striker. Paul and I always knew that, but in our FA Youth Cup-winning team, we played him at left-back to help broaden his outlook on the game. We felt it would make him more aware of the defensive side of the game and force him to work harder to get into the positions he favoured.

From a purely technical viewpoint, Stephen McPhail is even more gifted than Harry. Stephen is one of a number of boys unearthed by our wonderful Irish scout, Paddy Hillier, whose group of players in our 1996–97 youth squad also included Maybury, Lynch, Boyle, Nicky Byrne and Kevin Doyle. I often tell Paddy that he must have been wearing a shamrock on the day he came across Stephen. I find it difficult to think of any player in England with Stephen's first-touch, vision and passing skills. From the day I started working with him, he impressed me as a young midfielder with a great knowledge of how the game should be played, i.e. when to pass the ball or retain it, when to knock it long or short; and he could see openings that no other players could see. That is still the case.

I am struggling to think of a better pass in recent years than the thirty-yard ball by Stephen that set up Jimmy Floyd Hasselbaink for his goal in the 5–0 win over Derby at Pride Park during the 1997–98 season. With so many players in our team going forward, having someone who can pick them out as well as Stephen can is very much a bonus. Harry, Stephen's left-wing attacking partner, certainly benefited from this in that FA Youth Cup-winning season. When I recently asked Harry to name the best player he has ever played with, he immediately replied, 'Stephen'. For someone from the Irish Republic, Stephen has been paid the even bigger compliment of being favourably compared with Liam Brady.

However, throughout his career so far, he has been dogged by a lack of pace and mobility. He has always found it difficult to match the athleticism of other midfielders and therefore, while everyone recognises his skill, there have long been doubts about his ability to get on the ball often enough to be able to exploit it. It is something that he has had to work on ever since I have known him, but especially since he started playing for the first team. My heart goes out to him at times because nobody could ever accuse him of lack of effort in training or matches – he works his socks off. Harry has no problems at all with the physical side of the game and sometimes needs to be pushed. Stephen pushes himself.

Not being able to match the physical qualities of the opposition was no problem to Liam Brady. But the game has changed a lot since his day, and especially midfield play. You only have to look at Arsenal's Patrick Vieira and Manchester United's Roy Keane, and the number of runs they make from one box to the other, to see this. You have to be able to keep up with them physically to get the upper hand on them. It is a question of being able to impose your will on them. I can relate to Stephen about this because when I played at left-back under Allan Clarke, I was not as quick as I had been and I am sure opposing teams felt that we would be in trouble if their wingers could get at me. I never let that happen because I kept pushing forward, so that the wingers had to spend most of their time chasing me.

Harry and Alan Maybury were the oldest members of that youth group, so they were the first to break into the first team. In the 1995–96 season, Howard Wilkinson selected Harry in his starting line-up for two Premiership matches and Alan made one appearance. I had no hesitation in putting Harry's name forward when George Graham, on succeeding Howard the following season, asked me to recommend youth players whom I considered ready to start getting experience with his team. That season, Harry, a member of George's first-team squad on a few occasions, made one Premiership appearance as a sub, as did McPhail and Boyle.

Some people, notably Paul Hart, would have liked to see George give such players more opportunities because his team was hardly bristling with attacking talent and, according to him, he did not have as much to spend as one might have thought. In an article in the *Observer* he claimed:

> When I went to Elland Road, I had £5 million to spend and I needed ten new players. There was a lot of surgery to be done and unpleasant decisions to be made. A lot of players had to go and some shrewd buying was needed to get others in.

Our scoring ability had been a worry for some time. Towards the end of his Leeds career, Howard had been helped by the brilliance of Tony Yeboah – a scorer of great goals as well as a great goalscorer. The Ghanaian international, signed by Howard from Eintracht Frankfurt in January 1995 for £3.4 million, went on to get 12 league goals in 16 matches in partnership with Brian Deane to help us qualify for the Uefa Cup. The following season, he scored 12 goals in 22 matches, but Tony did not have a great deal of support. One major disappointment in that department was Swedish international Tomas Brolin whom Howard signed in November 1995 for £4.5 million.

Tomas, who was to earn the dubious distinction of being labelled Leeds' worst-ever signing, was nowhere near fit enough. He scored four goals in his 22 matches that season and when George Graham arrived, he was pushed into the background. It was the same with Tony Yeboah, who was initially hampered by a long-term injury and then had a falling out with George over the manager's complaints about his commitment and level of consistency.

It was a difficult first season for George, as one in which his famous ability to make his teams hard to score against came in very handy. We scored only 28 Premiership goals, but, fortunately, conceded no more than 38. That defensive record was due mainly to the great saves produced by Nigel Martyn. Indeed, Nigel, was given an enthusiastic pat on the back by Bill Fotherby. In his review of the season, Bill, who had succeeded Leslie Silver as chairman, wrote, 'Nigel Martyn has kept us in the Premiership and that could be worth between £6 and £8 million to this club.'

Despite the league and Cup success of our youth team, it was also a difficult season for Paul Hart. His relationship with George was nothing like what it had been with Howard. George disagreed with Paul's independence and influence. The rift between them meant that they hardly consulted with each other. For his part, Paul felt that George looked upon him as Howard's man, and for that reason did not trust him. Paul even feared that this might affect the development of the youth-team players. He worried that his conflict with George would make it harder for him to get his players into the first team while George was in charge. Thus during the summer, Paul left to take up the same position at Nottingham Forest.

There was a change for me, too, because when David Williams resigned as reserve-team coach to take charge of the youth team at Manchester United, George appointed me to replace him. One bonus in the move for me was that, as our reserve games did not clash with those of the first team, George made me part of his dug-out personnel for the Premiership and Cup matches. Another was that I was involved in the next stage of the development of the likes of Harry Kewell and Stephen McPhail.

12

FROM GEORGE TO DAVID

I WILL hardly go down in history as one of the best managers who strode into a British dug-out, but at least I can claim to have won a league title. It came in the 1997–98 season when George Graham steered us to fifth place in the Premiership and qualification for the Uefa Cup – a tremendous improvement on our fortunes in the two previous seasons – and my team won the Pontins Reserve League. This was never going to cause Sir Alex Ferguson or anybody else to look anxiously over their shoulders, but I was as proud of that achievement as I had been of our success with the youth squad, if not more so.

Of all the teams in a professional football club, the second eleven tends to be the most unsettled. It comprises an ever-changing mix of senior professionals who have been dropped from the first team and need to improve or maintain their fitness levels, and youth players deemed to have made sufficient progress to start being tested at another level. In our 24 matches, I used as many as 38 players. Most experienced players will confirm that it is far from easy to motivate yourself in reserve-team football. Apart from the comparatively low crowds, some of the big clubs play their home matches in rather less glamorous settings than do the first team in the Premiership. In those days, our home venue for reserve games was Halifax Town. It is now York City. Manchester United play at Bury.

To varying degrees, all the senior players selected for my team moaned about George, and not being in the first-team picture.

They did not like being with the reserves, which was understandable. But I got on well with them; while George was the bad guy, I was the good guy. When you are in charge of a reserve team, you represent the ideal shoulder to cry on. They want you to sympathise with them for not being in the first team. They are your pals. Even so, I was lucky because none of them went into a deep enough sulk to prevent him trying to do a good job for me. I thought this reflected a lot of credit on standards that George and David O'Leary were setting. It also reflected much credit on the teenagers who combined stints in the reserves with giving the club another good season in the FA Youth Cup, this time reaching the semi-finals.

Being forced to work with kids can be viewed as something of a come-down by senior players. It is especially difficult to handle when they have to train with them – something that is liable to happen when the manager or coach wants to work on the shape of his first team and those not involved have to go into other groups to ensure that they get the work they need as well. But both training and playing with our kids was no hardship for the experienced pros for the simple reason that all those kids could play. Technically, they were very much on the same wavelength, so the experienced players, far from finding matches frustrating, got a lot of enjoyment from them.

This was hardly surprising considering that the member of our FA Youth Cup-winning side who played the highest number of reserve games that season was Stephen McPhail (18). Others who were conspicuous by their presence were Wesley Boyle (17), Lee Matthews, Alan Maybury (12) and Jonathan Woodgate (11).

As for those recognised as first-team squad members, Tomas Brolin – for all the headaches he was causing George in his attempts to get him off our payroll and for all the distractions of the media commitments he seemed to have in Sweden – scored four goals in his three matches for me. He played in our first two matches of the season, scoring twice in the 3–0 home win over Manchester United and again in the 3–2 victory over Tranmere.

Others who did well for me were two Scottish players, Derek

Lilley and David Hopkin, who were bought by George from Morton and Crystal Palace respectively. David, in particular, gave the younger players a lot of support and encouragement. Although he played just eight matches for me, I will always be thankful for the way he put aside his disappointment over not being in the first team in favour of helping others. He and Derek each scored twice in our 5–0 win over third-placed Blackburn in our last match, which enabled us to beat Manchester United to the title by two points. Derek, with a total of 13 goals in 22 matches, was our top scorer.

George also had players who did an exceptional job for him that season, Lucas Radebe for example. When Lucas and his fellow South African international Phil Masinga were signed by Howard Wilkinson, it was Phil who attracted most of the attention, being an attacking player. But while Phil faded, and was sold to Bari just before Howard was sacked, Lucas, who had taken some time to settle down and then been hit with a cruciate ligament injury, went from strength to strength. Lucas has said that he responded to George because George showed more confidence in him than Howard had done.

'When George Graham joined Leeds, everything started to open up for me,' he recalled. 'His arrival was an opportunity for me and everyone at Leeds to make a fresh start.'

Under George, he emerged as probably our most dominant figure at the back and it has been the same story since David O'Leary became manager. I think a great deal of Lucas both as a person and a footballer. After some of the things that happened to him in South Africa – notably being accidentally hit by a bullet which went into his back and passed out of his body through his thigh – nothing seems to upset him. He is very appreciative of the ways in which his life has changed since he came to Leeds. He is a fantastic ambassador for his country, and for football.

It was George who first made him captain, a decision that led to Lucas being described as the African Tony Adams. In addition to his relationship with Nelson Mandela – who had Lucas by his side on a visit to Leeds in 2001 and described him as one of his heroes – you get a good idea of how much he is fêted in his own country when you go to one of the Internet websites devoted to him. On one, the opening page tells us: 'There is no King but O'Leary, and Lucas is his Knight.' Describing him as 'the world's greatest defender', his admirer adds, 'He is as the wind – you do not see him yet you feel his presence. He is as the night – he stalks, he is everywhere. He is as water – he adapts to his situation, even a bullet cannot destroy him.' Lyrical stuff, and at Leeds everyone is happy to maintain Lucas's image. Referring to the fact that Lucas's previous club was Kaiser Chiefs, David still refers to him as 'The Chief'.

Another of Howard's signings who responded well to George in the 1997–98 campaign was Rod Wallace. But by far the biggest boost for George was the form of the remarkable figure who was Wallace's striking partner – Jimmy Floyd Hasselbaink. By any criteria, the Dutch striker whom George bought from Portugal's Boavista for £2 million before the start of the season, was a fantastic signing. Jimmy was our top scorer with 22 goals (16 in the League) that season, and he maintained his position the following season. Moreover, when he forced the club to sell him, we received £12 million for him from Atletico Madrid. It was in Spain that Jimmy's scoring ability was best illustrated; even in a team who were relegated, he was still able to find the net 24 times in 34 games. Needless to say, having moved to Chelsea for £15 million, he became their top scorer as well.

He will get goals regularly in any team because of his immense physical power and his single-mindedness. I suppose the closest equivalent to him among English strikers would be Alan Shearer, although in view of his phenomenal shooting power, Leeds fans probably feel that he has even more in common with Peter Lorimer. All strikers want to score goals, but none of the front men I have ever worked with wanted to score as badly as Jimmy does. At Leeds, this is what put him ahead of Tony Yeboah, who was also a wonderful scorer but nevertheless lacked Jimmy's drive. If there was a hint of a scoring chance for him, he would go flat out to take it, irrespective of his other options. He was almost unstoppable. Players need to be very strong characters to adopt Jimmy's approach, shrugging aside complaints about their selfishness. Like a lot of Dutch footballers, Jimmy was opinionated and exuded an air of arrogance.

I always felt that Jimmy could work a bit harder off the ball. When he used to come into the dressing room and moan about not having received good enough service, something that he was liable to do on the rare occasions when he struggled to make an impact, I would say, 'Well, you didn't work hard enough to get yourself into the game.'

I got on well with Jimmy; I found that, if you said something that upset him, he was never one to bear a grudge. I was therefore surprised that when our chairman, Peter Ridsdale, offered his hand to Jimmy after our 2–0 victory over Chelsea at Elland Road, Jimmy deliberately ignored the gesture and walked away. Apparently, he blames Peter for the bad publicity he attracted when he decided to leave Leeds at the start of the 1999–2000 season. It is generally believed that Jimmy put in a transfer request because he felt he should be the highest paid player in the Premiership, not just at Leeds, and we would not pay him the £60,000 a week he was demanding. Jimmy claimed that Peter's public comments on the situation presented a misleading picture. Rightly or wrongly, most people felt that Jimmy was being greedy and trying to hold the club to ransom. The reaction of the fans was typified by a television commercial on Sky Sports, which showed a distressed Leeds supporter scratching a Hasselbaink sticker from his car window in disgust.

As it turned out, the loss of Jimmy was not the blow to us that it was expected to be. In a way, the centre-forwards who have followed him, notably Michael Bridges and Mark Viduka, have both suited us better than he did. Both have been on a par with him in terms of his scoring record but at the same time, both are better leaders of the line and are more adept at bringing other people into the scoring picture – a big asset in view of the bolder attacking style of our team under David O'Leary.

Mark Viduka, in particular, is a wonderful orchestrator of the play in the last third of the field. He really does get as much pleasure from setting up chances for others as he does from sticking the ball in the net himself.

George Graham made himself every bit as unpopular with the fans as Hasselbaink did when he left Leeds for Tottenham after two months of the 1998–99 season. After all, Leeds had given him the opportunity to get his career back on the right track following his eighteen-month Football Association suspension from the game. George insisted that his decision to move back to the south was sparked by his desire to be closer to his girlfriend Susan (now his wife) and his family, but at the time it was tempting to suggest that this had always been his plan and he had used Leeds to get back on his feet. George did not live far from me – like David, he had a house in Harrogate – and the impression I got whenever we bumped into each other there was that he was very happy living in the town.

It was not as if Leeds were looking like relegation candidates. We had made a solid, if unspectacular start with two wins and five draws from the first seven Premiership matches, and got over our first Uefa Cup hurdle with a victory on penalties against Portugal's Maritimo. There was also the question of his willingness to join a club where, because of his links with Arsenal, many of the supporters were bitterly opposed to his appointment. There had been stories about the possibility of him going to Tottenham, to replace the much-maligned Christian Gross, for some time. Ironically, what was to prove our last league match under his management happened to be a 3–3 draw at Tottenham on 26 September. The reason why it stands out in my mind is the nature of the Tottenham fans' protest about his proposed appointment.

George did not travel back to Leeds with us after the game, preferring to spend the weekend in London, and as our coach swung out of the White Hart Lane gates into Tottenham High Road, the driver suddenly had to drop his speed to virtually crawling pace because of a man deliberately walking in front of the vehicle. There was no police escort to deal with the situation and no way in which the coach could get around him. He came to a stop outside a pub, which was the signal for a large group of fans to burst out and launch an attack on the vehicle. They threw bricks and stones at us, smashing some of the windows, and one man managed to open the coach door and almost get inside. Fortunately, the driver was able to see an escape route and take us through it.

The escape route for Leeds in finding the right replacement for George, initially an approach to Leicester for Martin O'Neill, proved no less impressive. Despite David O'Leary's inexperience in the job, which will have been even more worrying to his doubters in view of his short time as an assistant manager, this has been an inspired appointment.

One difference between George and David was that David took more of a chance with the youngsters coming through. David's attitude to playing inexperienced youngsters is similar to mine when I was manager. Like me, his views on this had been influenced by the fact that he had been brought into first-team football when he was a teenager. As he remarked, 'I have always said that if a player is good enough, he is old enough. Peter Lorimer was fifteen when he played in Leeds' first team, and if I had a fourteen year old who was good enough, I would play him. I do not see it as that much of a gamble because I am close to the players. I feel they relate to me. I played in the Arsenal first team at seventeen, for the Republic of Ireland at Wembley at eighteen and in a Cup final at nineteen. Obviously, the players have to be mentally strong, but it helps them that I know what they are going through and can help them through it.'

Up to David taking over in October 1998, only Harry Kewell, who had played in all our earlier matches that season (after twenty-six appearances in the previous campaign) could be classed as an established member of the side. Under David, places were promptly found for Jonathan Woodgate and Alan Smith – both for the first time – and Stephen McPhail. That season, David also gave debuts to Paul Robinson and Matthew Jones.

To suggest that David showed greater faith in these lads than George did is not entirely fair. It has to be borne in mind that you can do a lot of harm to players by subjecting them to the physical and mental demands of first-team football too early. Also, the likes of Woodgate, Smith and McPhail were better equipped to handle this under David if only because they were a bit older. George would have given them their chance sooner or later – he would have had to because of their ability. However, knowing how conservative George could be, I have my doubts that he would have thrown them all in at the deep end at the same time. I also have the feeling that they would not have blossomed as much under George.

As I said earlier, one of the strange characteristics about managers and coaches is that they can be totally different from what they were like as players. They have a tendency to be like Hamlets wanting to be clowns or vice versa. George, nicknamed 'Stroller' when he was an attacking midfielder with Arsenal and Chelsea because of his elegant, laid-back style, was not a player who appeared to bother too much about defence. But, as a manager, this has been his trademark. What you remember the most about almost all of his teams is their discipline and ability to maintain clean sheets. It was fascinating to watch him in training. The majority of his work was focused on organising the back four and ways in which life could be made easier for them through all the players working together in closing the opposition down and winning the ball further up the field.

It has also been fascinating to watch David. A centre-half he might have been but you could easily be forgiven for thinking that he had been a centre-forward because much of his training is geared to going forward and scoring goals. He does concern himself with the defensive side of the game but definitely encourages the players to use their attacking ability more than George did.

This is not the only way in which David has shown a more positive attitude. As George has acknowledged, he has taken Leeds on to a new level, and I cannot help thinking that this might have been because David had a more optimistic view of what the club were capable of achieving. It seems to me that George's decision to leave had something to do with his not truly believing that the club could be taken any higher in the foreseeable future, and that in terms of winning trophies, Tottenham had greater potential.

The decision was proved justified in that respect because in his first season at White Hart Lane, Tottenham won the League Cup. But Spurs faded and it all ended in bitterness and acrimony for George when his conflict with the chairman, Sir Alan Sugar, and the change in the ownership of Tottenham resulted in his being sacked.

When he looks at what has happened to David and Leeds, I wonder whether George regrets not staying where he was.

Perhaps the greatest irony of his situation at Tottenham compared with David's at Leeds concerns the money David has had to spend in the transfer market and the quality of his buys. While Sir Alan Sugar was often criticised for not being a true Tottenham supporter, and not allowing any football emotion to get in the way of his decisions, the reverse has been true of Leeds' chairman Peter Ridsdale.

In assessing the factors that have helped David make a success of the job, it is impossible to overlook Peter. In an era when so many of the men running football clubs come across as businessmen first, football lovers second, Peter is a manager's dream. He is a lifelong Leeds supporter. One of his clearest memories is of Leeds reaching the 1965 FA Cup final and of spending the night outside Elland Road in a sleeping bag, aged thirteen, to ensure he was among the first in the queue for a ticket. As he was a goalkeeper at school, his favourite Leeds player was Gary Sprake. Apparently, his late father, a salesman, had little interest in football. However, Peter set a better example to his children. When a matchday crèche was introduced at Elland Road in the 1980s, his son was among the first infants to be put in it. As one would expect of someone who has been devoted to the club for so long, his knowledge of the history of Leeds United and the players is little short of encyclopedic. Peter, whose business credentials were established in retail management with the Burton Group and, more specifically, the Top Man brand, must have thought he had found Utopia when he became Leeds chairman.

Some might well have looked upon this as letting a child loose in a sweetshop. His position of power has not changed him – he has remained no different from many other Leeds followers. On away trips, when the players go for a walk after arriving at our hotel, Peter likes nothing better than to don a tracksuit top and accompany them. He loves to get inside information about the team and I have quite a bit of fun with him over that. Occasionally, he will gently probe me about the side David intends to select, and I will say, 'Mr Chairman, if David wants you to know, I'm sure he will tell you.' Peter just smiles.

Like most other fans, he has opinions about the team and has no compunction about discussing them openly, even in situations where a lot of other chairmen might be more discreet.

He is unpretentious and approachable, and sensitive to the needs of the fans. I remember a newspaper article in which Peter, in response to the criticism that Leeds did not have a supporters' representative on the board, replied, 'We do – it's me.' A lot of chairmen make that point, but with Peter, it really is valid.

This side of Peter came to the attention of the public through the manner in which he dealt with the appalling murders of two Leeds followers in Istanbul before our Uefa Cup-tie with Galatasaray in 1999–2000. Upon hearing the news of the tragedy while having dinner with Galatasaray officials on the eve of the match, Peter earned enormous respect and admiration for immediately taking the responsibility of helping the families of the bereaved, and the five fans who had been injured. He was genuinely surprised at the plaudits this brought him. As he said in an interview with Jim White in the *Guardian*, 'I made a decision to take the lead – it's what I felt the chairman of a PLC should do. Nobody advised me to do it. In fact, if anyone did advise me, they told me not to do anything, to sit tight and see what happened. All I knew [when he first learned of the clashes between Leeds supporters and Turkish youths] was that we had someone dead and another in hospital dying. I simply behaved as I felt appropriate.'

I am told that Peter's willingness to make himself available for media interviews on important issues relating to the club has caused some Premiership chairmen to describe him, dismissively, as 'Publicity Pete'. But it comes back to Peter's sense of leadership and his appreciation of the principle that Leeds have a duty to communicate with their public.

The communication between him and David is clearly superb. As I said, Peter is a Leeds fan and, as such, he is prepared to allow his football heart to take him into areas where a lot of other chairmen would not dream of treading. Nothing is too good for the players as far as Peter is concerned. His pride in the club makes it important to him not only that we are the best but that we are seen to be the best.

Even Arsenal, perhaps the classiest of all English football clubs, were impressed last season when they were told that the Boeing 747 they chartered at great expense for their last Champions League match in Valencia – a specially designed VIP plane in which the seating has been reduced to about forty and the extra space used to provide every conceivable comfort for the players – had been used by us for all our away matches in Europe.

The greatest example of Peter's dreams of grandeur for his beloved Leeds was his willingness to sign Rio Ferdinand for a British record fee of £18 million at a time when it seemed that the transfer system would be scrapped and that Rio's value could be wiped out overnight. Even Arsenal and Chelsea, two clubs with the financial clout to take the gamble of signing him – and two clubs who would probably have been in an even better position to do so than Leeds, given their geographical location – seemed to look upon it as too big a risk to take. I think Rio has proved that this is their loss and our gain. The signing of Rio Ferdinand is a wonderful example of what you get when you have a passionate Leeds supporter at the head of the club, and a bold, enthusiastic manager who does not set any limits on his ambitions.

13

LIVING UP TO EXPECTATIONS

I HAD no quibbles with David O'Leary's appointment, and not just because of his decision to promote me to the position of assistant manager. Although I had not spent much time in his company, and appreciated that he was inexperienced, I felt that the club needed management continuity. As far as I was concerned, confirmation that he was the right man for the job was provided with his second team-talk.

David, who landed the job on a permanent basis in the third week of October 1998, after the club had spent three weeks trying to get Martin O'Neill from Leicester, had not been happy with his first briefing to the players. He was keen to let everyone know what he expected and he felt he had not got the message across in the way he wanted. This was more than offset by his second attempt, in a Derby hotel meeting room before our 2–2 draw at Pride Park on 31 October. Basically, David's message was that he badly wanted to win major honours and he wasn't going to settle for second best. He also stressed that he was going to do the job his way, and that if any player did not like this then, no matter who he was, he would be shown the door. It was as strong and articulate a speech as any I have heard from a new manager. In fact, it was difficult to believe that David, then forty-one, had never been a manager before.

This is still the case. Such is the aura of authority David exudes that anyone who does not know him could easily be forgiven for thinking that he had been in the job for many years.

As we have seen many times, great players do not necessarily make great or even good managers. In gaining the respect and support of players, someone with David's background – encompassing eighteen years at Arsenal, where he made a club record 558 league appearances, and playing for the Irish Republic in the World Cup finals – does start with an advantage. However, that can quickly evaporate if the people you are dealing with find any faults or weaknesses. In some ways, it is rather like a group of schoolchildren testing out a new teacher. In David's case, you have to remember that just a couple of years before he landed the job, he was a Leeds player, one of the boys. The way he has handled all this, through his knowledge of the game and his honesty and fairness with the players, makes it clear that he is a natural in the job.

David and I are both family men who share a love of good food and red wine. It's good to be with him socially because, with that Irish charm and sense of fun, he is great company. Apart from our different sporting tastes – outside soccer, his favourite sport is motor racing while mine is golf – we have different personalities. He is more emotional and demonstrative than I am, as you can see when he feels Leeds have been slighted or are the victims of an injustice. Our matches against the Gunners, for instance, tend to be exceptionally highly charged and David does find it difficult to detach himself from this atmosphere.

It seems strange to see him so passionate on behalf of Leeds when you look at his Arsenal background. The most well-known instance was when we beat Arsenal 1–0 at Elland Road in 2000–01. It was a stormy match, which produced a total of seven bookings, six for Arsenal. David was involved in two confrontations with Arsenal's Robert Pires, exchanging words with him after the French forward had been booked for a challenge on Lee Bowyer, and then blowing kisses at him and wishing him *au revoir* as the player passed him in the main entrance corridor. It caused Pires to lose his rag completely; from all accounts, one of his team-mates had to restrain him.

I also had something to say to someone from Arsenal – their manager, Arsene Wenger – but it was done in a more understated manner. There was a lot of ranting and raving going on as the teams and officials were walking through the dressing-room tunnel at the finish and Wenger was as uptight as anyone. He was complaining bitterly to me about all manner of perceived injustices to his players. I just said, 'Mr Wenger – can't you accept a defeat?' David liked that.

Having observed David at close hand, I would single out his relationship with his backroom staff – notably our chief coach Brian Kidd, reserve-team coach Roy Aitken and me – as one of his best qualities. David is very ambitious for both himself and the club, and therefore, while he is the one who ultimately makes all the decisions, he is more than happy for us to keep questioning his methods, not to mention each other's. He is self-confident and open-minded enough not to feel threatened by this. When David felt that he needed to step back from the day-to-day involvement with the players on the training field, and appointed Brian to fill the gap, he was quoted as saying, 'Brian's coaching ability was not the only reason why I chose him. I wanted a strong fellow who would question my tactics, not someone who just nods agreement with everything.' These are his guidelines for all of us.

It is often said that football is a game of opinions, and being from a race as opinionated and argumentative as the Scots, I cannot help but fully endorse that sentiment. I have lost count of the number of disputes I used to have with my fellow Glaswegian, Ian McNeill, when Ian was our chief scout under George Graham. The vast majority of our arguments, or discussions as I prefer to call them, were over players rather than tactics. We did agree on some things. Ian was definitely a kindred spirit of mine in recognising the importance of players who could take on opponents. As Chelsea's assistant manager, he had been instrumental in the club signing Pat Nevin. But more often than not, we were in conflict. I remember a particularly lively debate over Ian's view that the Dutchman, Clyde Wijnhard, one of George's last signings for Leeds, was a better striker than Alan Smith.

It has always worried me that, because of this side of our relationship, Ian might have felt – wrongly – that I had something to do with David's decision to release him in favour of promoting our assessor of opponents, Ian Broomfield, into his role. The truth is that I respected his right to voice his opinions and as far as I was concerned, the fact that we did not see eye to eye on various things did not affect our relationship in the slightest. I like to think that it was the same from his point of view.

This is the principle on which the relationship between David, Brian, Roy and myself is based, in the belief that it is healthy for the development of any club for people to have different views.

When Brian Kidd became head coach, one change he made that bothered me concerned our set-up when defending free kicks. Brian wanted all our players back well inside our penalty area, while I argued that we needed someone on the edge of the box to deal with situations where our failure to get the ball away cleanly presented the opportunity for an opponent to score with a long-range shot. As it turned out, David decided to go along with Brian on this, and it worked out well for us. But, as if to make sure that I didn't turn into a wallflower, he stressed, 'Never stop voicing your opinion.' It is his mantra to all of us.

David and I think the same way about most aspects of football, but it is only to be expected that there are some players he likes and I don't, and vice versa, and that we do not always see eye to eye on tactics. One example of this was our 2–1 Premiership win over Liverpool, probably our best performance of the 2000–01 campaign. We were 2–0 ahead by half-time, through goals by Rio Ferdinand and Lee Bowyer, and were so much in command that I saw no reason to change the way we had been playing. In the first half, Mark Viduka and Alan Smith, with Lee Bowyer and Harry Kewell supporting them down the flanks, had caused the Liverpool back four a lot of problems.

However, with Liverpool bringing on their substitutes, Gary McAllister and Vladimir Smicer, in place of Danny Murphy and Patrick Berger at the start of the second half to give themselves greater flair in the central attacking areas, David felt it was necessary for us to make some changes to counter this. Lee Bowyer was moved inside into a deeper position, and Alan Smith was switched to his position on the right flank. My own view was that we were in a strong enough position to maintain our control of the game without having to change our system and that the change might have the effect of allowing Liverpool to wriggle off the hook. One result of it was that Liverpool's left-back, Jamie Carragher, was able to come into the attacking picture more, knowing that there was no need for him to give his central defenders as much cover as before, and that when he moved forward, Alan Smith would have to track him.

Ultimately, I thought we were fortunate because shortly after Steve Gerrard reduced the arrears, Liverpool were reduced to ten men through Gerrard being sent off. Of course, no one can be sure that Liverpool would not have made life difficult for us anyway. But what I said will at least have given David something to think about. While he is very much the Boss, this is what he expects from us.

Another aspect of his success which I think merits special mention is his boldness in the transfer market. It is not realistic to expect the youth system of any club to produce all of its core players, particularly a club where the standards are as high as they are at Leeds, and David has filled in the gaps superbly. Generally, the players David has bought have been on a different level from the ones George purchased. One of the reasons why they have blended in so well with the home-grown lads, apart from their ability, is their ages. Most of David's buys, up to the end of the 2000–01 season, are in their early to mid twenties – the youngest are Rio Ferdinand and Robbie Keane at twenty-one – and they have been able to maintain and enhance the chemistry of the squad. Also, there has been plenty of scope for them to develop and for their market value to increase.

The drive for a club to reach the top has to come from the top, from the manager and the chairman, and the money David has been able to spend has sent out the most impressive of signals. It has helped raise the profile of the club to its highest point for almost thirty years. The higher you go, the more money you need to spend to maintain your success.

In his first season, David brought David Batty back to Leeds for £4.4 million. For the 1999–2000 season, the outlay on improving our squad was more than £25 million, on Eirik Bakke, Danny Mills, Michael Bridges, Michael Duberry, Darren Huckerby and Jason Wilcox. For the 2000–01 season, it was just over £35 million for Olivier Dacourt, Mark Viduka, Dominic Matteo and Rio Ferdinand – £46 million if you take into account the £11 million with which the club completed the permanent signing of Robbie Keane. The fees for Dacourt, Viduka and Ferdinand meant the club's transfer record was broken three times in the space of six months.

No matter how well Leeds might be faring, David takes the view that if he has a chance of buying someone who can make us even better, he will take it. So while some suggested that Rio was bought because of the uncertainty concerning Jonathan Woodgate's future (following the police charges brought against him, Lee Bowyer and Michael Duberry), the truth is that we would have signed him anyway.

David and I were aware of the fact that Rio, like so many players with an abundance of talent, was prone to the occasional moments of casualness. But he was easily the most complete central defender in Britain from a technical viewpoint, and we felt that in a team in which he would need to stretch himself more, his concentration was bound to improve. We also took into account that he was twenty, some way short of the age when a central defender can be expected to be at his peak and, of course, his special ability to make us more constructive on the ball at the back.

Rio has a tremendous thirst for football knowledge. He is forever asking questions about players and tactics, which I think is a great credit to the people who were involved with him at West Ham. His willingness to keep listening and learning has been borne out by the defensive versatility he has shown here. Before he came to Leeds, a number of the people I spoke to about him were of the opinion that he should always be used as a sweeper, in a role where he had two other central defenders with him and did not have anyone specifically to mark. At Leeds, he has shown that he is no less effective when operating in a flat back four. In fact, it has helped him to be in such a system. In terms of his defensive responsibilities, being less detached from his colleagues at the back has made his job more straightforward. Suffice it to say that the £18 million we paid for him does not look at all exorbitant today. There is not a team in the world that Rio could not play in.

As for the Leeds signings who preceded him, it was appropriate that David Batty should be the first, in December 1998. I could not have agreed more with the manager when he said that Batty should never have been allowed to leave. I was the one who signed him for the club as an apprentice professional in 1985, the year I was sacked. Everyone took a shine to him because he was so enthusiastic. We had a small gym at the end of the dressing-room corridor and David, who was very small, would come there two or three nights a week to build himself up. He broke into the team at eighteen, when Billy Bremner was manager, and went on to establish himself as a key figure under Howard Wilkinson. Howard's decision to sell him to Blackburn for £2.75 million in October 1993 was as unpopular with the fans as the sale of Eric Cantona had been. He was a player with whom they could easily identify because he was a Leeds lad and played with a passion that made it plain for all to see that he really cared about the club.

David O'Leary had good cause to appreciate what he contributed to the team in his midfield anchor role. David played ten league games for Leeds in the season that Batty left, and the first three of these were with Batty sitting in front of him to help protect him.

It is generally believed that Howard released him because the player needed a fresh challenge. Batty had become stereotyped as little more than a ball-winner and, with players such as Gary McAllister and Gordon Strachan taking on the bulk of the creative responsibility, I think he felt that he would get greater opportunities to show what he could do on the ball elsewhere. Indeed, David seemed to blossom in that department at Blackburn, displaying a composure and technical expertise with his passing that took a lot of people by surprise.

He has often been criticised for not being adventurous enough in his distribution, for too often playing the ball sideways or backwards, instead of forward. The same was said of Ray Wilkins, and even John Giles. However, players in this mould are great believers in that old adage about possession being nine-tenths of the law, and in the general principle of teams not giving the ball away cheaply. To a degree, I have to declare myself a member of that club, too.

If there has been a flaw in Batty's game, it is that he does not score enough goals. I find this very difficult to understand because he has the energy to make runs from the edge of our box into shooting positions at the other end, and is a wonderful striker of the ball. But no matter how many times you try to encourage him to have a go at goal more often, something happens inside his head to stop him. The boys tease him all the time over it, although as the practical joker in the squad – and one clever enough to avoid getting caught – he can always be relied upon to get his own back.

Of all the personal success stories in our rise under David O'Leary's management, Batty's is arguably the most inspiring. I felt he was producing the best form of his entire career when he sustained a calf injury in November 1999, which put him out of action for twelve months. It was discovered that his recovery from the injury was being hampered by the medication he had been taking for a heart problem following an earlier rib injury. A lot of people, me included, started to have doubts about whether he would play at the top level again.

It was partly because of the uncertainty about his future that the similarly combative Olivier Dacourt was bought from Lens in May 2000. Olivier had impressed us when playing for Everton, despite being sent off in one match against us. Olivier did well in Batty's absence, but he was probably the member of the team who benefited the most from Batty's comeback in December. It gave us the stability in the centre of midfield to allow Olivier to get forward more, and become our equivalent of Arsenal's Patrick Vieira.

They are a tremendous pair. Both have the physical power to keep forcing mistakes from the opposition and, having won the ball, the skill to set our own attack in motion. With David having wasted no time in making us one of the most attack-minded teams in the Premiership – and one of the most inexperienced – Batty's signing was very timely. Because of his background, the players responded to him immediately; and their youthful exuberance was good for him, too. He was thirty when he returned to Leeds and, in the context of our playing set-up, he was almost like the team's grandfather. He did not have the best of starts. The rib injury sustained on his debut, in the 2–0 home win over Coventry, caused him to miss the next ten matches and for much of that period our results were erratic. But he played in nine of the last eleven matches, in which – significantly – we were beaten only once and clinched fourth place. Given the boldness of our style of play at home, I thought David's defensive ability was particularly important to us at Elland Road. In the four other league matches he played there that season, only Manchester United managed to score (they got a 1–1 draw). Of the other games, we had a goalless draw against Liverpool, a 1–0 win over Arsenal and a 2–0 win over Tottenham.

Few can have expected us to finish as high as we did. It certainly seemed unlikely after David's opening four Premiership matches, which brought one defeat and three draws. Then in ninth place, we suddenly transformed ourselves with three wins on the trot and the confidence from that seemed to create a snowball effect. Since then, surprising people has become a Leeds habit. There were even more raised eyebrows the following season.

It began with two major question marks against us, neither of which was unreasonable in my view. The first revolved around the thought that teams would know more about our young players now. For all footballers, making the most of their initial first-team chances is one thing – maintaining their level of performance under the pressure of knowing that people expect them to play well as opposed to hoping that they can do so is quite another. The other doubt concerned the loss of Jimmy Floyd Hasselbaink.

But the youngsters kept going, and David took the squad on to another level via the transfer market. Thus, we finished third in the Premiership and clinched a place in the European Champions League qualifying competition; and we reached the semi-final of the Uefa Cup.

The obvious place to start in making sense of all this is with

Michael Bridges who was bought from Sunderland for £5 million in July 1999, a month short of his twenty-first birthday, and found himself stepping into the gap left by Hasselbaink. Someone who probably anticipated this not being a problem was Jack Hixon, the elderly north-east scout who had brought Michael to Sunderland and who was responsible for unearthing Alan Shearer and bringing him into league football with Southampton. Come to think of it, Shearer might well have predicted a great season for Bridges, too. Like Shearer, Michael had become attached to Newcastle as a schoolboy but was hampered by injury and allowed to drift away. Hixon, having left Southampton to join Sunderland, spotted him as a sixteen year old and ensured that whenever Michael needed any advice about his game, Shearer would be available to provide it. Whatever help Shearer was able to give, it was certainly beneficial. Although Michael had been used mainly as a substitute by Sunderland, largely because of the new lease of life that Niall Quinn was experiencing there, I think everybody accepted that he had as much all-round ability as any striker in the country and that his time would come.

Sunderland did not want to lose him, but when he finally told the club that he did not want to extend his contract beyond its existing expiry date in June 2000, they were forced to accept the inevitable. George Graham seemed certain to sign him for Tottenham and, in fact, Sunderland publicly announced the transfer, subject to a medical and the agreement of personal terms. The same day, David O'Leary and Peter Ridsdale stepped in to whisk Michael from under George's nose.

That night, while Michael was agreeing to come to Leeds, any football fan who happened to be in a fish restaurant in the north Yorkshire village of Asenby might well have thought that I had something to do with it. By the strangest of coincidences, Linda and I were having dinner there with the Sunderland chairman, Bob Murray, and his wife Sue, two of our closest friends. We got to know each other through mutual friends, Len and Teri McCormick. Len, a Yorkshire-based Liverpool supporter (with whom I have a standing £50 bet each season that Leeds will finish higher than his side in the table) is managing director of the Batleys Cash and Carry outlets. The company have a hospitality box at York racecourse and it was there that Bob and I first met.

When we go out together, we are both careful not to reveal too much about our clubs. Therefore, although Bob was aware that David and I thought a lot of Michael as a player, our conversations on the subject never went beyond that. The dinner in that north Yorkshire restaurant had been arranged before the start of Bob's negotiations with Tottenham and Leeds and, strange as it might seem, the situation with Michael was hardly discussed even then.

I think Michael plumped for Leeds partly because he felt we were the likelier of the two clubs to mount a serious challenge to the Premiership ascendancy of Manchester United, and also because we were so much closer to his north-east roots.

The decision proved to be a good one for both parties. Michael emerged as our top scorer in 1999–00 with 21 goals, 19 of them in 34 Premiership matches, and also set up plenty of opportunities for others. As I said earlier, the way our team had evolved meant that Michael's ability to hold the ball and bring others into the attacking play was not something to be sneezed at as far as we were concerned. As with Mark Viduka, it probably made him an even more important member of our team than Hasselbaink had been.

What a memory Michael's first season at Elland Road would have been for him, and us, if we had landed our first major honour for eight years. Manchester United, the eventual champions, finished 22 points ahead of us, but for some time, we had been the team in the driving seat. Once the season got into full swing, United or Leeds occupied the top spot. After a moderate start, with two wins, two defeats and a draw, a run of six successive Premiership wins (which was part of an even more impressive club-record ten-match winning run in all competitions) took us from sixth place to first. We held that position for all but a couple of weeks up to the start of February, and it was not until April that we dropped lower than second.

It was during that period that a dark cloud descended over the club through the tragic events in Istanbul. We had experienced two defeats on the trot, against Leicester and Chelsea, immediately before the trip to Galatasaray; and upon our return, the lingering feeling among everyone connected with the club that football was irrelevant made it unsurprising that the run should continue through further losses against Aston Villa and Arsenal.

There is little doubt that, this being a stage of the season when experience is particularly important, we were also affected by the absence of the injured David Batty. If there was one game where we could have done with his steadying influence, it was the home defeat by Arsenal on 16 April. In the first half, Ian Harte was sent off for a foul on Dennis Bergkamp. Arsenal were leading through a Thierry Henry goal, and in the last half an hour, Martin Keown, Kanu and Mark Overmars made it 4–0. That pushed us into fourth place, and at the end of April, with four matches to go, and Manchester United and Arsenal comfortably installed in the first two positions, it looked as if Liverpool would be third.

But their challenge for a Champions League place collapsed with three defeats and a draw against Chelsea (0–2), Leicester (0–2), Southampton (0–0) and Bradford (0–1), while we achieved wins over Sheffield Wednesday (3–0) and Watford (3–1) and draws against Everton (1–1) and West Ham (0–0) to pip them by two points.

David O'Leary summed it up perfectly when he said, 'I did not think we would make it. Three-quarters of the way across the ocean, the engines failed and we only just limped into port.'

On the last day, we were fortunate that Liverpool's opponents, Bradford, were fighting for their Premiership lives, whereas the West Ham team we had to face were in the middle of the table. Even so, it was difficult to believe that Liverpool, who had suffered just four previous away defeats, had been beaten at Bradford; and, of course, the irony of it was that David Wetherall, our former centre-half, scored the only goal.

Our game at West Ham could easily have gone either way. That it did not go West Ham's was due largely to Nigel Martyn, which seemed to me to emphasise how quickly a keeper can transform himself from hero to villain, and vice versa. The previous week, Nigel had taken a lot of stick for the mistake against Everton – in misjudging a Don Hutchison cross – which brought the Mersey-siders the 1–1 draw. Against West Ham, who were probably the better team on the day and created the best chances, Martyn produced a wonderful save from John Moncur in the second half.

As if the achievement of getting a shot at the European Champions League for the first time was not a big enough boost for the club, the other reason for celebration was the long Uefa Cup run which provided the know-how, and the confidence, necessary to believe that we could make a reasonable challenge at this level.

I have always believed that competitive matches in other countries are perfect bonding experiences for teams. Quite apart from the advantage of players being together for two or three days, a lot of these matches can be steps into the unknown for them and the more uncomfortable the environment, the more they tend to pull together. Chelsea's Dutch defender Mario Melchiot got quite carried away on the subject. Talking generally about Chelsea's need to improve their away record, he likened away matches to eleven colleagues going into strange and dangerous areas where they needed to stay together in order to protect themselves properly.

I could appreciate the point he was trying to make. The principle of players putting on a united front was very important to us in a Uefa Cup campaign that produced trips to Partizan Belgrade, Lokomotiv Moscow, Spartak Moscow, Roma, Slavia Prague and Galatasaray. It says much about the strength of character being developed in our squad that only Spartak Moscow and Galatasaray recorded home wins over us, and that the list of away successes included a goalless draw against Roma in the Olympic Stadium.

Of the thirty-six European ties in which I took part as a Leeds player the one that stood out as the most intimidating was the second leg of our Uefa Cup second-round match against Napoli in Naples in November 1968. We had won the first leg 2–0, and the attendance for the return was only 15,000. Nonetheless, the level of their hostility towards us, not to mention that of the Napoli players, was frightening. I cannot possibly be exaggerating about this – Norman Hunter looks back on that match as the only occasion he can ever recall being scared on a football field.

Under strict instructions from Don Revie not to allow ourselves to be provoked, we kept our cool quite well – some feat considering our players were being kicked all over the place and missiles were being hurled by the crowd. But, just before the end of normal time, with the aggregate score at 2–2, a Napoli player made the mistake of jumping at Paul Madeley and causing a horrible cut on his thigh. Paul was like me, one of the last people you would expect to foul anyone deliberately, even in retaliation. Thus, when he was battered, it was the last straw for Don. At the final whistle, when he was able to get us all together to give us instructions and advice for extra time, he gave us the go-ahead to take the law into our own hands. 'Right, that's it,' he said. 'I don't care about the result – just bury them.' It was the only time we had ever heard him say something like that and some of our lads had no compunction about following his instructions (I was one of the exceptions, natur-ally!). That period of extra time was like a war. With the teams still deadlocked, we went through on the toss of a coin. Not surpris-ingly, the Napoli fans were less than overjoyed about that. Our coach had to pass through a sort of wire cage on its way out of the stadium, which was just as well because it was raining bottles and coins.

The atmosphere for the match against Galatasaray in Turkey was similarly intimidating. One thing I will always remember about it was the line of riot police with batons forming a protective barrier for the players and officials as they came on to the pitch. The noise around the stadium was something else. For anyone who likes a passionate backdrop to matches, I would say that the one provided by that Galatasaray crowd is as stimulating as any you will find anywhere in the world.

The Galatasaray fans were packed into this relatively small ground like sardines. For the full ninety minutes, they never seemed to stop jumping up and down and singing and chanting, almost always in unison. It was as if every spectator had been wound up like a clockwork toy or had had a battery implant before the game. I have never known anything quite like it.

Whether the matches against Galatasaray should have gone ahead in the light of the fatal attacks on two of our supporters on the eve of the first leg is open to debate. The decision was not one that I would have liked to make, but on balance, I think Peter Ridsdale was right when he said, 'It is important to show the world that we will not allow the futility of violence and personal injury to cast a shadow over football in this country.'

Also open to debate is whether we would have beaten Galatasaray in normal circumstances. Although they were a good team, as they went on to emphasise by beating Arsenal in the final, the key to our 4–2 aggregate defeat concerned the chances we missed in the first leg which helped them keep their 2–0 lead and forced us to chase the game more than we would have wished in the second leg.

However, one thing I am sure about is that what we went through in Turkey and other places was one of the main reasons why we went so close to taking the greatest European football prize of all.

14

JUST THE
BEGINNING

W HEN Leeds were beaten 2–0 at home by Liverpool in the
FA Cup fourth round on 27 January 2001, I cannot imagine
any bookmakers being inundated with bets on our reaching the
last four of the European Champions League and finishing fourth
in the Premiership to qualify for the Uefa Cup again.

True, we were going well in the Champions League, having
reached the competition's winter break in the second phase with
an overall record of five wins and three draws in ten matches.
But we were tenth in the Premier League, and two days after
the Liverpool defeat, the contributions of two of our key players,
Jonathan Woodgate and Lee Bowyer, were reduced considerably
by the start of their trial at Hull Crown Court.

In the Premiership, we had won only nine of our twenty-three
matches and suffered nine defeats. What was especially worrying
was that five of those defeats had come at home, against Manchester City, Ipswich, West Ham, Aston Villa and Newcastle. Even
some of our wins were not particularly impressive, and David felt
that unless we improved, there was a danger of our declining
further and slipping into the relegation zone.

However, the position we were in then was understandable when
you looked at the number of players who had not been available
for selection. David Batty, Stephen McPhail, Jason Wilcox and
Harry Kewell had all missed the start of the season with long-term
injuries, and after a few weeks, we also lost Michael Duberry and
Michael Bridges for the rest of the season. It was not until

December that Batty and Kewell made their first appearances. Wilcox did not do so until November, while McPhail – outside an attempt at a first-team comeback in September – had to wait until the end of the season.

The loss of so many influential attacking players was a handicap for us in our matches at Elland Road, not just because of the talent of those players but the way in which others fed off them. For example, the unavailability of both Kewell and Wilcox had an effect on the form of left-back Ian Harte. Ian definitely missed Harry – the rapport between the two is similar to the one that Terry Cooper and I once had. Without someone like Harry causing defenders headaches in front of him, the scope for Ian to get forward and add to their misery was more limited.

I always felt that once we started getting some of our injured players back, we would be OK, and I was proved right. After that FA Cup-tie against Liverpool, we won eleven of our remaining fifteen Premiership matches, and our only defeat was at Arsenal. By the time the run started, it was also clear to me that our players really had the bit between the teeth in the European Champions League.

I have never subscribed to the view that British players generally lack the technical ability of their counterparts in other countries. We are just as skilful as they are – it is just that, because of the nature of our football, it does not show as much. In my experience, few continental teams relish facing English opposition, especially when that opposition does not try to play them at their own game. Our football is played at a higher tempo with teams putting a lot of pressure on opponents in virtually all parts of the field and therefore making it more difficult for them to use their skills. I never cease to be amazed at the number of continental teams who cannot cope with it. This was part of the secret of our successful Champions League run.

In a way, because of the radical changes to the format of the competition, our Champions League achievement was even more impressive than that of reaching the European Cup final in 1975. We needed to play eight games to get to that stage, whereas our run to the last four of the Champions League involved sixteen.

There were so many tremendous individual performances from so many different players that in trying to list them, I am struggling to know where to begin. Starting from the back, the memories that immediately spring to mind are of Paul Robinson, our twenty-one-year-old second-choice goalkeeper who had previously made just a handful of first-team appearances, and none of them in Europe, frustrating some of the best strikers in the world in our matches against Besiktas, Barcelona, Real Madrid and Lazio. Others that stand out are Dominic Matteo's stature as Rio Ferdinand's central defensive partner, a role he was originally pushed into because of the unavailability of others; Lee Bowyer making light of the pressure of his court case, and not being able to train properly during it, with the six goals that made him our top scorer in the Champions League proper; and Mark Viduka and Alan Smith tearing defences to pieces with their movement and ingenuity.

To the public, Dominic Matteo probably did not stand out as much as the others did, but I thought he was magnificent. We paid Liverpool £4.25 million for him at the start of the season, and he must rank as one of David's biggest bargains. Signed principally as cover for Ian Harte at left-back, he played a few games in that position when Ian went through a bad patch; and because of the injury problems of Harry Kewell and Jason Wilcox, he also did a good job for us on the left side of the midfield. But he really came into his own when, again because of injuries, he started operating alongside Rio at the heart of the defence. This is his best position as far as I am concerned. I think he is more effective when all the play is in front of him. He is strong, quick and good in the air; the major advantage of his being with Rio concerns the balance of one player being naturally left-sided and the other right-sided.

I can appreciate why England and Scotland were involved in a tug-of-war for Dominic's services. He was eligible to play for both countries – he was born in Scotland and has English parents and Italian grandparents. Craig Brown and Sven-Goran Eriksson both wanted to select him. Eriksson was so keen that even when Dominic decided to plump for Scotland – obviously, much to my delight –

his assistant, Tord Grip, phoned him a couple of times to try to persuade him to change his mind.

All this did wonders for Dominic's confidence, which was apparent to me in a change I noticed in him off the field. Some players can handle criticism better than others, and in my early dealings with Dominic, I must admit that I found that he could be a bit touchy about it. This was a trait for which Jack Charlton was noted among his Elland Road colleagues; big Jack was a stubborn character whose pride made it hard for him to accept the blame for anything. Dominic, much younger and less set in his ways, was not as inflexible as Jack was. Even so, if you felt there was something he could do better, you would have to be careful about how you put it to him. I think I can understand one of the reasons for this. Dominic had been at Liverpool for twelve years, since he was a fourteen-year-old schoolboy, and I should imagine that the adjustment to a new club, initially without having a role or position that he could call his own, was bound to involve some feelings of insecurity. But the self-assurance he gained through establishing himself as a key member of the side made him a different person by the end of the season.

This was driven home to me by a conversation we had following the 3–0 Champions League semi-final defeat in Valencia. The second goal just after half-time stemmed from a headed clearance by Dominic which broke back to Juan Sanchez on the right. Dominic's reaction was to retreat, to help protect our goal – which is a defender's natural instinct – and Sanchez cut in past David Batty and hit the ball past a wrong-footed Nigel Martyn from twenty-five yards. Being hyper-critical, I thought that the goal, which was effectively the killer one for us, might have been avoided if Dominic had raced forward to close Sanchez down. When I discussed this with him, he immediately agreed. In fact, I'd hardly got the words out of my mouth when he said, 'Eddie, I know – I knew as soon as I did it that I had made a mistake.'

No one could blame Dominic for the defeat and even with the goal, you could make a reasonable case for claiming that others were equally culpable. It is the same with every goal – somewhere down the line, you can always single out players who did something which contributed to it. It is the players who are willing to acknowledge all their mistakes, no matter how small they might be, the ones who are hard on themselves, who end up as great players as opposed to just good ones. This is the transformation Dominic is undergoing at Leeds. In view of the different positions and roles he filled last season, I thought his consistency was remarkable.

He was in good company. Another who maintained a particularly high standard was Lee Bowyer. I was delighted that Lee was voted the club's player of the year by our supporters. I find him the easiest of people to deal with in training. He does everything you ask him to do, and does not complain about anything. On top of this is his ability to keep bombing up and down the park, from one penalty box to the other, and the goals he scores as a consequence.

The wee man is one of football's freaks. Managers and coaches are always stressing the importance of players training hard and eating the right food, but their arguments – all perfectly sound – are liable to collapse when you look at Lee. His diet is not exactly what you would expect from a highly tuned athlete – he loves fast food, and especially McDonald's hamburgers and fries. It has become a standing joke among the players. On European trips, you immediately know that the town or city has a McDonald's outlet by the cheer that emanates from the back of our coach when it passes one.

Adding to the sense of wonderment over the extraordinary energy that Lee shows on the field is the knowledge that he does not need to train as most other players. Indeed, he can get by for a while without doing any real training at all. This was the case throughout the eight-week court case in which he was involved last season. The trial meant that he could play in our home European ties only, and even then, he was never able to get to the ground before 6.30 p.m. The rest of the team would have a pre-match meal at a hotel and would not see Lee until they arrived in the dressing room. There was always a touch and go element about his availability to play for us during the week; when we played Everton at Goodison, we even flew him across in a helicopter.

A lot of people were amazed by Lee's performances, given the strain of the court case. But he looked upon playing for Leeds as an escape from those pressures. Our matches, and particularly our European ties, provided an outlet for all the stress he was experiencing off the field, and I think that was one of the reasons why his physical contribution was so high.

Lee alone would have been more than enough for opposing teams to cope with, but they also had Mark Viduka and Alan Smith giving them headaches as well. Mark and Alan make an intriguing pair, especially to David O'Leary, Brian Kidd and me because we have the responsibility of getting the best out of them. Mark needs to be wound up, whereas Alan has to be calmed down.

Mark has as much going for him as any centre-forward in the world. It is difficult to believe that David paid just £6 million for him. His talent is awesome; as he stands 6ft 2ins and weighs 14 stone, the same can be said of his physical strength. He is probably the strongest player I have worked with. He is also one of the most laid-back. He is so relaxed that sometimes he gives you the impression of having just fallen out of bed. He seems to have a broader view of life than a lot of other professional footballers. When I look at the path of his football career – born in Australia, he played in Croatia with Dinamo Zagreb and in Scotland with Celtic before coming to England – I am almost tempted to suggest that it is part of a grand plan to live and work in as many countries as he can before returning home. He strikes me as being the archetypal happy-go-lucky Australian back-packer. No matter how much success he achieves with Leeds, it would never surprise me if he came in one day and told us he was moving on to another country.

He has a great attitude to life – there is not much that seems to bother him. That is seen in his style of play. One of the paradoxes concerning a lot of big men in the game is that they tend to be disconcertingly mild-mannered and find it difficult fully to exploit their power. Older generations of Leeds fans will readily recall this being a characteristic of John Charles, our great player of the 1950s who was given the nickname 'The Gentle Giant'. I would not go so far as to describe Mark as such. Nonetheless, he does not use his power as much as he could.

I thought that Arsenal's Martin Keown was rash beyond belief in our match at Highbury last season when he provoked Mark by blatantly catching him with an elbow (an action that led to Mark stamping on him). He was very lucky that Mark quickly regained his self-control. Had the pair been in a boxing ring, Keown would have needed at least three of his team-mates to help get Mark off him. As David Batty once remarked to me, 'If I had to fight Mark, and he was in a bad mood, I think I would need to get a gun and shoot him.'

Mark does not waver from a physical challenge, but occasionally, you have to present him with one. Before a match, David or I will often warn him about the opposing centre-half attempting to establish a physical mastery over him. For example, before we played Tottenham last season, David asked me to have a word with him in the dressing room about Sol Campbell.

'Campbell's a big, strong lad,' I told him. 'David is a bit concerned that he is going to knock you all over the place.' Mark just smiled.

'We'll see,' he said. Mission accomplished.

This sort of motivation is the last thing that Alan Smith needs. Most of our dealings with him are devoted to urging him to keep a cool head. It is no secret that Alan's fiery temperament, which led to him being sent off three times in 2000–01, is something of a problem. He is still only twenty-one, but his tendency to blow up when things are not going well for him has been prevalent ever since he joined the club as a schoolboy. In training, he has even been known to cross swords with David Batty. As for competitive matches, there are games where I do so much shouting at him to cool down that I end up hoarse.

One of the difficulties in getting the message across is that when the red mist descends Alan is not usually aware of doing anything wrong. When you draw his attention to it from the dug-out, he will occasionally look at you with an expression of puzzlement, as if to say, 'What are you picking on me for?' It will be the same story when you mention it to him after the game. After one foul he committed, it was only when I showed him a video of it that he acknowledged that the offence was as foolish as I'd said it was. It can be so agonising; when Alan was sent off in the last minute against Valencia for a reckless challenge on Rodriguez Vicente, I could see it coming some time before he got to the Spaniard, but was powerless to do anything that might have stopped him.

One way in which David and I are trying to get Alan to improve this facet of his game is to keep reminding him of how being sent off and suspended can rebound on the team. In striving to make him more conscious of the need to remain available for selection, we felt that the greater competition for first-team places up front as a result of signing Robbie Keane in December 2000 would also help.

After his rush of blood to the head against Valencia, I thought there was a big lesson for Alan in Michael Owen's performance in the FA Cup final against Arsenal. Owen hardly got a kick for most of the match but he kept his self-discipline and composure and ended up scoring the late goals that gave them their 2–1 victory.

I believe that Alan is potentially as good a striker as Owen, if not an even better one. Like Mark, he has tremendous all-round ability and his work-rate and his finishing are outstanding. In every training session geared to finishing, he can always be relied upon to be the player with the best hits to misses ratio. The one criticism I can make of him is that he is not selfish enough. We are always trying to encourage him to have more attempts at scoring instead of setting up others.

The paradox about Alan is that his temperament can be viewed as his strength as well as his weakness. There is an element of the daredevil in his make-up. When I started working with him, it came as no surprise to learn that he had been the British BMX champion as a schoolboy. He is liable to be too brave for his own good, and go for balls that he has precious little chance of winning.

That inevitably leads to sharp body contact with opponents and that is where a lot of the trouble starts for him. It would be wrong to make excuses for him but most of his indiscretions stem from frustration. They are manifestations of the enormous pressure he puts himself under in his determination to prove himself.

He provided a perfect insight into this before the start of 2000–01. He had not been looking impressive in training and with Mark Viduka having joined the club, and Michael Bridges having been our top scorer the previous season, it seemed that he might struggle to get a place in our starting line-up. Before we played Huddersfield in a friendly, David asked me to have a chat with him about this. As I was doing so – on the pitch before the kick-off – David came on to the field and walked over to us. Alan, with no trace of anger or resentment, told him, 'I am a better player than Viduka and Bridges put together, and I am going to prove it to you.' Instead of throwing his toy out of the pram, as some highly acclaimed young strikers might have done, Alan looked upon it as a challenge that was going to bring the best out of him. You can understand why the Leeds fans love him. They adore him for the same reasons that they adore David Batty.

Top-class players do not need much advice on how to get on the same wavelength, they do it instinctively, and Alan and Mark had no problems at all in establishing a rapport with each other. At one stage in the season, we thought about putting them in wide positions to stretch opposing defences across the field and create more space for team-mates bursting through from deep positions. That is how Manchester United's strikers tended to operate. But the idea was shelved, partly because our central midfield players were not the types who could really benefit from the system and partly because of the understanding Mark and Alan had developed. Both as a pair and individually, they put central defenders under enormous pressure, and it seemed inappropriate to put them in areas in which they would be isolated from each other.

The class that Mark and Alan gave us up front was shown from the very start of our European campaign, when we beat TSV 1860 Munich 3–1 on aggregate in the Champions League qualifying matches. It could be argued that the victory over the Germans was our greatest achievement. Those were matches in which our European adventure could easily have been over before it had properly begun.

They were played at a time when our injury crisis was at its most acute; and in the first leg, both Olivier Dacourt (who, like Mark Viduka, was making his debut) and Eirik Bakke ruled themselves out of the return by being sent off. In that game, our new striking partnership gave us a taste of things to come just before half-time. Mark got a touch to a long Nigel Martyn kick and, with a German defender making a hash of clearing it, Alan nipped in to put us ahead. Late in the second half, a foul on Alan as he tried to apply the finishing touch to a pass by Mark led to Ian Harte making it 2–0. Then we lost Olivier and Erik, and our chances of maintaining our lead in the second leg were further undermined by Munich scoring in the last minute.

David O'Leary's description of the second leg in Munich's Olympic Stadium as the most difficult test of his career was justified. One of the things I remember about the match is that when we arrived at the stadium, the stands were empty except for two figures with a big Leeds banner sitting in the top tier. They turned out to be my son Nicholas and son-in-law Mark, who had thought that the kick-off time was an hour earlier than it was. When the match started, in front of a packed house of 56,000, it became clear that we would need all the support we could get.

Munich put us under a lot of pressure, and we were lucky not to lose our aggregate lead just before half-time when Thomas Hassler's free kick hit the bar. By half-time, Munich seemed to be favourites, mainly because of their right-side attacking player, Harald Cerny. Exceptionally quick and direct, he had given Ian Harte an uncomfortable time in the opening forty-five minutes. But for the second half, David O'Leary dealt with that problem by putting Ian on the right and switching right-back Danny Mills, more of a natural defender than Ian, to the left. After one minute of the restart, Mark Viduka and Alan Smith came up with a solution of their own. Mark showed tremendous determination to beat a couple of Munich defenders to the ball, and when it broke to Alan, his striking partner dispatched it into the net. Nigel Martyn did the rest with a string of excellent saves, including a brilliant one-handed one from Daniel Borimirov. Danny Mills and Michael Duberry also distinguished themselves by somehow managing to clear the follow-up effort from Agostino off the line.

Having got our invitation to the big Champions League party, our first match in Group H against Barcelona in front of a crowd of 85,000 in the Nou Camp Stadium was even more harrowing. If people needed any evidence to support the view that we were out of our depth in Champions League company, our 4–0 defeat by Barcelona was it. Here again, we did not have anything like a full-strength squad to choose from; and it is no disgrace to be turned over by a team including Rivaldo, Patrick Kluivert and Dani up front and the likes of Emmanuel Petit on the bench. Manchester United and Chelsea had both been walloped by the brilliant Catalan team in the Champions League.

What hurt was that we made it easy for them by showing them too much respect. It is the last thing that any team can afford to do against opposition of Barcelona's calibre Those sides can immediately sense any apprehension the opposition may feel and once they get that message, they are not slow to capitalise on it and go for the jugular. Rivaldo enjoyed himself as much as anyone that night, repeatedly being allowed to drift off the front and either run at us with the ball or bring others into the play. He scored a great first goal after nine minutes and Frank de Boer made it 2–0 eleven minutes later. At that point, David and I were both wishing that the referee could blow his final whistle. We were relieved that Barcelona got two more goals only – courtesy of Kluivert in the last fifteen minutes – because it could easily have been six or seven.

Afterwards, we sat down with the players in the dressing room and talked to them about their approach and what was needed in European football. The main part of the talk concerned the importance of believing in themselves and not allowing teams to walk all over them. One of the common denominators about the leading European Cup teams is that they all have world-class strikers who can get goals out of nothing, and David and I tried to make the players realise that sitting back and allowing them to come on to us was tantamount to soccer suicide. We had to defend a lot higher up the pitch, to keep them as far away from our goal as possible and, of course, put ourselves in a position where we could trouble their defence as well.

They absorbed the lesson superbly, and Mark Viduka and Alan Smith played a crucial part in the improvement. They never gave defenders a moment's peace. In quickly closing defenders down they made it hard for teams to play the ball from the back in the way they wanted to. In a number of instances, the opposition's attempts to get at us were killed at source. No less of a problem to defenders was the pair's movement and willingness to take them on and attack the space behind them.

By the time we met Barcelona again, at Elland Road, we had beaten AC Milan 1–0 at home and put another four points in the bag with a 6–0 win and goalless draw against Besiktas. Again, Barcelona had more of the game, but they found us a different team from the one they had outclassed in Spain. Knowing that victory would guarantee a place for us in the next phase, we had the start we wanted with Lee Bowyer's superb goal from a free kick after just five minutes, and for all the pressure Barcelona put on us, they had to wait until the fourth minute of stoppage time to equalise, through Rivaldo.

The following month, that spot in the last sixteen was clinched by our 1–1 draw with AC Milan in Italy in our final game, a result which put Barcelona out of the competition.

In our next phase, Group D, we did even better by collecting a total of nine points (four against Lazio and six against Ander-lecht) and booking our place in the knock-out quarter-final stage with two matches to spare.

As in the last round, we began with a defeat by a star-studded Spanish team followed by victory over a star-studded Italian one. The Spanish team in question were the European Cup-holders, Real Madrid, who beat us 2–0 at Elland Road. For the first hour, I thought we held our own, but once Real seized the initiative with goals by Fernando Hierro, their captain, and Raul in the space of two minutes midway through the second half, they could have gone on to put as many past us as Barcelona did.

Watching Real was a great experience for our fans, just as it was for our players. The Real star who attracted the most attention was inevitably Luis Figo, the world's most expensive player. Paul Robinson made a tremendous save from him (albeit at the expense of a corner from which Real got their first goal) and Lucas Radebe also distinguished himself with a last-ditch sliding tackle as the Portuguese international moved in to a shooting position inside the penalty area.

We could have no complaints about that defeat, especially when it was followed by what many considered to be the best of all our Champions League victories, over Sven-Goran Eriksson's Lazio in the Olympic Stadium in Rome. Lazio were the Italian champions, and like Real, they did not exactly seem to have stinted themselves when it came to buying high-profile foreign players. Their Foreign Legion list included the Argentinian trio of Hernand Crespo (who had been bought by the Italian club for the previous world record transfer fee of £35 million), Juan Sebastian Veron and Diego Simeone, plus Chile's Marcelo Salas.

I am sure this will be the game that Harry Kewell remembers the most, given that it was his first match in the Champions League – and the fright he had beforehand. The day before the game, Harry was among a group of players who went on a shopping trip, and when they met up to return to the hotel in our hired mini bus, Harry showed them a jacket he had bought in one of the city's exclusive designer shops. When they asked him how much he had paid for it, Harry replied, 'Forty million lira – about £1,500.' Apparently, when they told him that, in fact, it had cost him £10,000, Harry's face went whiter than our shirts. One can be fairly certain that any record for covering the distance between the mini bus and the shop will have been broken by Harry in his rush to return the jacket and get the debit on his credit card wiped out.

The shock clearly did not do him much harm. Ten minutes from the end against Lazio, Harry was involved in the outstanding move that brought us the only goal, starting it with a pass to Alan Smith from the left. Alan pushed it across to Mark Viduka who totally outwitted the Lazio defence with an audacious backheel to give Alan his scoring chance.

Mark was brilliant that night against Alessandro Nesta and that description could also be applied to the performances he and Alan Smith produced in the 4–1 win over Anderlecht in Brussels, which put us through to the last eight. We completed our Group D programme with an unlucky 3–2 defeat by Real Madrid and a 3–3 draw against Lazio. Another great attacking performance – the 3–0 win over Deportivo La Coruna at home – put us within what appeared to be easy reach of the semi-finals. Deportivo were completely overpowered that night, particularly in the central midfield area where they were always struggling to contain David Batty and Olivier Dacourt. Deportivo did have one player who seemed to be able to match them, tackle for tackle – the Brazilian, Emerson, who knew what to expect from his experiences of playing in England with Middlesbrough. But it was like trying to defend the Alamo for him, and Deportivo could easily have lost by a heavier margin.

Strange as it might seem, when looking at our collapse in the second leg, I don't think having a three-goal lead helped us. Deportivo got the start they wanted with their penalty goal after nine minutes and, with nothing to lose, threw everything at us. The thought of the previously unthinkable happening – losing the lead – got to us. But when Deportivo made it 2–0 near the end, they started panicking as well. Instead of continuing to probe for clear-cut openings, they were shooting from virtually anywhere. We regained our composure whereas they lost theirs.

This was the third time we had lost in Spain; and Valencia finally ended our European dream when they made it four in the semi-final second leg. You had to admire Valencia's expertise at the back, and Gaizka Mendieta's skill in midfield, but Valencia were not as good a team as Real Madrid or Barcelona. Despite being held to a goalless draw at Elland Road, where Valencia's goalkeeper, Santiago Canizares, distinguished himself with his remarkable save from Dominic Matteo's header, I still thought we could get through. I continued to be optimistic even after Uefa announced their ban on Lee Bowyer for stamping on an opponent in the heat of the previous match; and after Valencia's controversial opening goal scored by Juan Sanchez in sixteen minutes.

That goal did not change anything for us; because of the away-goal rule, one was still all we needed to establish an aggregate lead. In the last twenty minutes of the first half, it looked increasingly likely that we would get it. We were putting Valencia under pressure, and their coach, Hector Cuper, and their fans were clearly getting more and more agitated. At half-time, everybody in our dressing rooms was delighted with the way things were going. All the players were convinced that we were going to score.

Unfortunately, I think this caused us to lose sight of the likelihood of Valencia lifting themselves for the start of the second half, and the importance of keeping our concentration at the back. You cannot afford any slackness at all against teams with Valencia's know-how, as we found out. Just three minutes into the second half, we were 2–0 down. All our discipline went out of the window. As a contest, the game was over.

Valencia, having lost to Real Madrid in the final the previous season, had to settle for second place again, against Bayern Munich. These were teams who were at their peak, whereas Leeds have yet to reach that stage. For us, the defeat in Spain was not the end; it was the beginning. I can honestly see no reason why the club should not establish the same sort of record that was achieved in the Revie years. I think it goes without saying that nothing would give me greater pleasure than to be part of it.

INDEX